P9-DMH-996

A12900 359693

WITHDRAWN

ILLINOIS CENTRAL COLLEGE
PS3511.I9Z698
C.1   STACKS
F. Scott Fitzgerald,

A12900 359693

PS
3511   MIZENER
.I 9   F. Scott Fitzgerald
Z698
c.1

WITHDRAWN

Illinois Central College
Learning Resource Center

TWENTIETH CENTURY VIEWS

The aim of this series is to present the best in contemporary critical opinion on major authors, providing a twentieth century perspective on their changing status in an era of profound revaluation.

Maynard Mack, *Series Editor*
Yale University

F. SCOTT FITZGERALD

F. SCOTT FITZGERALD,

A COLLECTION OF CRITICAL ESSAYS ,

Edited by
Arthur Mizener, e d

ILLINOIS CENTRAL COLLEGE
LIBRARY · INSTRUCTIONAL MATERIALS CENTER

A SPECTRUM BOOK

Prentice-Hall, Inc., *Englewood Cliffs, N.J.*

06649

PS
3511
.I9
Z698
c.1

FITZGERALD, FRANCIS SCOTT KEY.

Current printing (last digit):

13 12 11 10 9 8 7 6 5

© 1963 BY PRENTICE-HALL, INC.

ENGLEWOOD CLIFFS, N. J.

All rights reserved. No part of this book may be reproduced in any form, by mimeograph or any other means, without permission in writing from the publishers.

LIBRARY OF CONGRESS CATALOG CARD NO.: 63-9306

Printed in the United States of America

C 32084

Table of Contents

THE GREAT GATSBY

LATE WORK

F. SCOTT FITZGERALD

Introduction

by Arthur Mizener

Almost from the start of his career—at least from the publication of *This Side of Paradise* in 1920—Scott Fitzgerald was a popular and successful writer. During his professional career, a period of just about twenty years, he produced something like 160 short stories, mostly for the high-priced magazines. (During a period of just about the same length Hemingway wrote his "first forty-nine stories," as his publishers optimistically called them when they brought them together in a book in 1938.) Of the four novels Fitzgerald published during these twenty years, two—*The Great Gatsby* (1925) and *Tender Is the Night* (1934)—were more successful than serious books usually are, and two—*This Side of Paradise* (1920) and *The Beautiful and Damned* (1922)—were bestsellers. This success, and Fitzgerald's financial and psychological dependence on it, had an important effect on the character of his work and a striking effect on his reputation.

His early success combined with his personal expectations to determine his relations with his society; more than any other gifted writer of his generation, he was committed to and lived in his time, so that for him the tension between his own serious standards as a writer and the conventional standards of the magazine audience was very great. The effects on his work of this tension between his gift and his commitment were both good and bad. On the one hand, it meant that he wrote a great deal which, if it was not out-and-out hackwork, was the expression of a carefully limited range of his understanding. On the other hand, it gave to his best work the quality that distinguished it most strikingly from the work of other good writers of his time, that is, the normality of its conception of life and the sense of intimacy it creates in his readers.

But the very fact that such a normal conception of life was rare among the writers of his time—as it perhaps is among writers at most times—meant that his work was regarded with some doubt by his fellow writers and by the critics. One of the most unfortunate consequences of the clumsiness with which American society and its intellectual community have handled their relations with one another is the way they have blundered when a gifted man who can communicate with his society has come along. Fitzgerald was very much a victim of this clumsiness; during his lifetime he was under constant pressure from his audience to write less honestly and at the same time rarely taken seriously by writers and critics he himself respected.

This Side of Paradise was—with some justification—violently attacked by serious critics and, what was much worse for Fitzgerald, treated by them as if it were hardly literature at all. H. L. Mencken, the most influential critic of the time, pronounced *The Great Gatsby* "no more than a glorified anecdote," and the well-known reviewer, Isabel Paterson, called it "a book for the season only." Peter Quennell described *Tender Is the Night* as "a rather irritating type of *chic*." Only a few critics, and those mostly Fitzgerald's personal friends, took his work seriously during his lifetime, and even they gave a good deal of their attention to lecturing him about the way he was wasting his talent. His good friends Edmund Wilson and John Peale Bishop, both of whom wrote carefully and responsibly about his work, were very stern with him on this point;[1] Hemingway took him so severely to task in a letter about *Tender Is the Night* that he felt it necessary to apologize by adding, "About this time I wouldn't blame you if you gave me a burst. Jesus its marvellous to tell other people how to write, live, die, etc." The exceptions to this general attitude, like the admirable reviews of Malcolm Cowley, James Thurber, John Chamberlain, and Dennis Harding (in *Scrutiny*),[2] were rare.

It was not until the 1940's, when Fitzgerald was dead and the careful editorial work of Edmund Wilson had made available *The Last Tycoon, The Great Gatsby,* half a dozen of Fitzgerald's best stories, and the fascinating personal material of *The Crack-Up,* that critics generally began to concern themselves seriously with Fitzgerald. There had been a small flurry—again mostly the work of old friends—at the time of his death, in December, 1940, when *The New Republic,* then under Malcolm Cowley's literary editorship, produced a group of obituary comments by Dos Passos, Glenway Wescott, and Budd Schulberg, and *The New Yorker* contributed a short but devastating note on *The Herald-Tribune*'s inaccurate obituary. But until Mr. Wilson did his work, the established view of Fitzgerald remained the one that Westbrook Pegler expressed with his usual excess of vulgarity at the time of Fitzgerald's death, when he described Fitzgerald as the representative figure of a "group or cult of juvenile crying-drunks." As late as 1939, The Modern Library dropped *The Great Gatsby* because it failed to sell.

But between Fitzgerald's death and the publication of *The Crack-Up* in 1945, the reputation of *The Great Gatsby*—and along with it, of Fitzgerald's work in general—gradually increased; by 1945, Lionel Trilling

---

[1] See, for example, Edmund Wilson's essay, pp. 80-81 below.
[2] See pp. 143-145 below for Mr. Harding's review of *Tender Is the Night.*

could fairly say in his introduction to New Directions' reissue of *Gatsby* that "Fitzgerald is now beginning to take his place in our literary tradition." Thus, when *The Crack-Up* appeared that same year, Fitzgerald received the kind of thoughtful and perceptive attention that is represented in this book by the essays of Lionel Trilling, William Troy, and Andrews Wanning. There was a similar concentration of serious criticism in 1951, when two full-length books about Fitzgerald were published (three, if one counts Budd Schulberg's *The Disenchanted* a book about Fitzgerald). The essays in this book by Edwin Fussell, Malcolm Cowley, Leslie Fiedler, Tom Burnam, and D. S. Savage are products of that time.

Since then Fitzgerald's work has had the same kind of attention from critics that the work of the other important writers of the twenties has had, as a glance at the annual bibliographies in *PMLA* will show, and nearly half the essays in this book were produced after 1951.

II

If the unusual combination of serious and popular writer in Fitzgerald has had a marked effect on the development of his reputation, it had an even more important effect on the character of his work itself. He was, to begin with, only partially successful in living as a writer with the tension between the two sides of his nature. His best work was frequently rejected; "Outside the Cabinet-Maker's" was turned down by seven magazines before it was finally accepted by *The Century Magazine*. It constantly exacerbated him that, as he once wrote his agent and friend, Harold Ober, "a cheap story like *The Popular Girl* [*The Saturday Evening Post*, February 11 and 18, 1922] written in one week while the baby was being born brings $1500.00 & a genuinely imaginative thing into which I put three weeks real enthusiasm like *The Diamond in the Sky* [the working title of "The Diamond as Big as the Ritz," eventually published in *The Smart Set*, June, 1922] brings not a thing."

Part of the time he deliberately wrote what the high-priced magazines wanted, what he called, speaking of the stories in *Flappers and Philosophers*, "passably amusing stories, a bit out of date now, but doubtless the sort that would then have whiled away a dreary half hour in a dental office." He was never casual about such stories; he worked on them conscientiously and "there was," as he wrote in his Notebooks, "one little drop of something—not blood, not a tear, not my seed, but me more intimately than these, in every story, it was the extra I had." But again and again, to the very end of his life, he would be carried away by the delight of writing out of his full understanding of life without thinking about the needs of the magazines at all. Less than a year before his death, when he began the actual writing of *The Last*

Tycoon, he was filled once more with the old, irrepressible excitement; you can hear it in the letter he wrote his daughter: "Scottina: . . . Look! I have begun to write something that is maybe great. . . . It may not *make* us a cent but it will pay expenses and it is the first labor of love I've undertaken since the first part of 'Infidelity.' "

But considering the difficulties of the situation, Fitzgerald, despite his complaints about the magazines and his self-criticism, did manage a good deal of the time to satisfy both impulses of his nature, to write from a familiar point of view about the actual world and to write something that was "maybe great." His best work in fact grows out of his precise understanding of his time, out of a concentration on the actualities of his world unequalled in the work of any contemporary. He lived, as Malcolm Cowley once put it, in a room full of clocks and calendars, haunted by the minute particulars that represented any given year and its attitudes because the precise quality of the feelings associated with these particulars was so vivid to him. His work is full of brilliant, casual observations of them—of the sound of " 'Three O'Clock in the Morning,' a neat sad little waltz of that year [1922]" that could be heard floating out of the door of Gatsby's house late at night after a party, of the feel of the year (1927) when "a widespread neurosis began to be evident, faintly signalled, like a nervous beating of the feet, by the popularity of cross-word puzzles," of the impression made by those who "drift here and there unrestfully wherever people played polo and were rich together."

This is not social history or even nostalgically evocative social history; if it is history at all, it is the history of a consciousness. What Lionel Trilling says of *The Great Gatsby* is true of all Fitzgerald's best work: "It keeps fresh *because* it is so specifically conscious of its time . . . . its continuing power comes from the courage with which it grasps a moment in history as a great moral fact." (My italics.) But if we are to understand the "great moral fact" embodied in the moment of history Fitzgerald's best work grasps, we need some knowledge of that moment. Indeed, we need this kind of knowledge for all writers who are, like Fitzgerald, partly novelists of manners. According to Boswell, Doctor Johnson once "observed, that all works which describe manners, require notes within sixty or seventy years, or less." Anyone who has, for example, tried to convey to students of a later generation the wonderful absurdity of the conversation between Bill Gorton and Jake Barnes in Chapter XII of Hemingway's *The Sun Also Rises* knows how necessary such knowledge is. Very little of what Hemingway means comes through to the reader who does not know enough to see the point of imagining Mencken and Frankie Frisch at Holy Cross, or Bishop Manning at Loyola, or Wayne B. Wheeler at Notre Dame—or, possibly, at Austin Business College. What is true of Hemingway is even truer of Fitzgerald, who lived far more intimately than Hemingway the life of his times.

That life was, as I have tried to suggest, his means of conveying his understanding of life; as he himself well knew, it was "my material . . . all I had to deal with."

III

It is not easy to get a real sense of the life of the twenties because the decade has been so heavily exploited by the easy, vulgar, sentimental nostalgia of magazines like *Life*. Too many people think they know that the twenties were a silly, happy age when everyone was busy getting drunk in speakeasies or out of silver hip-flasks at Yale-Princeton games in the Bowl, or dancing to the pretentiously bad "jazz" of Paul Whiteman and George Olson, though no one of any intelligence in the period itself took this aspect of its life seriously. As Fitzgerald observed, it was— like every period—well supplied with foolish people, "people you didn't want to know [who] said, 'yes, we have no bananas.'"

In *The Sun Also Rises* Hemingway goes to some trouble to dissociate himself from such people by having Bill Gorton, fresh from America, say mockingly to Jake Barnes, "You're an expatriate. You get precious. Fake European standards have ruined you. You drink yourself to death. You become obsessed by sex. You spend all your time talking, not working. You are an expatriate, see? You hang around cafés." And Jake says, "It sounds like a swell life. When do I work?"—thus reminding us of all the responsibility and sheer hard work that is represented by the astonishing number of good books produced in that short decade.

The truth is that the 1920's was a time of great cultural change in America marked by an outburst of creative activity so vigorous that we are still a little stunned by it. Until the end of the first world war, the United States was a provincial nation, even—at least culturally—a colonial nation. Americans believed that, with very few exceptions, only Europeans could write significant books, and one of the results of their thinking so was that by and large only Europeans did. This provinciality is still clearly evident at the beginning of the twenties, even in those who felt themselves in rebellion against it. The world of Harding and Coolidge ("the heir," as Mencken called him, "of Washington, Lincoln, and Chester A. Arthur"), of Wayne B. Wheeler and his Anti-Saloon League, of Anthony Comstock's salacious-minded censoring of books, was obviously provincial. But we ought also to remember the widespread opinion among the rebellious intellectuals of the early twenties that James Branch Cabell's *Jurgen* (1919)—which was spectacularly suppressed—was the work of a subtle, worldly, and brilliant talent. That was very provincial, too, for *Jurgen* is an affected and superficial book, much more like the work of Jeffrey Farnol than anything else.

At the beginning of the twenties Fitzgerald was saying, with the portentous air of a man revealing the shocking realities of life, that the hero

of *This Side of Paradise* "saw girls doing things that even in his memory
would have been impossible: eating three-o'clock, after-dance suppers in
impossible cafés, talking of every side of life with an air half of earnestness, half of mockery, yet with a furtive excitement that Amory considered stood for a real moral let-down." Their mothers, he said, had no
"idea how casually their daughters were accustomed to be kissed." It
was all quite shocking, and the way *This Side of Paradise* was taken by
the general public as a revelation of the wickedness of The Younger
Generation shows that they thought it quite shocking too. Only a few
old intellectual roués like Heywood Broun dared to say of the book that
"there is too much footwork and too much feinting for anything solid
and substantial being accomplished. You can't expect to have blood
drawn in any such exhibition as that."

By the end of the 1920's Fitzgerald's attitude—and the general public's
—had changed almost beyond recognition. From the vantage ground of
1931, Fitzgerald could recall with remote, unshocked amusement how,
in the middle twenties, "a perfectly mated, contented young mother
[asked] my wife's advice about 'having an affair right away,' though she
had no one especially in mind, 'because don't you think it's sort of un-
dignified when you get much over thirty?'"

IV

The revolutionary change in manners that occurred during the
twenties—perhaps unequalled in American history except during the
period of the Civil War—was accompanied by a sudden flourishing of
talented writers. These are the writers whom Gertrude Stein somewhat
misleadingly named The Lost Generation—Fitzgerald, Hemingway,
Faulkner, Dos Passos, Lewis, and the rest. They were anything but
"lost" in the sense of being in uncertainty or doubt. It was, to be sure,
fashionable in the twenties among people you did not want to know to
talk about being disillusioned, but even the gloomy Mr. Eliot went out
of his way to disillusion those who imagined *The Waste Land* was meant
to express their alleged disillusionment; he said the idea was "nonsense"
and added acidly that "I may have expressed for them their illusion of
being disillusioned, but that did not form part of my intention."

The writers of the twenties were not disillusioned. They were only
released from what seemed to them the stifling restrictions of the previous
generation's narrow, hypocritical attitudes, into a freedom that was
heady with optimism. As Fitzgerald remarked afterwards, "it seemed
only a question of a few years before the older people would step aside
and let the world be run by those who saw things as they were—and it
all seemed rosy and romantic to us who were young then. . . ." This is
not the attitude of a lost generation, except in the sense that explorers

convinced that El Dorado is over the next mountain range may be said to be lost. It is rather the attitude of the first generation of a country that has become capable of imagining its own greatness. It is not easy to determine how much the work of these young writers had to do with causing the change in our manners that came about in the twenties and how much that change had to do with releasing their talents; in any event, the two things occurred together.

"There had been a war fought and won and the great city of the conquering people was crossed with triumphal arches and vivid with thrown flowers of white, red, and rose," as Fitzgerald said in 1920. This was the striking effect. With his eye for the only apparently insignificant detail that makes clear the imaginative source of such change, Fitzgerald also observed that "with Americans ordering suits by the gross in London, the Bond Street tailors perforce agreed to modify their cut to the American long-waisted figure and loose-fitting taste, *something subtle passed to America, the style of man.*" (My italics.)

A time had come when American writers could think it possible to make major works of literature out of American experience. Freed in fact from the provinciality of the previous generation and in imagination from a sense of the insignificance of their world, they set about with enthusiasm to clear away the grubby little world their parents had lived in and to imagine a new one. This new world was not, on the whole, conceived in social and political terms.

The political attitudes of intellectual people in the twenties were— except for a very small number of socialists—libertarian and individualistic rather than, in our sense, liberal. The most influential political voice of the period was Mencken's—"We didn't even remember anything about the Bill of Rights," Fitzgerald recalled, "until Mencken began plugging it." But Mencken was a conservative, even a reactionary, in his basic political feelings.

He was prepared to be arrested when Boston suppressed an issue of *The American Mercury* for printing an article about prostitution called "Box-Car Molly," and he spoke out strongly in favor of freedom of speech, even for Communists, even during the hysteria of the Palmer "Red Raids" that followed the first world war. But it is characteristic of Mencken that he did so by attacking—in the name of individual liberty and the Bill of Rights—collective attitudes of every color.

Let a lone Red arise to annoy a barroom full of Michigan lumberjacks, and at once the fire-alarm sounds and the full military and naval power of the nation is summoned to put down the outrage. But how many Americans would the Reds convert to their rubbish, even supposing them free to spout it on every street corner? Probably not enough, all told, to make a day's hunting for a regiment of militia. The American moron's mind simply doesn't run in that direction; he wants to keep his Ford even at the cost of losing the Bill of Rights.

That shows a talent amounting almost to genius for insulting everybody's sacred cow, for making all ideologies appear beneath contempt. Mencken thought them all absurd, just as he thought absurd the stock attitudes of the American businessman who, he said, "goes to bed every night with an uneasy feeling that there is a burglar under the bed, and gets up every morning with a sickening fear that his underwear has been stolen." It was perfectly consistent of Mencken to be, when the time came, a violent anti-New Dealer and to remain, despite his professional newspaperman's knowledge of American elections, convinced right up to the end that Alfred Landon would defeat Franklin Roosevelt.

The courage with which Mencken accepted the consequences of his almost anarchic individualism was bound to gain the respect and ad-miration of a generation filled with doubts about the democracy which —they had been told too often—they had fought a war to make the world safe for. "We had heard ["the words sacred, glorious, and sacrifice and the expression in vain"], sometimes standing in the rain almost out of earshot, so that only the shouted words came through, and had read them, on proclamations that were slapped up by billposters over other proclamations, now for a long time, and I had seen nothing sacred, and the things that were glorious had no glory and the sacrifices were like the stockyards at Chicago if nothing was done with the meat except to bury it," as Frederic Henry puts their feelings in *A Farewell to Arms*.

Most thoughtful people in the twenties were libertarians like Mencken, though many of those who agreed with him then turned out to be liberals rather than conservatives when a decision was forced on them by the Depression and the decade that followed. But even though many of them were, as Fitzgerald says in his Notebooks he was, "essentially Marxian" (in the quintessential sense in which many businessmen are today), few of them ever lost the libertarian feelings Mencken had en-couraged in them.[3]

Meanwhile, until late in the twenties when the Sacco-Vanzetti case aroused them, the question of politics hardly existed for them. Fitz-gerald caught their attitude perfectly when he said in 1931, after the question of politics had begun to trouble people in a big way, "The events of 1919 left us cynical rather than revolutionary, in spite of the fact that now we are all rummaging around in our trunks wondering where in hell we left the liberty cap—'I know I *had* it'—and the moujik blouse. It was characteristic of the Jazz Age that it had no interest in politics at all." How "the events of 1919" produced this effect on them is beautifully realized in "May Day" (1920), the story Fitzgerald wrote about them at the time. The characteristic attitude of the twenties to-

---

[3] There is a fine illustration of the conflict that went on in such people in Daniel Aaron's account of Malcolm Cowley's inner struggle during the thirties, when he was trying to cooperate with the Communists. See Professor Aaron's *Writers on the Left*.

ward the *volonté général* is clearly expressed by Anthony Patch in *The Beautiful and Damned* (1922):

> He tried to imagine himself in Congress rooting around in the litter of that incredible pigsty with the narrow and porcine brows he saw pictured sometimes in the rotogravure sections of the Sunday newspapers, those glorified proletarians babbling to the nation the ideas of high-school seniors! Little men with copy-book ambitions who by mediocrity had thought to emerge from mediocrity into the lustreless and unromantic heaven of a government by the people. . . .

V

The positive aspect of the twenties' attitude is implied in Anthony's meditation by the phrase, "lustreless and unromantic heaven." Perhaps better than any other writer of the time Fitzgerald expressed this positive feeling, this vision of a lustrous and romantic heaven that seemed "rosy and romantic to us who were young then," and the feeling that—when defeat came—it was because a stubbornly unimaginative society with an incurable preference for a meretricious life prevented people capable of imagining this heaven from achieving it. When Gatsby's life is finished, only Gatsby himself seems to Nick Carraway to have been all right, and what seems to him to blame for the disaster "is what preyed on Gatsby, what foul dust floated in the wake of his dreams. . . ."

With his "extraordinary gift for hope, [his] romantic readiness," his "heightened sensitivity to the promises of life," Gatsby constructed a Platonic conception of himself and a dream of a romantic heaven that he focused—almost deliberately, certainly with a full consciousness of what was happening—on Daisy Fay. "He knew that when he kissed this girl, and forever wed his unutterable visions to her perishable breath, his mind would never romp again like the mind of God." To this conception, and its embodiment, "he was faithful to the end." But it had, sadly enough, only "a vast, vulgar, meretricious beauty," because it was unavoidably made out of the materials Gatsby's society provided him. Perhaps no human being would have been adequate to that vision; certainly Daisy Fay and her kind were not. Gatsby could invent only the kind of heaven "that a seventeen year old boy would be likely to invent" in Fitzgerald's time, a world filled, for Gatsby, with "interesting people. . . . People who do interesting things. Celebrated people"—like "Mr. Buchanan, the polo-player," and Jordan Baker, that "great sportswoman" who would "never do anything that wasn't all right," though Tom Buchanan is in fact a vicious, self-deceived sentimentalist and Jordan Baker an incurable liar and cheat.

Until very near the end of his life Fitzgerald felt that life was unendurable without a belief in the possibility of realizing some romantic dream of a meaningful existence. In a letter to a friend about *Gatsby* he said that "the whole burden of this novel is the loss of those illusions that give such color to the world so that you don't care whether things are true or false so long as they partake of the magical glory." That is why, when Daisy destroys Gatsby's faith and his dream at last breaks up, he finds himself in "a new world, material without being real," and, in effect, chooses to die.

In expressing these feelings—the feeling that life is unendurable without a belief in the possibility of a meaningful existence, and the feeling that the world conspires to make such a belief impossible—Fitzgerald spoke for his own time and perhaps, in a broader sense, for all generations of Americans—as the ending of *The Great Gatsby,* with its overt reference to our American past, suggests he himself felt. In the twenties writers thought it was possible to tell the truth about the inner experience of Americans, to describe "the way it was," as Hemingway put it, and they thought American life in their time was such that, if they succeeded, their novels would be important. Their subject was the making of Americans, in a sense very different from the merely political one—the notion that Americans were "new men," the products of a novel social experiment—which had dominated men's imaginations in previous generations.

In these feelings, and to some extent at least because he succeeded in realizing them in his fiction with unusual intensity and that unwariness he recommended to writers in his Notebooks, Fitzgerald was, as Glenway Wescott said at the time of Fitzgerald's death, "our darling, our genius, our fool." The twenties were a time of greatness in American literature and a time of radical transformation in American society. For both these reasons it is well worth acquiring the understanding of their most representative writer that the essays in this book provide.

THE CAREER

F. Scott Fitzgerald

by *Lionel Trilling*

" 'So be it! I die content and my destiny is fulfilled,' said **Racine's** Orestes; and there is more in his speech than the insanely bitter irony that appears on the surface. Racine, fully conscious of this tragic grandeur, permits Orestes to taste for a moment before going mad with grief the supreme joy of a hero; to assume his *exemplary* role." **The** heroic awareness of which André Gide speaks in his essay on Goethe **was** granted to Scott Fitzgerald for whatever grim joy he might find in it. It is a kind of seal set upon his heroic quality that he was able to utter his vision of his own fate publicly and aloud and in *Esquire* with **no** lessening of his dignity, even with an enhancement of it. The several essays in which Fitzgerald examined his life in crisis have been gathered together by Edmund Wilson—who is for many reasons the most appropriate editor possible—and published, together with Fitzgerald's notebooks and some letters, as well as certain tributes and memorabilia, in a volume called, after one of the essays, *The Crack-Up*. It is a book filled with the grief of the lost and the might-have-been, with physical illness and torture of mind. Yet the heroic quality is so much here, Fitzgerald's assumption of the "exemplary role" is so proper and right that it occurs to us to say, and not merely as a piety but as the most accurate expression of what we really do feel, that

"F. Scott Fitzgerald." From *The Liberal Imagination: Essays on Literature and Society* (New York: The Viking Press, Inc., London: Martin Secker & Warburg Limited, 1951) by Lionel Trilling. Copyright © 1945 by Lionel Trilling. Reprinted by permission of the author, The Viking Press, Inc., and Martin Secker & Warburg Limited.

Nothing is here for tears, nothing to wail
Or knock the breast, no weakness, no contempt,
Dispraise, or blame, nothing but well and fair,
And what may quiet us in a death so noble.

This isn't what we may fittingly say on all tragic occasions, but the original occasion for these words has a striking aptness to Fitzgerald. Like Milton's Samson, he had the consciousness of having misused the power with which he had been endowed. "I had been only a mediocre caretaker . . . of my talent," he said. And the parallel carries further, to the sojourn among the Philistines and even to the maimed hero exhibited and mocked for the amusement of the crowd—on the afternoon of September 25, 1936, the New York *Evening Post* carried on its front page a feature story in which the triumphant reporter tells how he managed to make his way into the Southern nursing home where the sick and distracted Fitzgerald was being cared for and there "interviewed" him, taking all due note of the contrast between the present humiliation and the past glory. It was a particularly gratuitous horror, and yet in retrospect it serves to augment the moral force of the poise and fortitude which marked Fitzgerald's mind in the few recovered years that were left to him.

The root of Fitzgerald's heroism is to be found, as it sometimes is in tragic heroes, in his power of love. Fitzgerald wrote much about love, he was preoccupied with it as between men and women, but it is not merely where he is being explicit about it that his power appears. It is to be seen where eventually all a writer's qualities have their truest existence, in his style. Even in Fitzgerald's early, cruder books, or even in his commercial stories, and even when the style is careless, there is a tone and pitch to the sentences which suggest his warmth and tenderness, and, what is rare nowadays and not likely to be admired, his gentleness without softness. In the equipment of the moralist and therefore in the equipment of the novelist, aggression plays an important part, and although it is of course sanctioned by the novelist's moral intention and by whatever truth of moral vision he may have, it is often none the less fierce and sometimes even cruel. Fitzgerald was a moralist to the core and his desire to "preach at people in some acceptable form" is the reason he gives for not going the way of Cole Porter and Rodgers and Hart —we must always remember in judging him how many real choices he was free and forced to make—and he was gifted with the satiric eye; yet we feel that in his morality he was more drawn to celebrate the good than to denounce the bad. We feel of him, as we cannot feel of all moralists, that he did not attach himself to the good because this attachment would sanction his fierceness toward the bad—his first impulse was to love the good, and we know this the more surely because we perceive that he loved the good not only with his mind but also with his **quick** senses and his youthful pride and desire.

He really had but little impulse to blame, which is the more remarkable because our culture peculiarly honors the act of blaming, which it takes as the sign of virtue and intellect. "Forbearance, good word," is one of the jottings in his notebook. When it came to blame, he preferred, it seems, to blame himself. He even did not much want to blame the world. Fitzgerald knew where "the world" was at fault. He knew that it was the condition, the field, of tragedy. He is conscious of "what preyed on Gatsby, what foul dust floated in the wake of his dreams." But he never made out that the world imposes tragedy, either upon the heroes of his novels, whom he called his "brothers," or upon himself. When he speaks of his own fate, he does indeed connect it with the nature of the social world in which he had his early flowering, but he never finally lays it upon that world, even though at the time when he was most aware of his destiny it was fashionable with minds more pretentious than his to lay all personal difficulty whatever at the door of the "social order." It is, he feels, *his* fate—and as much as to anything else in Fitzgerald, we respond to the delicate tension he maintained between his idea of personal free will and his idea of circumstance: we respond to that moral and intellectual energy. "The test of a first-rate intelligence," he said, "is the ability to hold two opposed ideas in the mind, at the same time, and still retain the ability to function."

The power of love in Fitzgerald, then, went hand in hand with a sense of personal responsibility and perhaps created it. But it often happens that the tragic hero can conceive and realize a love that is beyond his own prudence or beyond his powers of dominance or of self-protection, so that he is destroyed by the very thing that gives him his spiritual status and stature. From Proust we learn about a love that is destructive by a kind of corrosiveness, but from Fitzgerald's two mature novels, *The Great Gatsby* and *Tender Is the Night,* we learn about a love— perhaps it is peculiarly American—that is destructive by reason of its very tenderness. It begins in romance, sentiment, even "glamour"—no one, I think, has remarked how innocent of mere "sex," how charged with sentiment is Fitzgerald's description of love in the jazz age—and it takes upon itself reality, and permanence, and duty discharged with an almost masochistic scrupulousness of honor. In the bright dreams begins the responsibility which needs so much prudence and dominance to sustain; and Fitzgerald was anything but a prudent man and he tells us that at a certain point in his college career "some old desire for personal dominance was broken and gone." He connects that loss of desire for dominance with his ability to write; and he set down in his notebook the belief that "to record one must be unwary." Fitzgerald, we may say, seemed to feel that both love and art needed a sort of personal defenselessness.

The phrase from Yeats, the derivation of the "responsibility" from the "dreams," reminds us that we must guard against dismissing, with easy words about its immaturity, Fitzgerald's preoccupation with the bright charm of his youth. Yeats himself, a wiser man and wholly fulfilled in his art, kept to the last of his old age his connection with his youthful vanity. A writer's days must be bound each to each by his sense of his life, and Fitzgerald the undergraduate was father of the best in the man and the novelist.

His sojourn among the philistines is always much in the mind of everyone who thinks about Fitzgerald, and indeed it was always much in his own mind. Everyone knows the famous exchange between Fitzgerald and Ernest Hemingway—Hemingway refers to it in his story, "The Snows of Kilimanjaro" and Fitzgerald records it in his notebook—in which, to Fitzgerald's remark, "The very rich are different from us," Hemingway replied, "Yes, they have more money." [1] It is usually supposed that Hemingway had the better of the encounter and quite settled the matter. But we ought not be too sure. The novelist of a certain kind, if he is to write about social life, may not brush away the reality of the differences of class, even though to do so may have the momentary appearance of a virtuous social avowal. The novel took its rise and its nature from the radical revision of the class structure in the eighteenth century, and the novelist must still live by his sense of class differences, and must be absorbed by them, as Fitzgerald was, even though he depise them, as Fitzgerald did.

No doubt there was a certain ambiguity in Fitzgerald's attitude toward the "very rich"; no doubt they were for him something more than the mere object of his social observation. They seem to have been the nearest thing to an aristocracy that America could offer him, and we cannot be too simple about what a critic has recently noted, the artist's frequent "taste for aristocracy, his need—often quite open—of a superior social class with which he can make some fraction of common cause— enough, at any rate, to account for his own distinction." Every modern reader is by definition wholly immune from all ignoble social con-

---

[1] Mr. Trilling has apparently taken this anecdote from Edmund Wilson's footnote in *The Crack-Up* (New Directions, 1945), p. 125, though in Mr. Wilson's version Fitzgerald says, "The rich," not "The very rich." This anecdote originated in Hemingway's story, "The Snows of Kilimanjaro," though Hemingway does not there claim that he and Fitzgerald actually exchanged the remarks. "He remembered . . . how [Scott Fitzgerald] had started a story once that began, 'The very rich are different from you and me.' And how someone had said to Scott, 'Yes they have more money.' " Near the beginning of "The Rich Boy" (1926) Fitzgerald had written, "Let me tell you about the very rich. They are different from you and me." When "The Snows of Kilimanjaro" appeared, Maxwell Perkins wrote Fitzgerald: "I was present when that reference was made to the rich, and the retort given, and you were miles away." Of Fitzgerald's observation about the rich, Mr. Trilling has said, in "Manners, Morals, and the Novel," "But the truth is that after a certain point quantity of money does indeed change into quality of personality: in an important sense the very rich *are* different from us. . . . Fitzgerald was right, and almost for that remark alone he must surely have been received in Balzac's bosom in the heaven of novelists." [A.M.]

siderations, and, no matter what his own social establishment or desire for it may be, he knows that in literature the interest in social position must never be taken seriously. But not all writers have been so simple and virtuous—what are we to make of those risen gentlemen, Shakespeare and Dickens, or those fabricators of the honorific "de," Voltaire and Balzac? Yet their snobbery—let us call it that—is of a large and generous kind and we are not entirely wrong in connecting their peculiar energies of mind with whatever it was they wanted from gentility or aristocracy. It is a common habit of writers to envision an actuality of personal life which shall have the freedom and the richness of detail and the order of form that they desire in art. Yeats, to mention him again, spoke of the falseness of the belief that the "inherited glory of the rich" really holds richness of life. This, he said, was a mere dream; and yet, he goes on, it is a necessary illusion—

> Yet Homer had not sung
> Had he not found it certain beyond dreams
> That out of life's own self-delight had sprung
> The abounding glittering jet. . . .

And Henry James, at the threshold of his career, allegorized in his story "Benvolio" the interplay that is necessary for some artists between their creative asceticism and the bright, free, gay life of worldliness, noting at the same time the desire of worldliness to destroy the asceticism.[2]

With a man like Goethe the balance between the world and his asceticism is maintained, and so we forgive him his often absurd feelings—but perhaps absurd as well as forgivable only in the light of our present opinion of his assured genius—about aristocracy. Fitzgerald could not always keep the balance true; he was not, as we know, a prudent man. And no doubt he deceived himself a good deal in his youth, but certainly his self-deception was not in the interests of vulgarity, for aristocracy meant to him a kind of disciplined distinction of personal existence which, presumably, he was so humble as not to expect from his art. What was involved in that notion of distinction can be learned from the use which Fitzgerald makes of the word "aristocracy" in one of those serious moments which occur in his most frivolous *Saturday Evening Post* stories: he says of the life of the young man of the story, who during the war was on duty behind the lines, that "it was not so bad—except that when the infantry came limping back from the trenches he wanted to be one of them. The sweat and mud they wore seemed only one of those ineffable symbols of aristocracy that were forever eluding him." Fitzgerald was

---

[2] George Moore's comment on Æ's having spoken in reproof of Yeats's pride in a quite factitious family line is apposite; "Æ, who is usually quick-witted, should have guessed that Yeats's belief in his lineal descent from the great Duke of Ormonde was part of his poetic equipment."

perhaps the last notable writer to affirm the Romantic fantasy, descended from the Renaissance, of personal ambition and heroism, of life committed to, or thrown away for, some ideal of self. To us it will no doubt come more and more to seem a merely boyish dream; the nature of our society requires the young man to find his distinction through cooperation, subordination, and an expressed piety of social usefulness, and although a few young men have made Fitzgerald into a hero of art, it is likely that even to these admirers the whole nature of his personal fantasy is not comprehensible, for young men find it harder and harder to understand the youthful heroes of Balzac and Stendhal, they increasingly find reason to blame the boy whose generosity is bound up with his will and finds its expression in a large, strict, personal demand upon life.

I am aware that I have involved Fitzgerald with a great many great names and that it might be felt by some that this can do him no service, the disproportion being so large. But the disproportion will seem large only to those who think of Fitzgerald chiefly through his early public legend of heedlessness. Those who have a clear recollection of the mature work or who have read *The Crack-Up* will at least not think of the disproportion as one of kind. Fitzgerald himself did not, and it is by a man's estimate of himself that we must begin to estimate him. For all the engaging self-depreciation which was part of his peculiarly American charm, he put himself, in all modesty, in the line of greatness, he judged himself in a large way. When he writes of his depression, of his "dark night of the soul" where "it is always three o'clock in the morning," he not only derives the phrase from St. John of the Cross but adduces the analogous black despairs of Wordsworth, Keats, and Shelley. A novel with Ernest Hemingway as the model of its hero suggests to him Stendhal portraying the Byronic man, and he defends *The Great Gatsby* from some critical remark of Edmund Wilson's by comparing it with *The Brothers Karamazov.* Or again, here is the stuff of his intellectual pride at the very moment that he speaks of giving it up, as years before he had given up the undergraduate fantasies of valor: "The old dream of being an entire man in the Goethe-Byron-Shaw tradition . . . has been relegated to the junk heap of the shoulder pads worn for one day on the Princeton freshman football field and the overseas cap never worn overseas." And was it, that old dream, unjustified? To take but one great name, the one that on first thought seems the least relevant of all—between Goethe at twenty-four the author of *Werther,* and Fitzgerald, at twenty-four the author of *This Side of Paradise,* there is not really so entire a difference as piety and textbooks might make us think; both the young men so handsome, both winning immediate and notorious success, both rather more interested in life than in art, each the spokesman and symbol of his own restless generation.

It is hard to overestimate the benefit which came to Fitzgerald from his having consciously placed himself in the line of the great. He was a "natural," but he did not have the contemporary American novelist's belief that if he compares himself with the past masters, or if he takes thought—which, for a writer, means really knowing what his predecessors have done—he will endanger the integrity of his natural gifts. To read Fitzgerald's letters to his daughter—they are among the best and most affecting letters I know—and to catch the tone in which he speaks about the literature of the past, or to read the notebooks he faithfully kept, indexing them as Samuel Butler had done, and to perceive how continuously he thought about literature, is to have some clue to the secret of the continuing power of Fitzgerald's work.

The Great Gatsby, for example, after a quarter-century is still as fresh as when it first appeared; it has even gained in weight and relevance, which can be said of very few American books of its time. This, I think, is to be attributed to the specifically intellectual courage with which it was conceived and executed, a courage which implies Fitzgerald's grasp —both in the sense of awareness and of appropriation—of the traditional resources available to him. Thus, *The Great Gatsby* has its interest as a record of contemporary manners, but this might only have served to date it, did not Fitzgerald take the given moment of history as something more than a mere circumstance, did he not, in the manner of the great French novelists of the nineteenth century, seize the given moment as a moral fact. The same boldness of intellectual grasp accounts for the success of the conception of its hero—Gatsby is said by some to be not quite credible, but the question of any literal credibility he may or may not have becomes trivial before the large significance he implies. For Gatsby, divided between power and dream, comes inevitably to stand for America itself. Ours is the only nation that prides itself upon a dream and gives its name to one, "the American dream." We are told that "the truth was that Jay Gatsby of West Egg, Long Island, sprang from his Platonic conception of himself. He was a son of God—a phrase which, if it means anything, means just that—and he must be about His Father's business, the service of a vast, vulgar, and meretricious beauty." Clearly it is Fitzgerald's intention that our mind should turn to the thought of the nation that has sprung from its "Platonic conception" of itself. To the world it is anomalous in America, just as in the novel it is anomalous in Gatsby, that so much raw power should be haunted by envisioned romance. Yet in that anomaly lies, for good or bad, much of the truth of our national life, as, at the present moment, we think about it.

Then, if the book grows in weight of significance with the years, we can be sure that this could not have happened had its form and style not been as right as they are. Its form is ingenious—with the ingenuity, however, not of craft but of intellectual intensity. The form, that is, is not the result of careful "plotting"—the form of a good novel never is— but is rather the result of the necessities of the story's informing idea, which require the sharpness of radical foreshortening. Thus, it will be

observed, the characters are not "developed": the wealthy and brutal
Tom Buchanan haunted by his "scientific" vision of the doom of civilization, the vaguely guilty, vaguely homosexual Jordan Baker, the dim
Wolfsheim, who fixed the World Series of 1919, are treated, we might
say, as if they were ideographs, a method of economy that is reinforced
by the ideographic use that is made of the Washington Heights flat, the
terrible "valley of ashes" seen from the Long Island Railroad, Gatsby's
incoherent parties, and the huge sordid eyes of the oculist's advertising
sign. (It is a technique which gives the novel an affinity with *The Waste
Land,* between whose author and Fitzgerald there existed a reciprocal
admiration.) Gatsby himself, once stated, grows only in the understanding
of the narrator. He is allowed to say very little in his own person. Indeed,
apart from the famous "Her voice is full of money," he says only one
memorable thing, but that remark is overwhelming in its intellectual
audacity: when he is forced to admit that his lost Daisy did perhaps
love her husband, he says, "In any case it was just personal." With that
sentence he achieves an insane greatness, convincing us that he really is
a Platonic conception of himself, really some sort of Son of God.

What underlies all success in poetry, what is even more important
than the shape of the poem or its wit of metaphor, is the poet's voice.
It either gives us confidence in what is being said or it tells us that we do
not need to listen; and it carries both the modulation and the living
form of what is being said. In the novel no less than in the poem, the
voice of the author is the decisive factor. We are less consciously aware
of it in the novel, and, in speaking of the elements of a novel's art, it
cannot properly be exemplified by quotation because it is continuous and
cumulative. In Fitzgerald's work the voice of his prose is of the essence of
his success. We hear in it at once the tenderness toward human desire
that modifies a true firmness of moral judgment. It is, I would venture
to say, the normal or ideal voice of the novelist. It is characteristically
modest, yet it has in it, without apology or self-consciousness, a largeness,
even a stateliness, which derives from Fitzgerald's connection with tradition and with mind, from his sense of what has been done before and
the demands which this past accomplishment makes. ". . . I became
aware of the old island here that flowered once for Dutch sailors' eyes—
a fresh, green breast of the new world. Its vanished trees, the trees that
had made way for Gatsby's house, had once pandered in whispers to the
last and greatest of all human dreams; for a transitory enchanted
moment man must have held his breath in the presence of this continent,
compelled into an aesthetic contemplation he neither understood nor
desired, face to face for the last time in history with something com-
mensurate to his capacity for wonder." Here, in the well-known passage,
the voice is a little dramatic, a little *intentional,* which is not improper
to a passage in climax and conclusion, but it will the better suggest in
brief compass the habitual music of Fitzgerald's seriousness.

Fitzgerald lacked prudence, as his heroes did, lacked that blind instinct of self-protection which the writer needs and the American writer needs in double measure. But that is all he lacked—and it is the generous fault, even the heroic fault. He said of his Gatsby, "If personality is an unbroken series of sucecssful gestures, there was something gorgeous about him, some heightened sensitivity to the promises of life, as if he were related to one of those intricate machines that register earthquakes ten thousand miles away. This responsiveness had nothing to do with that flabby impressionability which is dignified under the name of "the creative temperament"—it was an extraordinary gift for hope, a romantic readiness such as I have never found in any other person and which it is not likely I shall ever find again." And it is so that we are drawn to see Fitzgerald himself as he stands in his exemplary role.

Scott Fitzgerald—
the Authority of Failure

by William Troy

Of course, in any absolute sense, Scott Fitzgerald was not a failure at all; he has left one short novel, passages in several others, and a handful of short stories which stand as much chance of survival as anything of their kind produced in this country during the same period. If the tag is so often attached to his name, it has been largely his own fault. It is true that he was the victim, among a great number of other influences in American life, of that paralyzing high-pressure by which the conscientious American writer is hastened to premature extinction as artist or as man. Upon the appearance of *The Crack-Up*, a selection by Edmund Wilson of Fitzgerald's letters, notebooks and fugitive pieces, it was notable that all the emptiest and most venal elements in New York journalism united to crow amiably about his literary corpse to this same tune of insufficient production. Actually their reproaches betrayed more of their own failure to estimate what was good and enduring in his writing than his acknowledgeable limitations as an artist. If Fitzgerald had turned out as much as X or Y or Z, he would have been a different kind of writer—undoubtedly more admirable from the standpoint of the quasi-moral American *ethos* of production at any cost, but possibly less worth talking about five years after his death. And it might be said that Fitzgerald never hovered so close to real failure as when he listened from time to time, with too willing an ear, to these same reproaches.

But Fitzgerald brought most of it on himself by daring to make failure the consistent theme of his work from first to last. (Similarly Virginia Woolf used to be accused by the reviewers of being a sterile writer because she made sterility her principal theme.) It is perhaps only adumbrated in *This Side of Paradise*; for the discovery of its hero Amory Blaine that the world is not altogether his oyster is hardly the stuff of high tragedy. The book is interesting today as a document of the early twenties; nobody who would know what it was like to be young and

"Scott Fitzgerald—the Authority of Failure," by William Troy. From *Accent* (Autumn 1945). Copyright 1945 by the Estate of William Troy; Leonie A. Troy, Administratrix. Reprinted by permission of the Estate of William Troy; Leonie A. Troy, Administratrix.

privileged and self-centered in that bizarre epoch can afford to neglect it. But it can also be read as a preliminary study in the kind of tortured narcissism that was to plague its author to the end of his days. (See the article called "Early Success" in the Wilson collection.) *The Beautiful and Damned* is a more frayed and pretentious museum-piece, and the muddiest in conception of all the longer books. It is not so much a study in failure as in the *atmosphere* of failure—that is to say, of a world in which no moral decisions can be made because there are no values in terms of which they may be measured. Hardly is it a world suited to the purposes of the novelist, and the characters float around in it as in some aquamarine region comfortably shot through with the soft colors of self-pity and romantic irony. Not until *The Great Gatsby* did Fitzgerald hit upon something like Mr. Eliot's "objective correlative" for the intermingled feeling of personal insufficiency and disillusionment with the world out of which he had unsuccessfully tried to write a novel.

Here is a remarkable instance of the manner in which adoption of a special form or technique can profoundly modify and define a writer's whole attitude toward his world. In the earlier books author and hero tended to melt into one because there was no internal principle of differentiation by which they might be separated; they respired in the same climate, emotional and moral; they were tarred with the same brush. But in *Gatsby* is achieved a dissociation, by which Fitzgerald was able to isolate one part of himself, the spectatorial or aesthetic, and also the more intelligent and responsible, in the person of the ordinary but quite sensible narrator, from another part of himself, the dream-ridden romantic adolescent from St. Paul and Princeton, in the person of the legendary Jay Gatsby. It is this which makes the latter one of the few truly mythological creations in our recent literature—for what is mythology but this same process of projected wish-fulfillment carried out on a larger scale and by the whole consciousness of a race? Indeed, before we are quite through with him, Gatsby becomes much more than a mere exorcizing of whatever false elements of the American dream Fitzgerald felt within himself: he becomes a symbol of America itself, dedicated to "the service of a vast, vulgar and meretricious beauty."

Not mythology, however, but a technical device which had been brought to high development by James and Conrad before him, made this dissociation possible for Fitzgerald. The device of the intelligent but sympathetic observer situated at the center of the tale, as James never ceases to demonstrate in the Prefaces, makes for some of the most priceless values in fiction—economy, suspense, intensity. And these values *The Great Gatsby* possesses to a rare degree. But the same device imposes on the novelist the necessity of tracing through in the observer or narrator himself some sort of growth in general moral perception, which will constitute in effect *his* story. Here, for example, insofar as the book is Gatsby's story it is a story of failure—the prolongation of the adolescent incapacity to distinguish between dream and reality, between the terms demanded of life and the terms offered. But insofar as it is the narrator's story it is a successful transcendence of a particularly bitter and harrowing set of experiences, localized in the sinister, distorted, El Greco-like Long Island atmosphere of the later twenties, into a world of restored sanity and calm, symbolized by the bracing winter nights of the Middle Western prairies. "Conduct may be founded on the hard rock or the wet marshes," he writes, "but after a certain point I don't care what it's founded on. When I came back from the East last autumn I felt that I wanted the world to be in uniform and at a sort of moral attention forever; I wanted no more riotous excursions with privileged glimpses into the human heart ever recurring." [1] By reason of its enforced perspective the book takes on the pattern and the meaning of a Grail-romance—or of the initiation ritual on which it is based. Perhaps this will seem a farfetched suggestion to make about a work so obviously modern in every respect; and it is unlikely that Fitzgerald had any such model in mind. But like *Billy Budd, The Red Badge of Courage,* or *A Lost Lady*—to mention only a few American stories of similar length with which it may be compared —it is a record of the strenuous passage from deluded youth to maturity.

Never again was Fitzgerald to repeat the performance. *Tender Is the Night* promises much in the way of scope but it soon turns out to be a backsliding into the old ambiguities. Love and money, fame and youth, youth and money—however one shuffles the antitheses they have a habit of melting into each other like the blue Mediterranean sky and sea of the opening background. To Dick Diver, with a mere change of pronoun, may be applied Flaubert's analysis of Emma Bovary: *"Elle confondait, dans son désir, les sensualités du luxe avec les joies du coeur, l'élégance des habitudes et les délicatesses du sentiment."* And it is this Bovaryism on the part of the hero, who as a psychiatrist should conceivably know more about himself, which in rendering his character so suspect prevents his meticulously graded deterioration from assuming any real significance. Moreover, there is an ambiguous treatment of the problem of guilt. We are never certain whether Diver's predicament is the result of his own weak judgment or of the behavior of his neurotic wife. At the end we are strangely unmoved by his downfall because it has been less a tragedy of will than of circumstance.

Of *The Last Tycoon* we have only the unrevised hundred and thirty-three pages, supported by a loose collection of notes and synopses. In an unguarded admission Fitzgerald describes the book as "an escape into a lavish, romantic past that perhaps will not come again into our time." Its hero, suggested by a well-known Hollywood prodigy of a few years ago, is another one of those poor boys betrayed by "a heightened sensitivity to the promises of life." When we first meet him he is already a sick and disillusioned man, clutching for survival at what is advertised in

---

[1] The "ever recurring" of this sentence is not in *The Great Gatsby.* [A.M.]

the notes as "an immediate, dynamic, unusual, physical love affair." This is nothing less than "the meat of the book." But as much of it as is rendered includes some of the most unfortunate writing which Fitzgerald has left; he had never been at his best in the approach to the physical. Nor is it clear in what way the affair is related to the other last febrile gesture of Stahr—his championship of the Hollywood underdog in a struggle with the racketeers and big producers. Fortuitously the sense of social guilt of the mid-thirties creeps into the fugue, although in truth this had been a strong undertone in early short stories like "May Day" and "The Rich Boy." It is evident that Stahr is supposed to be some kind of symbol—but of what it would be hard to determine. From the synopses he is more like a receptacle for all the more familiar contradictions of his author's own sensibility—his arrogance and generosity, his fondness for money and his need for integrity, his attraction toward the fabulous in American life and his repulsion by its waste and terror. "Stahr is miserable and embittered toward the end," Fitzgerald writes, in one of his own last notes for the book. "Before death, thoughts from *Crack-Up*." Apparently it was all to end in a flare-up of sensational and not too meaningful irony: Stahr, on his way to New York to call off a murder which he had ordered for the best of motives, is himself killed in an airplane crash, and his possessions are rifled by a group of schoolchildren on a mountain. If there is anything symbolic in this situation, could it be the image of the modern Icarus soaring to disaster in that "universe of ineffable gaudiness" which was Fitzgerald's vision of the America of his time?

Inquiry into what was the real basis of Fitzgerald's long preoccupation with failure will not be helped too much by the autobiographical sketches in *The Crack-Up*. The reasons there offered are at once too simple and too complicated. No psychologist is likely to take very seriously the two early frustrations described—inability to make a Princeton football team and to go overseas in the last war. In the etiology of the Fitzgerald case, as the psychologists would say, the roots run much deeper, and nobody cares to disturb them at this early date. His unconscionable good looks were indeed a public phenomenon, and their effect on his total personality was something which he himself would not decline to admit. The *imago* of the physical self had a way of eclipsing at times the more important *imago* of the artist. But even this is a delicate enough matter. Besides, there were at work elements of a quite different order—racial and religious. For some reason he could never accept the large and positive influence of his Celtic inheritance, especially in his feeling for language, and his hearkening back to the South has a little too nostalgic a ring to be convincing. Closely related to this was the never resolved attitude toward money and social position in relation to individual worth. But least explored of all by his critics were the permanent effects of his early exposure to Catholicism, which are no less potent because rarely on the surface of his work. (The great exception is "Absolution," perhaps the finest of the short stories.) Indeed, it may have been the old habit of the confession which drove him, pathetically, at the end, to the public *examen de conscience* in the garish pages of *Esquire* magazine.

To add to his sense of failure there was also his awareness of distinct intellectual limitations, which he shared with the majority of American novelists of his time. "I had done very little thinking," he admits, "save within the problems of my craft." Whatever he received at Princeton was scarcely to be called an education; in later years he read little, shrank from abstract ideas, and was hardly conscious of the historical events that were shaping up around him. Perhaps it is not well for the novelist to encumber himself with too much knowledge, although one cannot help recalling the vast cultural apparatus of a Tolstoi or a Joyce, or the dialectical intrepidity of a Dostoievski or a Mann. And recalling these Europeans, none of whom foundered on the way, one wonders whether a certain coyness toward the things of the mind is not one reason for the lack of development in most American writers. Art is not intellect alone; but without intellect art is not likely to emerge beyond the plane of perpetual immaturity.

Lastly, there was Fitzgerald's exasperation with the *multiplicity* of modern human existence—especially in his own country. "It's under you, over you, and all around you," he protested, in the hearing of the present writer, to a young woman who had connived at the slow progress of his work. "And the problem is to get hold of it somehow." It was exasperating because for the writer, whose business is to extract the unique quality of his time, what Baudelaire calls the quality of *modernité,* there was too much to be sensed, to be discarded, to be reconciled into some kind of order. Yet for the writer this was the first of obligations, without it he was nothing—"Our passion is our task, and our task is our passion." What was the common problem of the American novelist was intensified for him by his unusually high sense of vocation.

In the last analysis, if Fitzgerald failed, it was because the only standard which he could recognize, like the Platonic conception of himself forged by young Jay Gatsby in the shabby bedroom in North Dakota, was too much for him to realize. His failure was the defect of his virtues. And this is perhaps the greatest meaning of his career to the younger generation of writers.

"I talk with the authority of failure," he writes in the notebooks, "Ernest with the authority of success. We could never sit across the same table again." It is a great phrase. And the statement as a whole is one neither of abject self-abasement nor of false humility. What Fitzgerald implies is that the stakes for which he played were of a kind more difficult and more unattainable than "Ernest" or any of his contemporaries could even have imagined. And his only strength is in the consciousness of this fact.

The Function of Nostalgia:

F. Scott Fitzgerald

by Wright Morris

"Can't repeat the past?" he cried incredulously. "Why of course
you can!"   —Jay Gatsby

The "subject" of Wolfe, Hemingway, and Faulkner, however various
the backgrounds, however contrasting the styles, pushed to its extremity,
is nostalgia. But it was left to F. Scott Fitzgerald, the playboy, to carry
this subject to its logical conclusion. In fictional terms this is achieved in
The Great Gatsby. In personal terms it is achieved in *The Crack-Up*.

Thomas Wolfe's nostalgia, his cry of *"Lost, lost, lost—"* was a cliché
he neither transformed nor examined, but Fitzgerald made of it a form of
consciousness. Nostalgia, quite simply, is *all* there is. In plumbing this
sentiment to its depths, rather than merely using or abusing it, Fitzgerald dropped to the deep, dead-end center of the American mind. He
let his line out deeper than Hemingway and Twain, deeper than the
Mississippi and the Big-Two Hearted River, down to that sunken island
that once mythically flowered for Dutch sailors' eyes.

That was where the dream began, he tells us, that still pandered to
men in whispers: that was where man held his breath in the presence
of this brave new world. It was Fitzgerald, dreaming of paradise, who was
compelled to an aesthetic contemplation that made of nostalgia, that
snare and delusion, a work of art.

Through all he said, even through his appalling sentimentality, I was
reminded of something—an elusive rhythm, a fragment of lost words, that
I had heard somewhere a long time ago. For a moment a phrase tried to
take shape in my mouth and my lips parted like a dumb man's, as though
there was more struggling upon them than a wisp of startled air. But they
made no sound, and what I had almost remembered was uncommunicable
forever.

"The Function of Nostalgia: F. Scott Fitzgerald." From *The Territory Ahead* (New
York: Harcourt, Brace & World, Inc., 1958) by Wright Morris. Copyright © 1958 by
Wright Morris. Reprinted by permission of the author.

That elusive rhythm, that fragment of lost words, that ghostly rumble among the drums are now, thanks to Fitzgerald, a part of our inheritance. Those who were never there will now be there, in a sense more compelling than those who were there, since they will face it, and grasp it, in the lucid form of Fitzgerald's craft. Like Gatsby, he, too, believed in the green light, in the orgiastic future that recedes before us, leading by a strange circumambulation back into the past, back to those dark fields of the republic where the Big Two-Hearted River flows into the Mississippi, and the Mississippi flows, like time, into the territory ahead. Time and the river flow backward, ceaselessly, into the mythic past. Imperceptibly, the function of nostalgia reduces the ability to function.

The power and sources of nostalgia lie beyond the scalpel. Nostalgia sings in the blood, and with age it grows thicker, and when all other things fail it joins men in a singular brotherhood. Wherever they live in the present, or hope to live in the future, it is in the past that you will truly find them. In the past one is safely out of time but not out of mind.

Nostalgia is a limbo land, leading nowhere, where the artist can graze like a horse put to pasture, feeding on such clover of the past as whets the appetite. The persuasive charm of Fitzgerald is that this clover, which he cups in both hands, is almost chokingly sweet. We dip our faces into the past as into the corridor of that train, homeward bound at Christmas, the air scented with luggage, coonskin coats, and girls with snow melting in their hair. But it has a greater virtue still. It is inexhaustible. It is the artist—not the vein of nostalgia—that gives out or cracks up.

As a man steps from the wings of his own imagination to face the music, the catcall facts of life, Fitzgerald stepped forward in *The Crack-Up* to face the audience. It is a *performance*. He knows the crowd is openly snickering at him. For this curtain call, however, which nobody asked for, an apologetic *apologia pro vita sua,* he has reserved the few lines, implicit but unspoken, in his books. Self-revelation as revealing as this, many found contemptible. Not that he had cracked up—that was commonplace—but that in cracking up he had owned up to it. Nor would that have really mattered if, in owning up, he hadn't owned anything. But Fitzgerald *knew*. That was the hell of it. He was the first of his generation to know that life was *absurd*.

It is fitting that Fitzgerald, the aesthete of nostalgia, of the escape clause without question, should be the first American to formulate his own philosophy of the absurd. But nostalgia, carried to its conclusion, leads nowhere else. Had he been of the temperament of Albert Camus, he might have been the first to dramatize the idea that the only serious question is suicide. Fitzgerald sensed that. In admitting to the concept that life is absurd he confronted the one idea totally alien to American life.

Therein lies the to-be or the not-to-be, the question of suicide. He goes on to tell us, in a further installment, why he had lost the ability to function. He had become *identified* with the objects of his horror and his compassion. He was in the shadow of the hallucinative world that destroyed Van Gogh. He points out that when Wordsworth came to the conclusion that "there had passed away a glory from the earth," he was not compelled to pass away with it, nor did Keats, dying of consumption, ever give up his dream of being among the great poets.

Fitzgerald had been able, for many years, to hold certain opposing ideas in his mind, but when he had lost the ability to *function* he had cracked up. The myth of Sisyphus became his personal myth. While he had the resources, he was able to function in spite of the futility of the situation, but when he had overdrawn these resources, he cracked up. He lay at the bottom of the incline, the rock on top of him.

Some time before World War II made it fashionable, Fitzgerald had discovered the philosophy of the absurd. Different from the philosophers themselves, he lived and died of it. He had come, alone and prematurely, on a fact that was not yet fashionable: he had come on the experience rather than the cliché. The absurd, for Fitzgerald, was truly absurd, though nothing is ever *truly* absurd if enough clever people seem to believe in it.

The Crack-Up is a report from the limbo of the All-American mind. At the point where these two opposing dreams cross, the dreamer cracks up. Such crack-ups are now common, the Nervous Breakdown now joins the All-American in a fraternity that goes deeper than his gold lodge pin. But only Fitzgerald, twenty years ago, was both sufficiently aware and sufficiently honest to look through this crack into the limbo of the mind and report what he saw.

Those deformed souls in Dante's hell, the Diviners, each so strangely twisted between the chin and the chest that they had to come backward, since seeing forward was denied them, symbolize the schizoid state of the American mind. In this confusion of dreams it is the orgiastic future that engages our daytime talents and energy, but the dark fields of the past is where we take refuge at night. The genius and progressive drive of a culture that is both the reproach and the marvel of the world is crossed with a prevailing tendency to withdraw from the world and retire into the past.

The ability of most Americans to *function*—as artists, citizens, or men of business—resides in their capacity to indulge in one of these conflicting dreams at a time; to be all for the future, that is, or all for the past. Sometimes the rhythm is that of an alternating current, the past and the present playing musical chairs, but when they meet in the mind at the same moment, that mind is apt to lose its ability to function. It cracks up.

No more curious or revealing statement than *The Crack-Up* exists in our literature. After such knowledge Rimbaud wrote *A Season in Hell,* then stopped writing, and Dostoevski gave us his *Notes from Underground.* The author of Gatsby, reduced to "clowning it" in the pages of *Esquire,* had to strike a "tone" that would permit him to commit hara-kiri in public. It is this tone, plus the setting of *Esquire,* that gave the statement its curious reputation. The sober-minded need not take it "seriously." What Fitzgerald *knew* can be discounted because of *where* and *how* he said it. Most readers found, as Fitzgerald had predicted, such self-revelation contemptible, and dismissed the testimony of *The Crack-Up* as an ill-bred example of self-pity. It is the *giving up,* rather than the cracking up, that we find inadmissible.

The author of *The Great Gatsby,* stripped of his luck and his illusions, neither had the guts to keep it to himself nor the talent to forge new ones. In this complaint there is some justice. It is an indictment, however indirect, of the limbo of Nostalgia. But where others merely lost themselves, Fitzgerald knew where he was lost. He knew what they did not know—that from this maze there was no way out. It was neither fatigue nor the aimless wandering, but the paralysis of will that grew out of the knowledge that the past was dead, and that the present had no future. The Good, that is, in the last analysis, might not prevail. It led him to a conclusion not unlike that reached by Twain in *What is Man?*

So what? This is what I think now: that the natural state of the sentient adult is a qualified unhappiness.

Does it seem a tame monster—after the sense of horror—to be frightened by? Qualified unhappiness, if we examine it, is the opposite of *un*qualified happiness. It is the opposite, that is, of Jay Gatsby, of the Goethe-Byron-Shaw medley of Fitzgerald, of J. P. Morgan and Beauclerk, and St. Francis of Assisi, of all those giants who were now relegated, as Fitzgerald tells us, to the junk heap—the same junk heap where we will find the shoulder pads worn for one day on the Princeton football field, and that overseas cap never worn overseas.

It seems a little hard to believe—hard in the sense that we would rather not believe it—but Master Hemingway, whose nostalgia is carefully de-mothed before he wears it, bears witness to those things in *Death in the Afternoon.* Speaking of the Good Old Days, those times when men were men and bulls were tremendous, he sums up the past, the mythic past, in these words:

Things change very much and instead of great athletes only children play on the high-school teams now . . . they are all children without honor, skill or virtue, much the same as those children who now play football, a feeble game it has become, on the high-school team and nothing like the great, mature, sophisticated athletes in canvas-elbowed jerseys, smelling vinegary from sweated shoulder pads, carrying leather head guards, their moleskins clotted with mud, that walked on leather-cleated shoes that printed in the earth along beside the sidewalk in the dusk, a long time ago.

The irony of this passage neutralizes the charge of sentiment that it carries. Hemingway mocks it: Fitzgerald admits to its crippling effects. It seems manly to mock; it seems unmanly to acknowledge the effects. Sure, we felt that way long ago, but certainly we are not suffering from it *now*. It is this knowledge, knowledge that we *are* suffering, that deprives Fitzgerald, in spite of his power, of the manly persuasion the reader derives from Hemingway. It is classically summarized in Fitzgerald's observation that "the rich are different from us," and Hemingway's characteristic rejoinder, "Sure, they've got more money." [1]

That kind of answer, that kind of simplification, understandably pleases the athlete in each of us, grown old, who feels that he has put such childish things behind him, and is not dying of them. Fitzgerald knew otherwise. Not only Tom Buchanan, but every American, in his fashion, went through life with invisible goal posts on his shoulders, torn from the green sod on an afternoon of never-to-be-forgotten triumph.

But was this unqualified happiness? It takes some doing; it takes the total recall of what the *ambiance* of such a dream is like, one wherein the towers of Princeton, the Triangle Club, the football shoulder pads, and the overseas cap are all transmuted by the dreamer into pure gold. On the night the world changed, Fitzgerald tells us, he hunted down the specter of womanhood and put the final touch to the adolescent season in hell. On just the other side, a mere year or two later, was paradise.

It was not the vein that played out in Fitzgerald—since nostalgia is inexhaustible—but when he knew *where* he was, when he grasped the situation, he stopped mining it. In this sense, as in many others, he reminds us of James. As a man he continues to indulge in it, but as an artist he knew it was finished. He did not know, however, that art can sometimes begin where life stops. He was too profoundly and incurably committed to life itself.

"I have now at last become a writer only," he said, but he had been suckled too long on the sweep pap of life, and the incomparable milk of wonder, to be more than a writer in name only, resigned to that fact.

> . . . just as the laughing stoicism which has enabled the American negro to endure the intolerable conditions of his existence—so in my case there is a price to pay. I do not any longer like the postman, nor the grocer, nor the editor, nor the cousin's husband, and he in turn will come to dislike me,

---

[1] See the note on this anecdote on p. 14 above. Mr. Morris' version of it apparently derives from Edmund Wilson also. [A.M.]

so that life will never be very pleasant again, and the sign *Cave Canem* is hung permanently just above my door.[2]

Knowing better as an artist could not salvage him as a man. The depths of nostalgia, the slough of its despair, offered him no key to the facts of the absurd. They merely became absurd in their turn, like everything else. Having drawn on the resources he no longer possessed, and having mortgaged his remains, body and soul, he did what his countrymen now do by the thousands—he cracked up. He was different in the sense that he knew what had happened—and owned up to it.

Both *The Great Gatsby* and *Tender Is the Night* are full of personal revelation and prophecy. It is why they have such haunting immediacy when read today. The issues are still alive in anyone who is still alive. The cost of consciousness, like the expense of greatness, sometimes defies accounting, but we can see it more clearly in the life of Fitzgerald than in his works. In the life it *showed*. He was not a subtle craftsman on that plane. He was one of the lost, the truly lost; his flight established the classic itinerary, including that final ironic genuflection on the bright tan prayer rug of the Riviera.

If we reflect that Fitzgerald, while writing *Gatsby*, might have been one of the playboys in *The Sun Also Rises*—one of them, not merely with them, observing—his achievement is almost miraculous. The special charm of *Gatsby*, its durable charm, is that of recollection in tranquillity. The enchantment itself seems to come from the distance the narrator stands from the experience. The book has a serene, almost elegiac air; there is nothing frenetic or feverish about it, and the fires of spring, no longer burning, have filled the air with the scent of leaf smoke. The dark fields of the republic are bathed in a moonlit, nostalgic haze.

Fitzgerald was not yet thirty, but he was aware how well he had written. But the *meaning* of the book, its haunting tonal range, opening out into the past and portending the future, went considerably beyond both intentions and performance, into prophecy. This lucid moment of balance, when he was both fully engaged with living, yet aesthetically detached, may account for the higher level of performance than he achieved in *Tender Is the Night*. The later book is wiser, consciously wiser; the sun that had been rising is now setting, and Dick Diver is plainly stigmatized with the author's sense of his own predicament. But both books, however different in conception, close in such a manner that they blend together. The final scenes have a fugue-like harmony—an invocation in the one, a requiem in the other, to the brooding fertile

---

[2] In the original, the first sentence of this passage reads: "And just as the laughing stoicism which has enabled the American negro to endure the intolerable conditions of his existence has cost him his sense of the truth—so in my case there is a price to pay." [A.M.]

god of nostalgia, dearer than life *in* life, and, at the moment of parting, sweeter than death.

Where else, we might ask, in the literature of the world has the landscape of nostalgia, created by the author, served as the refuge for both the author and his characters? Dick Diver, having had his enchantment, having listened to the dream that pandered in whispers, and having been compelled to an aesthetic contemplation he has finally come to understand, returns to the dream of West Egg, knowing the green light will be missing from Daisy's dock, knowing that the future now stands behind him, with its tail in its mouth.

So he drifts from Buffalo to Batavia, from Geneva, New York, to Hornell, where that dream of a girl, Nicole, finally lost track of him. But Fitzgerald was too honest, now, to kill him off, or to let him die. He also knew too much to let the reader see him alive. So he deposited him in that limbo where there is neither a past nor a future, the world of nostalgia where he was an aimless drifter himself. Up ahead, but not too far ahead now, faint but persistent as the music from Gatsby's parties, the blinking marsh lights of *The Crack-Up* were all that shimmered in the dark fields of the republic.

> My own happiness in the past often approached such an ecstacy that I could not share it even with the person dearest to me but had to walk it away in quiet streets and lanes with only fragments of it to distill into little lines in books. . . .

What sort of happiness was this? *Un*qualified happiness, of course. The kind Gatsby had the moment he kissed Daisy, seeing, at the same moment, out of the corner of his eye that the blocks in the sidewalk seemed to form a ladder to the stars. At that moment the incomparable milk of wonder overflowed his cup of happiness, and Fitzgerald was able to distill it into more than a few little lines. In *Gatsby* this gift of hope is made flesh, and the promise is still one that Americans live by.

But the quiet streets and lanes of nostalgia soon turn upon themselves, a labyrinth without an exit, both a public madness and a private ecstacy. The strings of reminiscence tangle on themselves, they spin a choking web around the hero, and he must either surrender himself, without a struggle, or risk cracking up. Fitzgerald ran the risk. He did not, with Wolfe's adolescent bellow, try to empty the house of its ghosts by shouting, nor did he, like Faulkner, generate his escape with an impotent rage. He simply faced it. But he faced it too late. Having dispensed with his resources, he cracked up. The artist in him, as self-aware as Henry James, went on plying its hand, sharpening all the old pencils, but the man within him had died of nostalgia. The sign of *Cave Canem* that hung above his door meant exactly what it said.

Fitzgerald: The Horror
and the Vision of Paradise

by John Aldridge

"Amory saw girls doing things that even in his memory would have been impossible:" wrote the young Fitzgerald in *This Side of Paradise,* "eating three o'clock after-dance suppers in impossible cafés, talking of every side of life with an air half of earnestness, half of mockery, yet with a furtive excitement that Amory considered stood for a real moral let-down. But he never realized how widespread it was until he saw the cities between New York and Chicago as one vast juvenile intrigue." [1]

It was an oddly innocent intrigue that Amory-Fitzgerald reported. The girls almost always lost their curiosity after the first kiss. "I've kissed dozens of men," said one typically. "I suppose I'll kiss dozens more." The young men, even with the advantages of "sunk-down" sofas and innumerable cocktails, were usually content with shy claspings and sentimental poetry. It was an intrigue of manners merely, conducted by glittering children who could hardly bear to be touched; and it was the creation of a young man's innocence at a time when all things seemed larger than life and purer than a childhood dream.

This was the surface of Fitzgerald's world. Beneath it, almost undetectable even to Fitzgerald himself, was something else, something that the dawn light of eternal morning failed to penetrate and that stood between Amory Blaine, the enchanted voyager in Paradise, and the full possession of his enchantment. At Myra St. Claire's bobbing party he and Myra had slipped away from the others and gone to the "little den" upstairs at the country club. There they had kissed, "their lips brush[ing] like young wild flowers in the wind." But "sudden revulsion seized Amory, disgust, loathing for the whole incident," and he "desired franti-

"Fitzgerald: The Horror and Vision of Paradise." From *After the Lost Generation* (New York: McGraw-Hill Book Co., Inc., 1951) by John W. Aldridge. Copyright © 1951 by John W. Aldridge. Reprinted by permission of the author and McGraw-Hill Book Co., Inc.
[1] From *This Side of Paradise* by F. Scott Fitzgerald, published and copyright, 1920, Charles Scribner's Sons, New York. Fitzgerald wrote, ". . . that even in his memory would have been impossible: eating three-o'clock, after-dance suppers. . . ." [A.M.]

cally to be away." Later at college he had gone with a classmate and two girls on a Broadway holiday. Toward the end of the evening when they arrived at the girls' apartment, he was repelled by the laughter, the liquor, and his partner's "side-long suggestive smile," and for a terrifying moment he saw a deathlike figure sitting opposite him on the divan. Still later, when he, a friend, and a girl were caught in a hotel room by house detectives, Amory saw above the figure of the girl sobbing on the bed "an aura, gossamer as a moonbeam, tainted as stale, weak wine, yet a horror, diffusely brooding . . . and over by the window among the stirring curtains stood something else, featureless and indistinguishable, yet strangely familiar. . . ."

Fitzgerald tells us that for Amory "the problem of evil . . . had solidified into the problem of sex." [2] There are, to be sure, obvious sexual overtones to these visions, overtones that indicate a disturbing preoccupation with sexual guilt in Fitzgerald. But they indicate as well even deeper disturbances in Paradise itself; in fact, they are the same horrors which came to the older Fitzgerald in the night as he lay awake with insomnia, and they bring with them the same conviction of failure which prefigured his tragic "crack-up" and death. Indeed, they are horrors that touch at the core of Fitzgerald's work and are implicit in his vision, his "tragic sense," of the life of his time. For the beautiful there is always damnation; for every tenderness there is always the black horror of night; for all the bright young men there is sadness; and even Paradise has another side.

It is both an innocent and a haunted Paradise that Fitzgerald reveals in his first book; but it is not a perfect revelation of either. Amory's "enormous terrified revulsion" is an as-yet-uncentralized emotion. Amory is made to feel his horror, but at no time is it projected into the terms of the narrative. Perhaps it was a thing which Fitzgerald found inexpressible, which he could not understand in himself and could not, therefore, portray. But it is clear that in the very middle of his enchantment he was performing an act of exorcism, as if to free himself of ghosts that were even then speaking to him of the tragedy that was to be his and his time's.

The distance between Amory Blaine and Anthony Patch of *The Beautiful and Damned* is marked by Fitzgerald's growing comprehension of his theme and an increase in his power to detach from the personal and make dramatic the issues which were only imperfectly realized in the earlier novel. But more than anything else the novel is a record of Fitzgerald's emerging disenchantment with the Paradise ideal, a disenchantment which is paced so precisely by Anthony's drift toward ruin that it is almost as if Fitzgerald had been able to assert it finally only after Anthony had discovered it for him.

---

[2] Mr. Aldridge has misplaced the ellipsis in this quotation; it should read, "the problem of evil had solidified . . . into the problem of sex." [A.M.]

Through the entire first third of the book Anthony is merely a slightly older version of Amory. There are even signs that he might have come to nothing more than Amory's rather pompous realization of himself, the suffering, betrayed, but somehow purer young man who, at the end of *This Side of Paradise,* went forth to meet the world crying, "I know myself, but that is all." There is the difference, however, that where wealth for Amory was the gateway to the Paradise of his fancy, wealth for Anthony is a means of escaping the horror of life and of cheating the business system out of his soul. All of Anthony's sensibilities rebel at the thought that he might someday have to give up his notion of the utter futility of all endeavor and go to work. As long as he has wealth he can "divert himself" with pleasure, settle himself in that comfortable routine in which "one goes once a week to one's broker and twice to one's tailor," and hold himself aloof from that "air of struggle, of greedy ambition, of hope more sordid than despair, of incessant passage up and down, which . . . is most in evidence through the unstable middle class." [3] There is the further and very important difference that where Amory lost the girl he loved Anthony marries her.

Significantly, the disaster which overtakes this marriage is never actually centered in the marriage itself. Fitzgerald's acute "environmental sense" has by now become attuned to the destructive impulses of his time, with the result that the internal currents that sweep Anthony and Gloria along to greater and greater dissension are persistently less important than the disruptive circumstances which surround them. The spiritual breakdown, for example, which is represented in the wild parties, the furious drinking and spending of their class, counterpoints their failure to find in each other more enduring resources; but it is doubtful if without the attraction of the parties, the drinking, and the spending, they would have been quite so demoralized or so quickly damned. The horror is now on the exterior. It is a sense, vague and diffusive, of prevalent disaster; but the forms it takes, while indirectly the result of the increasing tensions within the marriage, stem from those other circumstances of which the marriage is merely an accident.

The summer house which Anthony and Gloria lease shortly after they are married becomes intolerable because of the poisonous associations that accumulate inside it. "Ah, my beautiful young lady," it seems to say to Gloria, "yours is not the first daintiness and delicacy that has faded here under the summer suns. . . . Youth has come into this room in palest blue and left it in the grey cerements of despair. . . ." But despair is still only "a somber pall, pervasive through the lower rooms, gradually . . . climbing up the narrow stairs. . . ." The nightmare episode during the party when Gloria runs insanely through the darkness to escape a fear that is only partially identified with Joe Hull is an-

---

[3] From *The Beautiful and Damned* by F. Scott Fitzgerald, published and copyright, 1924, Charles Scribner's Sons, New York.

other manifestation of that nameless dread which has come to reside at the Patches'. But Maury Noble, who discourses that same night on the meaninglessness of life and the nonexistence of God, is as much to blame. And what can be said of the songs—

> I left my blushing bride
> She went and shook herself insane
> So let her shiver back again

and

> The panic has come over us
> So ha-a-s the moral decline[4]

—which rise above these phantasms like the chorus of death itself? The crumbling structure is not only a marriage. It is Fitzgerald's vision of Paradise as well, going down in the dissolution of an age.

With the destruction of this ideal Fitzgerald's Jazz Age romance comes to an end. He might well say now with Anthony who, having won his inheritance at the price of his sanity and youth, boards a ship for Italy —"I showed them. It was a hard fight, but I didn't give up and I came through!" There is deep significance for Fitzgerald in this embarkation, this new pursuit of his vision into another world. It is part of the recurrent cycle of his generation; and it is the direction of his own final development. But to Fitzgerald in his passage from golden illusion to the bitterness of loss to ultimate exile and return there is one more step to take—and he takes it in his story of Jay Gatsby and the failure of the American Dream.

The Great Gatsby is by all odds Fitzgerald's most perfect novel. The gain in dramatic power which began to be evident in *The Beautiful and Damned* is climaxed now in a moment of insight in which self-understanding strikes and discovers its revelation in art. All the channels of Fitzgerald's sensibility seem to have anticipated their end in Gatsby; and all the dissident shapes that obstructed the progress of his search seem to find their apotheosis in Gatsby's romantic dream.

This dream of a past recapturable, of a youth and a love ceaselessly renewed, contrasts oddly with the milieu in which it is placed; yet it is obviously Fitzgerald's intended irony that a man like Gatsby should carry the burden of his own earlier enchantment at the same time that Gatsby's fate should emphasize its futility. It is because his dream is unworthy of him that Gatsby is a pathetic figure; and it is because Fitzgerald himself dreamed that same dream that he cannot make Gatsby tragic. Gatsby has all Fitzgerald's sympathy and all Fitzgerald's mistrust.

---

[4] Mr. Aldridge has slightly misquoted these songs; see *The Beautiful and Damned*, pp. 435 and 238. [A.M.]

He is thus Fitzgerald's most potent assertion of Paradise at the same time that he is his most emphatic farewell to it.

The events leading up to the opening of the novel resemble Fitzgerald's typical Jazz Age story. Gatsby, the simple, Midwestern youth, falls in love with Daisy, the beautiful rich girl. There is the brief, wholly idyllic affair which is abruptly terminated by the war. There is Daisy's quiet and conventional marriage to Tom Buchanan and Gatsby's return to the memory of a love which, as it has fed on itself, has reached obsessive proportions and become more real than any obstacle time or circumstance can put in its way. There are the years of struggle during which Gatsby painfully constructs the personality and the fortune which will make him deserving of Daisy; and there is the final achievement—the magnificent house in West Egg looking across the bay to the green light at the end of the Buchanan's dock. It is at this point that Gatsby is introduced; and it is immediately afterward that the flaws in his calculations become clear.

Gatsby's plan depends for its success upon Daisy's discontent with her marriage and her willingness to exchange it for a life of love. But Daisy's discontent, like her sophistication, is a pose, something picked up from "the most advanced people," part of the sham and deception of her world. "The instant her voice broke off, ceasing to compel my attention, my belief, I felt the basic insincerity of what she had said," Nick Carraway tells us. "I waited, and sure enough, in a moment she looked at me with an absolute smirk on her lovely face, as if she had asserted her membership in a rather distinguished secret society to which she and Tom belonged." [5] Daisy was born into that society, and she has been corrupted by it. That fact, so early revealed to us but unknown to Gatsby, sets the key for the principal irony of the novel.

Gatsby's story is, in a sense, Fitzgerald's parody of the Great American Success Dream. Gatsby, surrounded by the tinsel splendor of his parties, dressed in his absurd pink suits, protected from social ostracism by the fabulous legend he has constructed around himself, is still the naïvely ambitious boy who wrote in that schedule of childhood the formula of success—"Rise from bed. . . . Study electricity. . . . Work. . . . Practice elocution, poise and how to attain it. . . . Study needed inventions." The purchase of love and happiness is part of that formula; and if Gatsby had not been destroyed by a corruption greater than his own, it is probable that he would have arranged that too. But it was his misfortune to have believed too strenuously and loved too blindly. "Gatsby believed in the green light, the orgiastic future that year by year recedes before us. It eluded us then, but that's no matter—tomorrow we will run faster, stretch out our arms farther. . . . And one fine morn-

---

[5] From *The Great Gatsby* by F. Scott Fitzgerald, published and copyright, 1925, Charles Scribner's Sons, New York. Mr. Aldridge has omitted a sentence from the middle of this quotation. [A.M.]

ing— So we beat on, boats against the current, borne back ceaselessly into the past."

Scott Fitzgerald also believed in the "green light." He believed in the Buchanans, and he believed in Gatsby; and it was inevitable that he should end by disavowing both. If *The Beautiful and Damned* saw the emergence of his disenchantment with Paradise, *The Great Gatsby* was the final projection in art of that disenchantment and the beginning of a new phase in his career. The man who wrote *Tender Is the Night* almost nine years later had left even disenchantment behind. There was no dream now. There was only horror and sickness. The destructive element had at last completely broken through the privacy of the haunted mind and become part of the larger spectacle of an entire age short-circuiting itself to ruin.

"It occurred to me," remarked Nick Carraway in *The Great Gatsby,* "that there was no difference between men, in intelligence or race, so profound as the difference between the sick and the well." In the years between that novel and *Tender Is the Night* Fitzgerald had ample opportunity to test the truth of this observation; for they were years of ebbing vitality and doubt for him as well as for his time. The interval was marked by Fitzgerald's growing identification of himself with the life around him, by a greater and greater immersion in its sickness, and a progressive failure of self-control. The "age of excess" had told on him from the start; a process of "over-extension of the flank," of "burning the candle at both ends," [6] had begun as far back as Princeton, when he had been invalided out in his junior year, and had continued through the writing of his early books. There was always a hint of fever glow, of deep and excessive withdrawals at the bank of talent, about Fitzgerald's work. *Gatsby* may be said to have been a temporary recovery. But *Gatsby* was written during that fragile moment when the drive of youth meets with the intuitive wisdom of first maturity and before either the diseases of youth or the waverings of age begin to show through. Besides, *Gatsby* was the kind of book that had to be written; and perhaps the energy that went into the writing of it came to some extent from the book itself. But something in Fitzgerald died with Gatsby; when Gatsby's world fell to pieces and its glitter slowly dissolved, Fitzgerald was left with the pieces and the afterglow. He lived on in the afterglow; but it was by now a glow of sickness; and the pieces, when he fitted them back together, proved to be good only for a world as sick and bankrupt as he.

Tender Is the Night, then, is what Fitzgerald himself called "the novel of deterioration." It is written with a neurotic subtlety, crammed with tortured images and involuted patterns. It is like something out of a mental patient's diary and, by turns, like the clinical report of a

---

[6] ". . . an over-extension of the flank, a burning of the candle at both ends," *The Crack-Up,* p. 77. [A.M.]

patient who is doubling as his own psychoanalyst. The patterns of the earlier novels have now been broken down, rearranged, and absorbed into a new narrative form. Again the effect is a psychiatric formula—the mind unconsciously concealing the true object of its horror through a projection upon other objects which may or may not have originally pertained to that horror. But Fitzgerald fails to complete the process. Gloria Gilbert and Daisy Buchanan have become Rosemary Hoyt with her "virginal emotions" and her peculiarly American immaturity; but they have also become Nicole Diver, the enchanting and half-demented Jazz Daughter of Fitzgerald's new dissolute Paradise. Amory Blaine, Anthony Patch, and Tom Buchanan are all to be found in Dick Diver, but so too is Jay Gatsby. On all sides of these principals Fitzgerald has scattered the evidence of the general decay which he set out to depict. There is Nicole's incestuous relationship with her father; the corruption of the English Campions and Lady Carolines; the anarchism of Tommy Barban, who must be perpetually at war; the exhibitionism of Yale Man Collis Clay; the literary degeneracy of Albert McKisco; the self-indulgence of Abe North, whose moral suicide anticipates Dick Diver's own. But these forces, while satisfactorily realized in themselves, are not drawn together in the main situation of the novel, which is the story of the Divers.

Rosemary Hoyt takes over the "infatuation" element from the long line of deluded Fitzgerald males. She is delighted and fascinated by the Divers; their "special gentleness" and "far-reaching delicacy," the effortless command of the richness of life, seem to Rosemary to contain a purpose "different from any she had known." [7] They exert over her the kind of magic Thomas Wolfe glorified in the people "who have the quality of richness and joy in them . . . and communicate it to everything they touch." But Rosemary cannot penetrate the secret horror—that revolting scene which Violet McKisco came upon in the bathroom that night at the party—which is at the core of the Divers' relationship, nor can she know the price Dick has had to pay for his "amusing world" and his "power of arousing a fascinated and uncritical love." Rosemary is perhaps too hypnotized to care; her principal emotion is one of relief at having escaped through the Divers "the derisive and salacious improvisations of the frontier."

Yet Rosemary has come to Fitzgerald's last frontier, to the Divers who are "the last of their line" and whose ancestral curse it is to drift steadily but unaware toward ruin. Fitzgerald's familiar contrast between outward splendor and inner disintegration is particularly apt now to point up the Divers' underlying ambivalence: the glamour which is the thinnest

---

[7] What Fitzgerald actually wrote was, ". . . different from the rough and ready good fellowship of directors, who represented the intellectuals in her life. Actors and directors—those were the only men she had ever known. . . ." *Tender Is the Night*, p. 24. [A.M.]

sugar-coating of evil, the surface glitter which is the reflection of an incurable sickness of heart. Dick, the generous giver of his strength, first to the neurotic Nicole, then to all who demand it, is the shell of an illusion, the "exact furthermost evolution" of Fitzgerald's dream of the rich and the caricature of the emptiness he found at the center of that dream. At one time in his life Dick was faced with a choice between "the necessary human values," which he had learned from his father, and Nicole, whom he could not have without accepting her world of "charm, notoriety, and good manners." In the beginning, and in Dick's position as a doctor, Nicole was, as Arthur Mizener observed, a "professional situation"; it was his need to express his best impulses that made it a "human situation"; "wanting above all to be brave and kind, he . . . wanted, even more, to be loved." [8] So, as a doctor, he accepted the responsibility of Nicole's care, and, as a man, he accepted the responsibility of her love. And to her world and its increasing demands, to all the people who came to depend on him for all that they lacked in themselves, he gave his humanity. He was gay, charming, and polite. He gave until there was nothing left in him to give, until the impulses of his humanity were turned destructively upon himself and Nicole. Then, in a final act of will, realizing that Nicole's love for him was inseparable from her psychological dependence upon him, he broke that dependence and watched Nicole drift away from him forever. What he had failed to treat as a professional situation had been just that all along. The human situation had never existed outside himself.

This irony is deepened by the irony of the novel's setting. Europe, particularly the European Riviera, had been the last refuge of Fitzgerald's heroes. It was Amory Blaine's promise of the good life. It was Anthony Patch's escape from the vulgarity of the economic order. It was the hope of Paradise for Fitzgerald himself. But it was characteristic of Fitzgerald that he should find even this last oasis corrupt; and it was fitting that he should have Dick Diver renounce the scene of his corruption and return to America. Doctor Diver, uprooted and lost, seeking his sources through a succession of small, and progressively more obscure towns—Buffalo, Batavia, and Geneva, New York; and Scott Fitzgerald, turning his back on the East for the last time, facing west to Hollywood, the place of all our lost illusions.

The Last Tycoon is a brilliant fragment of the book Fitzgerald was writing when he died. Even with Edmund Wilson's scholarly interpretation of the notes that were left with the manuscript, we are given no more than an intimation of Fitzgerald's purpose; and even after we have read his synopsis and the opening chapters, we have always to bear in mind that both the plan and the writing would have been altered

---

[8] From *Tender Is the Night* by F. Scott Fitzgerald, published and copyright, 1934, Charles Scribner's Sons, New York. The end of this quotation should read, ". . . wanted, even more than that, to be loved." *Tender Is the Night*, p. 391. [A.M.]

considerably in the final version. Yet it is possible to visualize from
the material at hand the scope and promise of Fitzgerald's intention and
to weave *The Last Tycoon* at least partially into the context of the
earlier novels.

There is, first of all, the figure of the tycoon himself, Monroe Stahr.
Stahr, the last frontiersman, the embodiment of Fitzgerald's search for
values beyond all frontiers, has come to rest at last in Hollywood, where
the frontier has become a thing of cardboard and tinsel and the American Dream a corporation dedicated to the purveyance of dreams. In
Hollywood, Stahr's empire is as magnificent and powerful as the one
Gatsby envisioned; it is also as corrupt. But corruption has now become
an acceptable part of the social order. In fact, it is inevitable in a
nation "that for a decade had wanted only to be entertained." Yet,
because Stahr is wholly committed to his dream of power, he is, like
Gatsby, basically incorruptible.

To be incorruptible in Fitzgerald's world, however, is to be destroyed
by a larger corruptive force. Men like Gatsby and Stahr who subordinate
everything to their ambition have only one fear—the collapse of the system on which their ambition is based; and as the novel develops, it becomes clear that some such collapse is occurring around Stahr. As in
Tender Is the Night, the prophecy of doom is carried in the minor
figures who remain, for the most part, on the periphery of the action.
There is the ruined producer Manny Schwartz, whose suicide introduces the tragic theme in the opening section; Mr. Marcus, the industrial magnate who has lost his powers; the has-been actors and actresses,
all haunting the scene of their last triumphs; even Cecilia, who, in all
her innocence and youth, is somehow tainted. Then, too, there are the
debilitating effects on Stahr himself of the struggle which made him
a king—his fanatical disregard of his failing health, his morbid preoccupation with his dead wife, his almost deliberate "perversion of the
life force," as if he were consciously intent on death. Stahr, like the
Divers, is "the last of his line," and, like them, he embodies all the
strengths and weaknesses of a dynasty.

"Is *this* all?" asks Brimmer, the Communist organizer, as Stahr loses
his control. "This frail half-sick person holding up the whole thing?" [9]
And Fitzgerald himself might well have asked the same question; for
Stahr comes as a pathetic climax to his lifelong search for Paradise.
Looking back over the novels, however, we can see how the pattern of
this search resolves itself in Stahr; indeed, how there can be no other
possible resolution. Amory Blaine's infatuation with wealth set the key
for Anthony Patch's corruption by wealth. In Gatsby, Fitzgerald sounded
the futility of his dream only to reembrace the rich in Dick Diver and

[9] From *The Last Tycoon* by F. Scott Fitzgerald (edited by Edmund Wilson), published and copyright, 1941, Charles Scribner's Sons, New York. The second question
mark is Mr. Aldridge's. [A.M.]

discover the real futility of the spiritually bankrupt; and as Anthony, Gatsby, and Dick were destroyed, so Stahr prepares us for the final destruction, that ultimate collapse of self which comes after all dreams have died.

We can see too by what an inescapable process of disenchantment Fitzgerald arrived at Hollywood and his own crack-up. There have been his wanderings east from the "barbarian" St. Paul to the Princeton of *This Side of Paradise;* the New York parties of *The Beautiful and Damned;* the East Egg society of *The Great Gatsby;* and still east to the Paris and Riviera of *Tender Is the Night;* until Dick Diver's repatriation brings him abruptly back to the West once more. And as each place is left behind and the possibilities of place are diminished, the horrors accumulate until finally there is only enough will left for one last act of self-immolation—the return to the supreme lie of Monroe Stahr's world.

In completing the cycle of his life and art, Fitzgerald reproduced the design of an entire literary movement. But Fitzgerald was more than merely typical of that movement; he was its most sensitive and tormented talent and the prophet of its doom. With a sense of the destructive impulses of his time that can only be compared with Hemingway's, he yet lacked Hemingway's stabilizing gift—the ability to get rid of the bad times by writing of them. Fitzgerald never got rid of anything; the ghosts of his adolescence, the failures of his youth, the doubts of his maturity plagued him to the end. He was supremely a part of the world he described, so much a part that he made himself its king and then, when he saw it begin to crumble, he crumbled with it and led it to death.

But the thing that destroyed him also gave him his special distinction. His vision of Paradise served him as a medium of artistic understanding. Through it he penetrated to the heart of some of the great illusions of his time, discovering their falsity as if he were discovering his own. If that vision—like Hemingway's correlative of loss which it so much resembles—was limited, it was at least adequate to Fitzgerald's purpose; and it was a means of contact between his art and the experience of his time.

There is a certain quaintness about Fitzgerald's work today as there is about Hemingway's. But in Fitzgerald one has the sense of such a literal contemporaneity that it is almost impossible to read him without giving more attention to his time than to what he had to say about it. Mahjongg, crossword puzzles, Freud, bathtub gin, Warren G. Harding, and Fitzgerald are inextricably one; the time amounts to a consistent betrayal of the man. Yet the distance that separates his time from ours enables us to rediscover him in a fresh focus and to see in the important things he wrote that other dimension, always there, but obscured until now by the glitter of his surfaces. The emphasis now is on Fitzgerald's acutely penetrative side, his ability to manipulate the surfaces as if they were mirrors that reflect not only the contents of a room, the splendor of its occupants, but the concealed horrors of its essence—the ghosts hidden just behind the swaying arras, the disenchantment behind the bright masks of faces, the death to which everyone in the room has been spiritually mortgaged. The sense of impending catastrophe is never more deeply or terribly felt than when we are immersed, and seem almost destined to be drowned, in the welter of life with which Fitzgerald presents us: the end of the big party is always implicit in its beginning, the ugliness of age is always visible in the tender beauty of youth.

With this awareness, this assurance that Fitzgerald penetrated to the truth beneath his vision, it ceases to matter that his vision was, in many ways, frivolous and unbecoming or that, with all his insight, he often failed to perceive the implications of what he saw. What matters and will continue to matter is that we have before us the work of a man who gave us better than any one else the true substance of an age, the dazzle and fever and the ruin.

Fitzgerald's Brave New World

by Edwin Fussell

> Think of the lost ecstasy of the Elizabethans. "Oh my America, my
> new found land," think of what it meant to them and of what it
> means to us.
>
> (T. E. Hulme, *Speculations*)

I

The source of Fitzgerald's excellence is an uncanny ability to juxta-
pose the sensibilities implied by the phrase "romantic wonder" with
the most conspicuous, as well as the most deeply significant, phenomena
of American civilization, and to derive from that juxtaposition a moral
critique of human nature. None of our major writers is more romantically
empathic than this avatar of Keats in the era of Harding; none draws
a steadier bead on the characteristic shortcomings, not to say disasters,
of the most grandiose social experiment of modern times. Thence the
implacable moralist with stars (Martinis) in his eyes: worshipper, analyst,
judge, and poet. But it is not very illuminating to say that Fitzgerald
wrote the story of his own representative life, unless we are prepared to
read his confessions—and then his evaluation of those confessions—
as American history; and unless we reciprocally learn to read American
history as the tale of the romantic imagination in the United States.

Roughly speaking, Fitzgerald's basic plot is the history of the New
World (ironic *double entendre* here and throughout); more precisely,
of the human imagination in the New World. It shows itself in two
predominant patterns, quest and seduction. The quest is the search for
romantic wonder (a kind of febrile secular beatitude), in the terms pro-
posed by contemporary America; the seduction represents capitulation
to these terms. Obversely, the quest is a flight: from reality, from normality, from time, fate, death, and the conception of *limit*. In the social
realm, the pattern of desire may be suggested by such phrases as "the
American dream" and "the pursuit of happiness." Fitzgerald begins by

"Fitzgerald's Brave New World," by Edwin Fussell. From *ELH*, XIX (December
1952). Copyright © 1952 by Edwin Fussell. Reprinted by permission of the author and
The Johns Hopkins Press.

exposing the corruption of that dream in industrial America; he ends by discovering that the pursuit is universally seductive and perpetually damned. Driven by inner forces that compel him towards the personal realization of romantic wonder, the Fitzgerald hero is destroyed by the materials which the American experience offers as objects and criteria of passion; or, at best, he is purged of these unholy fires, chastened, and reduced.

In general, this quest has two symptomatic goals. There is, for one, the search for eternal youth and beauty, what might be called the historic myth of Ponce de Leon. ("Historic" because the man was really looking for a fountain; "myth" because no such fountain ever existed).[1] The essence of romantic wonder appears to reside in the illusion of perennial youth and grace and happiness surrounding the leisure class of which Fitzgerald customarily wrote; thus the man of imagination in America, searching for the source of satisfaction of his deepest aesthetic needs, is seduced by the delusion that these qualities are actually to be found in people who, in sober fact, are vacuous and irresponsible. But further, this kind of romantic quest, which implies both escape and destruction, is equated on the level of national ideology with a transcendental and Utopian contempt for time and history, and on the religious level, which Fitzgerald (whose Catholic apostasy was about half genuine and half imagined) persistently but hesitantly approaches, with a blasphemous rejection of the very conditions of human existence.

The second goal is, simply enough, money. The search for wealth is the familiar Anglo-Saxon Protestant ideal of personal material success, most succinctly embodied for our culture in the saga of young Benjamin Franklin. It is the romantic assumption of this aspect of the "American dream" that all the magic of the world can be had for money. Both from a moral, and from a highly personal and idiosyncratic Marxist standpoint, Fitzgerald examines and condemns the plutocratic ambitions of American life and the ruinous price exacted by their lure. But the two dreams are, of course, so intimately related as to be for all practical purposes one: the appearance of eternal youth and beauty centers in a particular social class whose glamor is made possible by social inequality and inequity. Beauty, the presumed object of aesthetic contemplation, is commercialized, love is bought and sold. Money is the means to the violent recovery or specious arrest of an enchanting youth.

In muted contrast, Fitzgerald repeatedly affirms his faith in an older, simpler America, generally identified as pre-Civil War; the emotion is

---

[1] It is a curious but far from meaningless coincidence that Frederick Jackson Turner used the image of "a magic fountain of youth" to evoke the creative and restorative powers of the unexhausted Western frontier. I am inclined to think Fitzgerald knew what he was about when he called *The Great Gatsby* "a story of the West." Traditionally in American writing "the West" means both the Western part of the United States and the New World, and especially the first as synecdoche of the other.

that of pastoral, the social connotations agrarian and democratic. In such areas he continues to find fragments of basic human value, social, moral, and religious. But these affirmations are for the most part subordinate and indirect; Fitzgerald's attention was chiefly directed upon the merchandise of romantic wonder proffered by his own time and place. Like the narrator in *Gatsby*, he was always "within and without, simultaneously enchanted and repelled by the inexhaustible variety of life." Through a delicate and exact imagery, he was able to extend this attitude of simultaneous enchantment and repulsion over the whole of the American civilization he knew. His keenest perception, and the one that told most heavily for his fiction, was the universal quality of the patterns he was tracing, his greatest discovery that there was nothing new about the Lost Generation except its particular toys. The quest for romantic wonder and the inevitable failure were only the latest in a long series.

Fitzgerald approached this major theme slowly and more by intuition than design. Or perhaps he had to live it, and then understand it, before he could write it. In a hazy form it is present in such early stories as "The Offshore Pirate" and "Dalyrimple Goes Wrong." It is allegorized in "The Diamond as Big as the Ritz" and fumbled in *The Beautiful and Damned*.

"May Day," significantly motivated by his first sharp awareness of class cleavages in American society, together with important cleavages of period in American history, is for the reader tracing Fitzgerald's gradual realization of this major theme the most rewarding production of his early career. Its formal construction on social principles ("Mr. In" and "Mr. Out") is obvious enough; what usually goes unnoticed is the way Fitzgerald's symbolic method extends his critique from the manners of drunken undergraduates to the pervasive malaise of an entire civilization. The hubris with which these characters fade from the story in a parody of the Ascension dramatically and comically pinpoints the materialistic hedonism, along with its traditional counterpart, a vulgar idealism, which Fitzgerald is already identifying as his culture's fatal flaw:

> Then they were in an elevator bound skyward.
> "What floor, please?" said the elevator man.
> "Any floor," said Mr. In.
> "Top floor," said Mr. Out.
> "This is the top floor," said the elevator man.
> "Have another floor put on," said Mr. Out.
> "Higher," said Mr. In.
> "Heaven," said Mr. Out.

Set against the story's controlling symbol, the universal significance of this passage frames its particular historical implications. The scene is an all-night restaurant, and the preliminary description emphasizes social and economic inequality, the brutalizations of poverty, the sick insouciance of unmerited riches. As a Yale junior is ejected for throwing hash at the waiters, "the great plate-glass front had turned to a deep creamy blue . . . Dawn had come up in Columbus Circle, magical, breathless dawn, silhouetting the great statue of the immortal Christopher [Christ-bearer], and mingling in a curious and uncanny manner with the fading yellow electric light inside." The final significance of this symbol can only be established after considering the conclusion of *The Great Gatsby* (and perhaps not even then; what, for example, about that oceanic "blue," or the failing efficacy of man-made illumination against the light of day, prior in time to the light it supersedes?). But the general intention is clear enough: Fitzgerald is measuring the behavior and attitudes of the Lost Generation with a symbol of romantic wonder extensive enough to comprehend all American experience, as far back as 1492. The contrast involves the ironic rejection of all that this present generation believes in, the immaturity and triviality of its lust for pleasure. But then, by a further turn of irony, the voyage of Columbus and his discovery of the Western Hemisphere is also the actual event forming the first link in the chain leading to the butt-end of contemporary folly. There is the further implication that some sort of conscious search is at the heart of American experience, but had never before taken so childish a form. What Fitzgerald is almost certainly trying to say with this image is: we are the end of Columbus' dream, and this is our brave new world.

II

With *The Great Gatsby* (1925), Fitzgerald first brought his vision to full and mature realization. Gatsby is essentially the man of imagination in America, given specificity and solidity and precision by the materials American society offers him. "If personality is an unbroken series of successful gestures, then there was something gorgeous about him, some heightened sensitivity to the promises of life, as if he were related to one of those intricate machines that register earthquakes ten thousand miles away." It is Gatsby's capacity for romantic wonder that Fitzgerald is insisting upon in this preliminary exposition, a capacity he goes on to define as "an extraordinary gift for hope, a romantic readiness" (the first phrase suggesting the central theological virtue, the second implying its parodic counterpart). With the simile of the seismograph, a splendid image of the human sensibility in a mechanized age, Fitzgerald has in effect already introduced the vast back-drop of American civilization against which Gatsby's gestures are to be interpreted. The image is as integral as intricate; for if Gatsby is to be taken as the product and manifestation of the seductive and corrupting motivations involved in "the American dream," he is also the instrument by means of which Fitzgerald will register the tremors that point to its self-contained possibilities of destruction, its *fault* (flaw), in the geological sense. "What preyed on Gatsby, what foul dust floated in the wake of his dreams" is the stuff of the novel, the social content of Fitzgerald's fictional world. But it is equally essential to realize that Gatsby, too, has been derailed by values and attitudes held in common with the society that destroys him. How else, indeed, might he be destroyed? Certainly, in such a world, the novel assures us, a dream like Gatsby's cannot possibly remain pristine, given the materials with which the original impulse toward wonder must invest itself. In short, Gatsby is somewhat more than pathetic, a sad figure preyed upon by the American leisure class. The novel is neither melodramatic nor bathetic, but critical. The unreal values of the world of Tom and Daisy Buchanan, to a very considerable degree, are Gatsby's values too, inherent in his dream. Gatsby from the beginning lives in an imaginary world, where "a universe of ineffable gaudiness spun itself out in his brain"; negatively, this quality manifests itself in a dangerous, and frequently vulgar, tendency toward sentimental idealizations: his reveries "were a satisfactory hint of the unreality of reality, a promise that the rock of the world was founded securely on a fairy's wing." (A variety of religious overtones emanates from the word "rock.") Gatsby's capacity for wonder is obviously corrupted by the meager and vicious nature of American culture. Potentially, he constitutes a tentative and limited indictment of that culture; actually, he is that culture's thoroughly appropriate scapegoat and victim. "He was a son of God . . . and he must be about His Father's business, the service of a vast, vulgar, and meretricious beauty." God the Father, or the Founding Fathers? In such ambiguity lurk the novel's deepest ironies.

Daisy finally becomes for Gatsby the iconic manifestation of this dubious vision of beauty. Little enough might have been possible for Gatsby at best, but once he "wed his unutterable visions to her perishable breath, his mind would never romp again like the mind of God." (Parody of the Incarnation.) Steadily and surreptitiously, Fitzgerald continues to suggest the idea of blasphemy in connection with Gatsby's Titanic imaginative lusts. But of course the focus of the novel must be sexual and social, for the implication *of* the religious implication is that Gatsby (that is to say American culture) provides mainly secular objects for the religious imagination to feed on, as it also provides tawdry images for the aesthetic imagination. After concentrating Gatsby's wonder on Daisy, Fitzgerald proceeds to an explicit statement of her thematic significance. Gatsby was "overwhelmingly aware of the *youth* and mystery that *wealth* imprisons and *preserves,* of the freshness of many clothes, and of Daisy, gleaming like silver, safe and proud above the hot struggles of the poor" (my italics). Her voice is mysteriously enchanting, the typifying feature of her role as *la belle dame sans merci,* and throughout the action serves to suggest her loveliness and desirability. But only Gatsby, in a rare moment of insight, is able to identify the causes of its subtle and elusive magic, upon which Nick Carraway meditates: "It was full of money—that was the inexhaustible charm that rose and fell in it, the jingle of it, the cymbals' song of it . . . High in a white palace the king's daughter, the golden girl . . ."

Possession of an image like Daisy is all that Gatsby can finally conceive as "success"; and Gatsby is meant to be a very representative American in the intensity of his yearning for success, as well as in the symbols which he equates with it. Gatsby is a contemporary variation on an old American pattern, the rags-to-riches story exalted by American legend as early as Crèvecoeur's *Letters from an American Farmer* (most mawkishly in the "History of Andrew, the Hebridian," significantly appended to the famous Letter III, "What is an American"), and primarily fixed in the popular mind by Benjamin Franklin. Franklin's youthful resolutions are parodied in those that the adolescent Gatsby writes on the back flyleaf of his copy of *Hopalong Cassidy,* a conjunction of documents as eloquently expressive of American continuities as of the progress of civilization in the new world.

The connection between Gatsby's individual tragedy and the tragedy of American civilization is also made, and again through symbol, with respect to historical attitudes. Gatsby's philosophy of history is summed up in his devotion to the green light burning on Daisy's dock. Nick first sees Gatsby in an attitude of supplication, a gesture that pathetically travesties the traditional gestures of worship. He finally discerns that the object of that trembling piety is precisely this green light which, until his disillusion, remains one of Gatsby's "enchanted objects." But only in the novel's concluding passage, toward which all action and symbol relentlessly tend, is the reader given the full implications of the green light as the historically-corrupted religious symbol ("Gatsby believed in the green light, the orgiastic future"). With no historical sense whatever, yet trapped in the detritus of American history, Gatsby is the superbly effective fictional counterpart of that native philistine maxim that "history is bunk." For those interested in such comparisons, he may also recall the more crowing moods of Emerson and Thoreau and the alleged "timelessness" of their idealistic visions and exhortations, now, alas, like Daisy who gleamed like silver, somewhat tarnished. For Fitzgerald, this contemptuous repudiation of tradition, historical necessity, and moral accountability, was deluded and hubristic. When he finally came to see —as he clearly did in *Gatsby*—that in this irresponsibility lay the real meaning behind the obsessive youth-worship of popular culture in his own day, he was able to identify Gatsby as at once the man of his age and the man of the ages, a miserable twentieth-century Ponce de Leon. His fictional world was no longer simply the Jazz Age, the Lost Generation, but the whole of American civilization as it culminated in his own time.

In the final symbol of the novel, Fitzgerald pushes the personal equation to national, even universal scope, in a way that recalls the method of "May Day." Fitzgerald is commenting on Gatsby's state of disillusion immediately before his death:

> He must have felt that he had lost the old warm world, paid a high price for living too long with a single dream. He must have looked up at an unfamiliar sky through frightening leaves and shivered as he found what a grotesque thing a rose is and how raw the sunlight was upon the scarcely created grass. A new world, material without being real, where poor ghosts, breathing dreams like air, drifted fortuitously about . . .

Such was the romantic perception of wonder, when finally stripped of its pleasing and falsifying illusions. Such was Fitzgerald's maturest vision of the United States of America, perhaps the most magnificent statement in all our literature of the cruel modernity of the "new world," its coldness, unreality, and absurdity nourished (if one may use so inappropriate a word) by that great mass neurosis known as "the American Dream." So Fitzgerald, the quintessential outsider-insider, moves to his final critique:

> And as the moon rose higher the inessential houses began to melt away until gradually I became aware of the old island here that flowered once for Dutch sailors' eyes—a fresh, green breast of the new world. Its vanished trees, the trees that had made way for Gatsby's house, had once pandered in whispers to the last and greatest of all human dreams; for a transitory enchanted moment man must have held his breath in the presence of this continent, compelled into an aesthetic contemplation he neither understood nor desired, face to face for the last time in history with something commensurate to his capacity for wonder.

The most obvious point to be made about this passage is its insistence that Gatsby's insatiable capacity for wonder could have, in the modern world, no proper objective. The emotion lingered on, generations of Americans had translated it into one or another set of inadequate terms, but Gatsby, like all his ancestors, though increasingly, was doomed by demanding the impossible. There is also the ironic contrast between the wonder of the New World (to its Old World discoverers) and what Americans (who all came from the Old World in the first place) have made of it; the same point Fitzgerald made in similar fashion with the Columbus image in "May Day." Finally, there is a more universal, an extrahistorical meaning implicit in the language of this passage—the hope that the new world could possibly satisfy man's inordinate, secular lusts (displaced religious emotions from the very outset) was "the last and greatest of all human dreams," seductive and unreal. The most impressive associations cluster around the word "pander," which implies the illicit commercial traffic among love, youth, and beauty, and which thus effectually subsumes most of the central meanings of the novel. In a later essay, Fitzgerald repeated with variations the "panders in whispers" phrase: New York City "no longer whispers of fantastic success and eternal youth," a fine instance of how the myths of Benjamin Franklin and Ponce de Leon came to be blended in his mind. The two parallel themes do, of course, meet in *The Great Gatsby;* indeed, they are tangled at the heart of the plot, for the most outrageous irony in Gatsby's tragedy is his belief that he can buy his dream, which is, precisely, to recapture the past. Unfortunately for this all too representative American, his dream "was already behind him, somewhere back in that vast obscurity beyond the city, where the dark fields of the republic rolled on under the night." It hardly needs saying that Fitzgerald chooses his language carefully, and that every word is loaded.

III

Tender Is the Night (1934) restates the essential theme and complicates it. If this novel seems somehow less successful than *Gatsby,* that is perhaps because the greater proliferation of thematic statement is not matched by a corresponding gain in clarity and control. But beneath the additional richness, and apparent confusion, the same general story can be made out. Dick Diver is like Gatsby the American as man of imagination. His chief difference from Gatsby is that he dispenses romantic wonder to others, in addition to living by and for it himself. Gatsby tries to purvey dreams, but doesn't know how. But to Rosemary Hoyt (of whom, more later) Dick's "voice promised that he would . . . open up whole *new worlds* for her, unroll an endless succession of magnificent possibilities" (my italics). Diver is the man with the innate capacity for romantic wonder, temporarily a member of the American leisure class of the 'twenties, an "organizer of private gaiety, curator of richly incrusted happiness." His intellectual and imaginative energies have been diverted from normal creative and functional channels and expended on the effort to prevent, for a handful of the very rich, the American dream from revealing its nightmarish realities.

Although Dick is given a more specific background than Gatsby, he is equally a product of his civilization and shares its characteristic deficiencies: "the illusions of eternal strength and health, and of the essential goodness of people; illusions of a nation, the lies of generations of frontier mothers who had to croon falsely that there were no wolves outside the cabin door." (The lies also of generations of American politicians, historians, publicists, fireside poets, and similar confidence-men, who had no such easy excuse.) This inherent romantic has been further weakened, though not quite destroyed, by the particular forms of sentimentality of his own generation: "he must press toward the Isles of Greece, the cloudy waters of unfamiliar ports, the lost girl on shore, the moon of popular songs. A part of Dick's mind was made up of the tawdry souvenirs of his boyhood. Yet in that somewhat littered Five-and-Ten, he had managed to keep alive the low painful fire of intelligence."

Such is the man, potentially noble like Gatsby, but with the fatal flaw of imagination common to and conditioned by the superficial symbols and motivations of his culture, who is brought against the conditions of temptation represented by Nicole. She is the granddaughter of a "self-made American capitalist" and of a German Count, and her family is placed in perspective by Fitzgerald's frequent analogies with feudal aristocracy. "Her father would have it on almost any clergyman," such as Dick's father; "they were an American ducal family without a title—the very name . . . caused a psychological metamorphosis in people." Yet behind this facade of glamor and power lies unnatural lust and perversion. Nicole's father, this "fine American type," has committed incest with his daughter—the very incarnation of the American vision of youth, beauty, and wealth—and made of her a psychotic for young Dr. Diver to cure. As Nicole says, " 'I'm a crook by heritage.' "

Through Nicole Fitzgerald conveys, as he had with Daisy, all that is sexually and socially desirable in youth and beauty: "there were all the potentialities for romantic love in that lovely body and in the delicate mouth. . . . Nicole had been a beauty as a young girl and she would be a beauty later." Apparently she is eternally youthful, and only at the end of the novel is it discernible that she has aged. Her face, which corresponds in sensuous utility to Daisy's voice, is lovely and hard, "her eyes brave and watchful, looking straight ahead toward nothing." She is an empty child, representative of her social class, of the manners and morals of the 'twenties, and of the world of values for which America, like Diver, was once more selling its soul. But it is chiefly Nicole's semblance of perpetual youth that allows Fitzgerald to exploit her as a central element in the narrative correlative he is constructing for his vision of American life. Occasionally he handles her in a way that goes beyond social criticism, entering, if obliquely and implicitly, the realm of religious apprehension:

> The only physical disparity between Nicole at present and the Nicole of five years before was simply that she was no longer a young girl. But she was enough ridden by the current youth worship, the moving pictures with their myriad faces of girl-children, blandly represented as carrying on the work and wisdom of the world, to feel a jealousy of youth.
>
> She put on the first ankle-length day dress that she had owned for many years, and crossed herself reverently with Chanel Sixteen.

(So Diver, at the end of the novel, but with full consciousness of the blasphemy, "blesses" the Riviera beach "with a papal cross," immediately before returning to the obscurity of small-town America. The malediction may by a later generation of readers be taken as Fitzgerald's also, whose equally obscure end was ironically to come in the most notorious of American small towns, Hollywood.) But while Fitzgerald could upon occasion thus extend the significance of his narrative, he never neglected to keep it firmly grounded in a specific social and economic world, and it is in this realm that most of his correspondences are established:

> Nicole was the product of much ingenuity and toil. For her sake trains began their run at Chicago and traversed the round belly of the continent to California; chicle factories fumed and link belts grew link by link in factories; men mixed toothpaste in vats and drew mouthwash out of copper hogsheads; girls canned tomatoes quickly in August or worked rudely at the Five-and-Tens on Christmas Eve; half-breed Indians toiled on Brazilian coffee plantations and dreamers were muscled out of patent rights in new tractors—these were some of the people who gave a tithe to Nicole, and as the whole system swayed and thundered onward it lent a feverish bloom to such processes of hers as wholesale buying, like the flush of a fireman's face holding his post before a spreading blaze. She illustrated very simple principles, containing in herself her own doom, but illustrated them so accurately that there was grace in the procedure.[2]

Yet even here religious nuance continues ("Christmas Eve," "tithe"); the simple principles Nicole illustrates are not only Marxian but also Christian. Still, if her principles are simple, their illustration is epic in scope and intention. The social ramifications of Fitzgerald's great novels are broad indeed; at their base are criminal injustice and inhuman waste, on a world-wide scale, and at their apex the American girl, the king's daughter, beautiful, forever young, and insane.

In the central scenes of temptation (Book 11, chapter v, in the original form), Fitzgerald quite deliberately allows Nicole to assume her full symbolic significance, thereby revealing unmistakably that the central action of *Tender Is the Night* must be read against the broadest background of American life. Throughout this chapter runs the *leitmotif* of the author's generalizing commentary, beginning with the passage: "the impression of her youth and beauty grew on Dick until it welled up inside him in a compact paroxysm of emotion. She smiled, a moving childish smile that was like all the lost youth in the world." This mood of pathetic nostalgia is quickly objectified in the talk of Dick and Nicole about American popular songs; soon Dick feels that "there was that excitement about her that seemed to reflect all the excitement of the

---

[2] Cf. Gatsby as seismograph. Probably it is dangerous to take too literally Fitzgerald's remark that he was "essentially Marxian"; it seems to me equally dangerous to ignore it altogether.

world." So ends the first of the two scenes that comprise this chapter. The second meeting opens on a similar key: "Dick wished she had no background, that she was just a girl lost with no address save the night from which they had come." This time they play the songs they had mentioned the week before: "they were in America now." And Fitzgerald drives the point home in his last sentence: "Now there was this scarcely saved waif of disaster bringing him the essence of a continent . . ."[3]

At first Dick laughs off the notion that Nicole's family has purchased him, but he gradually succumbs, "inundated by a trickling of goods and money." Once again, Nicole is the typifying object of her class and society, especially in the terms she proposes for the destruction of her victim's moral and intellectual integrity: "Naturally Nicole, *wanting to own him, wanting him to stand still forever*, encouraged any slackness on his part" (my italics). Although the pattern is more complex than in *Gatsby*, practically the same controlling lines of theme can be observed. The man of imagination, fed on the emotions of romantic wonder, is tempted and seduced and (in this case, nearly) destroyed by that American dream which customarily takes two forms: the escape from time and the materialistic pursuit of a purely hedonistic happiness. On the historical level, the critique is of the error of American romanticism in attempting to transcend and thus escape historical responsibility. On the economic level, the critique is of the fatal beauty of American capitalism, its destructive charm and recklessness. Thematically, the lines come together when Nicole attempts to own Dick and therefore to escape time—keeping him clear of it, too—as when Gatsby tries to buy back the past. On the religious level, if indeed there is one, the critique must be defined more cautiously: perhaps one can say that Fitzgerald intermittently insinuates the possibility that human kind are inveterately prone to befuddle themselves with the conspicuous similarities between the city of man and the city of God, paying scant attention to their more radical difference.

In Rosemary Hoyt, who brings from Hollywood to Europe the latest American version of the dream of youthful innocence, Fitzgerald has still another important center of consciousness. It is through her eyes, for instance, that Fitzgerald gives us his first elaborate glimpses of the Divers, and their hangers-on, at the Americanized Riviera. Because of Rosemary's acute but undisciplined perceptions, Fitzgerald can insist perpetually on the ironic tensions between the richest texture of social appearance and the hidden reality of moral agony: her "naïveté responded wholeheartedly to the expensive simplicity of the Divers, unaware of its complexity and its lack of innocence, unaware that it was all a selection of quality rather than quantity from the run of the world's bazaar; and that the simplicity of behavior also, the nursery-like peace

[3] Mr. Fussell means the last sentence of Chapter V of Book II. [A.M.]

and good-will, the emphasis on the simpler virtues, was part of a desperate bargain with the gods and had been attained through struggles she could not have guessed at." ("Nursery-like peace and good will" is a good example of how Fitzgerald's subtly paradoxical prose style incessantly supplies the kind of religious-secular befuddlement alluded to above.)

Rosemary manifests the effects of Hollywood sentimentality and meretriciousness on the powers of American perception and imagination. The image-patterns that surround her movements are largely concerned with childhood; she is "as dewy with belief as a child from one of Mrs. Burnett's vicious tracts." Immature and egocentric, she provides one more symbol of the corruption of imagination in American civilization; both deluded and deluding, she is without resources for escape such as are available to Nick Carraway and, to a considerably lesser extent, Dick Diver. It is Diver who sounds the last important note about her: "'Rosemary didn't grow up.'" That she is intended as a representative figure Fitzgerald makes amply clear in his embittered account of her picture "Daddy's Girl": "There she was—*so* young and innocent—the product of her mother's loving care . . . embodying all the immaturity of the race, cutting a new cardboard paper doll to pass before its empty harlot's mind."

Nicole and Rosemary are for this novel the objectified images of Fitzgerald's "brave new world." Only occasionally, and only in pathos, does Dick Diver escape the limits of this terrifying world. Once, the three of them are sitting in a restaurant, and Dick notices a group of "gold star mothers": "in their happy faces, the dignity that surrounded and pervaded the party, he perceived all the maturity of an older America. For a while the sobered women who had come to mourn for their dead, for something they could not repair, made the room beautiful. Momentarily, he sat again on his father's knee, riding with Moseby while the old loyalties and devotions fought on around him. Almost with an effort he turned back to his two women at the table and faced the whole new world in which he believed." Only as this illusion fades, to the accompaniment of an almost unbearable "interior laughter," does Dick Diver achieve a minimal and ambiguous salvation, a few shattered fragments of reality, including the anonymity of professional and social failure.

IV

For purposes of corroboration, one can add a certain amount of documentation from Fitzgerald's non-fictional writings, as collected in the posthumous volume *The Crack-Up* (1945). The point that most needs buttressing, probably, is that Fitzgerald saw in the quest for romantic wonder a recurrent pattern of American behavior. Such an attitude seems strongly implied by the works of fiction, but of course it is additionally reassuring to find Fitzgerald writing his daughter: "You speak of how good your generation is, but I think they share with every generation since the Civil War in America the sense of being somehow about to inherit the earth. You've heard me say before that I think the faces of most American women over thirty are relief maps of petulant and bewildered unhappiness" (p. 306). A brief sketch of a "typical product of our generation" in the *Note-Books* indicates further what qualities were involved in this "sense of being about to inherit the earth": "her dominant idea and goal is freedom without responsibility, which is like gold without metal, spring without winter, youth without age, one of those maddening, coo-coo mirages of wild riches" (p. 166). That this personal attitude, translated into the broader terms of a whole culture, represented a negation of historical responsibility, is made sufficiently clear in another *Note-Book* passage: "Americans, he liked to say, should be born with fins, and perhaps they were—perhaps money was a form of fin. In England, property begot a strong place sense, but Americans, restless and with shallow roots, needed fins and wings. There was even a recurrent idea in America about an education that would leave out history and the past, that should be a sort of equipment for aerial adventure, weighed down by none of the stowaways of inheritance or tradition" (p. 109). Still another passage, this time from one of the "Crack-Up" essays, makes it equally clear that Fitzgerald habitually saw the universal applicability of all he was saying about the ruling passions of America: "This is what I think now: that the natural state of the sentient adult is a qualified unhappiness. I think also that in an adult the desire to be finer in grain than you are, 'a constant striving' (as those people say who gain their bread by saying it) only adds to this unhappiness in the end—that end that comes to our youth and hope" (p. 84).

Fortunately, by some kind of unexplained miracle (perhaps nothing more mysterious than his deep-seated integrity as a writer), Fitzgerald did not have it in himself to be a cynic. For all the failure of futility he found in the American experience, his attitude was an attitude of acceptance, remarkably free of that sense of despair which Kierkegaard correctly prophesied as the typical sin of the moderns. There was always in him something of Jimmy Gatz's "extraordinary gift of hope," which enabled him to touch the subjects he touched without being consumed by them. (The tragedies of his personal life are another matter; I am speaking only of his heroism and integrity as an artist.) The exhaustion of the frontier and the rebound of the post-war expatriate movement marked for him the end of a long period in human history and it was really this entire period, the history of the post-Renaissance man in America, that he made the substance of his works. After exploring his materials to their limits Fitzgerald knew, at his greatest moments, that he had discovered a universal pattern of desire and belief and behavior, and that

in it was compounded the imaginative history of modern, especially
American, civilization. Thus (again from the *Note-Books*):

> He felt then that if the pilgrimage eastward of the rare poisonous flower
> of his race was the end of the adventure which had started westward three
> hundred years ago, if the long serpent of the curiosity had turned too
> sharp upon itself, cramping its bowels, bursting its shining skin, at least
> there had been a journey; like to the satisfaction of a man coming to die—
> one of those human things that one can never understand unless one has
> made such a journey and heard the man give thanks with the husbanded
> breath. The frontiers were gone—there were no more barbarians. The
> short gallop of the last great race, the polyglot, the hated and the despised,
> the crass and scorned, had gone—at least it was not a meaningless extinc-
> tion up an alley (p. 199).

There are dozens more such passages, in the non-fictional prose as in the
fictional; naturally, for Fitzgerald's subject, however broadly he came to
understand it, was in the first instance his own journey. He was by
nature almost incredibly sympathetic. He was also more knowledgeable
—both morally and intellectually—than he is generally credited with
being. To such an extent that his more enthusiastic readers are almost
tempted to say: if the polyglot gallop is not a meaningless cancellation of
itself, that is chiefly because Fitzgerald—and the few Americans who by
virtue of their imaginative grasp of our history can rightly be called his
peers—interposed a critical distance between his matter and his expression of it. There is perhaps more difference between an ordinary understanding of America and Fitzgerald's than between the gaudy idealizations of the Elizabethans and the equally comfortable cynicism of
twentieth-century London.

Fitzgerald and His Brethren

by Andrews Wanning

Complete candor in autobiography is very rare, for two reasons: because of the pride or inhibition or self-delusion of the man, or because of the dramatizing and myth-making faculty of the artist, even when dealing with himself. There is very little of the former in *The Crack-Up*, a remarkably interesting collection of the fragmentary autobiography of Scott Fitzgerald; there is some of the latter. There is also the discretion of the editor, whose concern for the living has turned a lot of the proper names into asterisks and evidently deleted a good deal more. Nevertheless the impression of a desperate effort at self-disclosure is one of the most striking things about this book. With the general wreck of his self-confidence, pride in his honesty with himself seems to have been the one concession Fitzgerald made to his vanity.

Many fascinating things emerge under this honorable scrutiny, and many of them have already been noticed by reviewers for the weeklies. What interests me most is the curious likeness uncovered between Fitzgerald and his fictional brethren—not necessarily in circumstances, but in a kind of basic underlying sensibility. The root of this lay, I should think, in a queer conflict in Fitzgerald himself: the conflict between Fitzgerald the snob and the worshiper of dazzle, and Fitzgerald the judge and the moralist.

Fitzgerald's liking for rich company has often enough been noted; but the sense in which it is basic in him, the sense in which wealth and glitter and the arrogance of position are almost his only symbols for earthly beatitude has been put bluntly by only one critic I know about— by Charles Weir in an article called *An Invite with Gilded Edges* in the *Virginia Quarterly*. Certainly Fitzgerald put it bluntly enough himself: great animal magnetism and money, he says in one of his notes, are the top things. In practice those among his characters who have great animal magnetism also either have, or get, money. There is probably no writer of our time whose imagery of the desirable is more consistently in terms of wealth, of diamonds, of pure material glitter. "Her voice is full of

"Fitzgerald and his Brethren," by Andrews Wanning. From the *Partisan Review*, (Fall, 1945). Copyright © 1945 by Partisan Review. Reprinted by permission of the author and the *Partisan Review*. The first part of this essay has been slightly revised. [A.M.]

money," says Gatsby of Daisy, thereby defining more than the source of his own fascination.

How did a man so sensitive as Fitzgerald come by what is almost a worship of money? First of all, I suppose, because nobody taught him anything else, and he was not an original thinker. He remembered of his college life most specifically that he was too light to play college football and that an attack of tuberculosis had cost him the presidency of the Triangle Club. He seems never to have got over the pang of these early failures to qualify as "the man most likely to succeed." Certainly he never learned in college that there was any form of success, even literary, not to be commercially or at least tangibly calculated.

But this, which is perfectly normal, does not quite explain the intensity of his feeling. The articles in *The Crack-Up* suggest the explanation: at twenty-two he endured the trauma of being poor—or at least genteel poor. After a "haughty career as the army's worst aide-de-camp" he got in an advertising agency. Here he lived a life curiously suspended between the rich friendships of Princeton and the painful reality of his salary. Poverty meant to him no actual privation; what it meant was the realization that others were much richer than he, and that it mattered. His autobiographical articles come back again and again to the portrait of his double life at this time: walking in now and then from his cheap bleak flat to the big parties, the handsome mansions, "ghost-like in the Plaza Red Room of a Saturday afternoon"; walking quickly "from certain places—from the pawn shop where one left the field glasses, from prosperous friends whom one met when wearing the suit from before the war." There was certainly a painful sense of insecurity and inferiority. Anyway, his New York adventure ended when the golden girl threw him over "on the basis of common sense." He must have had a partial breakdown; at any rate he went back home to St. Paul, convinced that he was a failure—there to hit the jackpot with *This Side of Paradise* and incidentally win back the golden girl.

After that, according to Fitzgerald, he was never "able to stop wondering where my friends' money came from, nor to stop thinking that at one time a sort of *droit de seigneur* might have been exercised to give one of them my girl." He describes himself as having a smouldering hatred for the leisure class, but its practical results seem to have been an envy and an admiration for the possibly not unattainable. The articles and notes in *The Crack-Up* are full of an acute sense of the gradations of class. He is always concerned as to whether he and Zelda were staying at the best, or the second best, or the bad hotel; with the relative fashion among relative groups of the watering places they frequented; with the social moving-up or moving down of the people he knew—and described. Even in the article the implicit snobbery has an almost sociological tone; in his creative work it is of course less blunt.

But all this is only the half of it, and it is the tension between this and the other half that makes, I think, the peculiar distinction of Fitzgerald both as stylist and as commentator. Behind the devotion to glitter is also the sense of the illusion of the felicity which it represents. "All the stories that came into my head," he observed quite accurately, "had a touch of disaster in them—the lovely young creatures in my novels went to ruin, the diamond mountains of my short stories blew up, my millionaires were as beautiful and damned as Thomas Hardy's peasants. In life these things hadn't happened yet, but I was pretty sure living wasn't the reckless, careless business these people thought." He put it another way in a letter to his daughter. "Sometimes I wish I had gone along with that gang [Cole Porter and Rodgers and Hart], but I guess I am too much a moralist at heart, and really want to preach to people in some acceptable form, rather than to entertain them."

The notion of Fitzgerald as a moralist is at first sight sufficiently astonishing. Certainly he was not an articulate moralist, with any conscious thought-out morality. He was not, as I said before, a thinker. In one of his later articles he confesses, a little pathetically, that other men were his intellectual, ethical and artistic consciences, and that "my political conscience had scarcely existed save as an element of irony in my stuff." He was, in short, a moralist by feeling and intuition; he had what I once heard described as a sense of smell. One of his values, he wrote in *The Crack-Up*, had been "a disregard of motives or consequences in favor of guess-work and prophecy."

As applied to the life of the rich, the sense of smell may have germinated in the smouldering resentment against the leisure class which he described and in the feeling of insecurity which dependence upon money had given him. But it made him, in any case, a fatalist as well as a moralist. One part of his nature told him that only the rich could be happy and gracious; but he knew by observation, experience and his peculiar intuition that even the rich were not. At the end of his life he wrote to his daughter, in about as explicit a moral concept as he ever expressed, the formulation he finally arrived at: the wise and tragic sense of life sees that "life is essentially a cheat and its conditions are those of defeat, and that the redeeming things are not 'happiness and pleasure' but the deeper satisfactions that come out of struggle." But that was long after the time of his first novels. In the twenties it is easier to recognize in his characters the attitude of Maury Noble, who wondered "at the unreality of ideas and at the fading radiance of existence."

Thinking of the tragic sense of life, Fitzgerald wrote in the account of his crack-up that "the test of a first-rate intelligence is the ability to hold two opposed ideas in his mind at the same time, and still retain the ability to function." But this is also, not accidentally, a definition of irony: the sense of something simultaneously affirmed and denied woven into the web of the style. With Fitzgerald the mark of his style is more specifically a nostalgic irony, and this is as much as anything the expression of the need to hold in the mind at once the two deeply ingrained but opposed ideas I have been describing. His style keeps reminding you, particularly in his earlier stuff, of his sense of the enormous beauty of which life, suitably ornamented, is capable; and at the same time of his judgment as to the worthlessness of the ornament and the corruptibility of the beauty. This irony of regret lies deep in the individual contour of phrase and assortment of words; if the felicity of its expression is no doubt not to be explained, it is still, it seems to me, the key to the consistency of the peculiar Fitzgerald tone.

You see it continually in the notebooks printed in this collection, where it emerges with the sharpness given to the focus of fragments. But the notebooks as a whole are a little disappointing; if the wise-cracks seem sometimes pretty thin and the descriptions have often the wilfulness and brittleness of visible tricks, it is probably because the irony is not sustained by a context, by the consistent congruity of an attitude. They remind you, in short, of how much the style in the novels interprets the essential subject matter.

The Great Gatsby is Fitzgerald's best novel because here the congruity of story and style and attitude is closest and most meaningful. Here he had a story whose central character not only symbolized his own conflicts and confusions, but made a moving commentary on a period and a country as well. The grandeur and pathos of Gatsby are that his enormous vitality, ambition and power of creation are all lavished on a "vast, vulgar, and meretricious beauty" unworthy of the emotion that cannot discover a worthier ideal. It is notable that the auditors clearly, and even Gatsby dimly, are aware of the corruption "concealing his incorruptible dream." The clearsightedness is Fitzgerald's commentary on himself: he wrote to John Peale Bishop at the time that Gatsby "started out as one man I knew and then changed into myself." Hence, I suspect, both the warmth and the compassion of the portrait of Gatsby. But if the feeling of the novel owes a good deal to its author's identity with his subject, its impact owes a lot too to its range; to the fact that Gatsby is not merely a disguise for Fitzgerald. Not only Gatsby and Fitzgerald have dreams nobler and finer than any tangible forms that are given them, or that they can find for them; more charged with emotion than the tangible forms justify. The tragedy of Gatsby was a fable for his America; it is not, I should say, by any means dead yet.

2

The price of writing within a generally realistic convention, particularly of the more personal sort, is that the writer's art must live on his own experiences and emotions while the business of writing interferes with his acquiring any more. Hence the reveries over childhood and youth so common in modern fiction. Reading over both *The Crack-Up* and the output it footnotes, one is struck again and again by how hard Fitzgerald worked whatever lodes were to be found in what was, after all, not a very varied upper middle-class life. It is not only in the recurrence of the ambiguous delight and disillusion. There are the milieux, for instance: how thoroughly and carefully he used every physical background with which he was familiar: the Middle West of St. Paul, Princeton, New York, Long Island, Zelda's South, the bars and the beaches of the rich in two continents. Of the limitations these imposed on him, Fitzgerald was thoroughly aware: "So many writers, Conrad for instance," he wrote to his daughter, "have been aided by being brought up in a métier utterly unrelated to literature. It gives an abundance of material and, more important, an attitude from which to view the world. So much writing nowadays suffers both from lack of an attitude and from sheer lack of any material, save what is accumulated in a purely social life. The world, as a rule, does not live on beaches and in country clubs."

Was sheer lack of material the reason for the falling-off in simple volume of output in the last fifteen years of Fitzgerald's life? It may have contributed. At any rate it is suggestive that between 1920 and 1925 he published three novels in which he used (or used up?) the backgrounds of his youth; that much later, in 1934, he drew on the international background of bars, beaches and asylums for *Tender Is the Night;* and that, ironically, the pot-boiling excursion to Hollywood gave him new material for his last serious work, the unfinished *Last Tycoon.*

But perhaps the drain on his emotions was even more serious. "I have asked a lot of my emotions," says one of the notes, "one hundred and twenty stories. The price was high, right up with Kipling, because there was one little drop of something—not blood, not a tear, not my seed, but me more intimately than these, in every story, it was the extra I had. Now it has gone and I am just like you now." Certainly there are signs of an emotional exhaustion in the later books. As others have noticed, there is never any really satisfactory reason given for Dick Diver's break-up in *Tender Is the Night.* But Fitzgerald's clearest implication is that Doctor Diver breaks up because he has cured Nicole by an almost physical transference of his own balance and will. Did Fitzgerald see Nicole as Diver's work of creation, did he transfer to him a feeling of the exhaustion of achievement? At any rate the reason seems to make better sense for Fitzgerald than it does for Doctor Diver.

As for *The Last Tycoon,* its promise, it seems to me, has been extravagantly over-estimated for the most generous reasons by his friends. It is true that it is about the only novel yet attempted to take Hollywood seriously; it is also true that Fitzgerald was certainly trying for what Dos Passos has called a wider "frame of reference for common humanity" than he had managed before. But it doesn't seem to come out right. In

The Great Gatsby Fitzgerald had started with personal dilemmas and a sort of self-examination and ended by creating a fable that had indeed Dos Passos' wider frame. In *The Last Tycoon* he apparently began with the frame and ended with the personal dilemmas and the self-protection willy-nilly dragging their way in. On any other basis the projected pattern is baffling. The serious theme of the novel, as evidenced first of all by the title, appears to be the modern conflict between the original craftsman of the whole and the mass-production assembly line. Why then did Fitzgerald choose to undercut his whole drama by letting us know that Stahr is a dying man? Why did he attach an apparently unrelated love affair which he regarded as "the meat of the book"? The love affair, no doubt, illuminates the last feverish gasping for life of a man with a "definite urge toward total exhaustion." But why have a hero so defeated in advance if you mean to deal evenly with a general theme? Unless Fitzgerald was again unwittingly projecting himself, I do not know the answer.

What seems particularly to have worried Fitzgerald about the book was the loss of the old emotion and sparkle; where the radiance and disillusion had balanced before, now the radiance was fading. "Where will the warmth come from in this?" he wrote of one of the scenes between Stahr and Kathleen. "My girls were all so warm and full of promise." The self-criticism was accurate; perhaps that is why after three years, even three years filled with sickness and pot-boiling, the novel was still only half-finished. It must have cost him an heroic effort to accomplish as much as he did. That effort was one of the two things that give to his last years a great dignity, if not the epic grandeur which he himself spoke of as a delusion. The other was his absorbing interest in his daughter. *The Crack-Up* reprints some of his wise and moving letters to her, particularly moving in the dedicated earnestness with which he strove by exposing his own failures to spare her his miseries.

It was, in any case, a sad life after the excitement of the first glory. Whether the outcome would have been any different if Fitzgerald had been working within a tradition less exacting of personal experience— one, for instance, where you could get along with a little reading for material provided you had human insight and imagination—can only be a matter of speculation. There were plenty of personal tensions in Fitzgerald's life beside those imposed by his writing. Still, it is worth remarking that other contemporaries have resorted to new participations in order to get at something other than "a purely social life." Dos Passos has been a periodic reporter between novels; and Hemingway the adventurer and political poseur may well be necessary to Hemingway the artist. Both, it may also be noted, have developed away from the novel of strictly individual dilemmas to some variety of the novel of social involvement.

My tentative point is that it is hard for a realistic writer to stay in business if he does not. All writing is of course to some extent a battening on one's self; and for all writers there must be a fear of repetition. But the demand that one make literature out of what one has actually lived is more exhausting than others; and modern American fiction, from Stephen Crane on (a perhaps ambiguous case), has had more than its share of abortive careers. "Books are like brothers," wrote Fitzgerald in his Note-Books. "I am an only child. Gatsby my imaginary eldest brother, Amory my younger, Anthony my worry, Dick my comparatively good brother, but all of them far from home. When I have the courage to put the old white light on the home of my heart, then. . . ." *The Crack-Up* makes the white light seem nearer home than Fitzgerald admitted; perhaps it would have been better for him if some of the brothers had been acquaintances or at least cousins. The old white light on the heart, it seems safe to say, is a particular focus with a higher price than most in human vitality and personality.

Third Act and Epilogue

by Malcolm Cowley

F. Scott Fitzgerald used to say that there were no second acts in American lives, but there was a second and even a third act in his own. After the glitter of his early success (he was a best-selling novelist at twenty-three), after the long disillusionment that was the theme of almost all his stories from *The Great Gatsby* in 1925 to *Tender Is the Night* in 1934, there was a crisis, a feeling of complete mental and physical exhaustion. That was the third act and it came near being the end of the play, but before his death in 1940, at the age of forty-four, there was a little-known epilogue in Hollywood that was a drama in itself.

The whole story, and especially the end of it, can be pieced together from *The Crack-Up,* a volume of Fitzgerald's literary remains that Edmund Wilson, his friend from Princeton days, has edited with the critical sense one might expect of him and not a little friendly discretion. The volume contains a number of autobiographical pieces, including some very good ones, that Fitzgerald wrote for various magazines; a series of extracts from his literary notebook; sixty-odd letters to his daughter and his close friends, a sampling short enough to make one wish for more; and a brief selection of letters to Fitzgerald and essays and poems about him. The book is obviously not intended for consecutive reading, but it makes excellent reading in snatches; you can open it almost anywhere and find lively writing and painfully honest self-judgment. Moreover, it deals with a novelist whose work and character, for all their shortcomings, have a way of holding our affection, like the life and work of Stephen Crane.

More than any other writer of these times, Fitzgerald had the sense of living in history. He tried hard to catch the color of every passing year: its distinctive slang, its dance steps, its songs (he kept making lists of them in his notebooks), its favorite quarterbacks, and the sort of clothes and emotions its people wore. He felt in the beginning that his own life was not merely typical but representative of a new generation; he could look inside himself and tell quite accurately how others would soon be

"Third Act and Epilogue" by Malcolm Cowley. From *The New Yorker,* (June 30, 1945). Copyright © 1945 The New Yorker Magazine, Inc. Reprinted by permission of the author and *The New Yorker.* The end of the article was revised by the author in 1951 to incorporate new material about Fitzgerald's last years in Hollywood.

thinking. Even in his later years he continued to be grateful to the Jazz Age because, he said, writing about himself in the third person, "It bore him up, flattered him, and gave him more money than he had dreamed of, simply for telling people that he felt as they did." He came to believe that he had helped to fix the patterns followed by people a little younger than himself. Thus, in one of his notebooks, he said of an unnamed relative that she was still a flapper in the nineteen-thirties. "There is no doubt," he added, "that she originally patterned herself upon certain immature and unfortunate writings of mine, so that I have a special indulgence for——as for one who has lost an arm or leg in one's service." He was a little wry about the Fitzgerald characters he kept encountering in life. One anecdote has been printed before, but it is worth repeating as he set it down in a notebook when he was living in Baltimore. It concerns a young man, a stranger, who telephoned Fitzgerald from a distant city, then from a city nearby, then from downtown, to announce his coming. At last the man drove up to the house, Fitzgerald noted, "with a great ripping up of garden borders, a four-ply rip in a new lawn, a watch pointing accurately and unforgivably at 3 A.M. But he was prepared to disarm me with the force of his compliment, the intensity of the impulse that had brought him to my door. 'Here I am at last,' he said, teetering triumphantly. 'I had to see you. I feel I owe you more than I can say. I feel that you formed my life.'"

Fitzgerald was himself the principal victim of his capacity for creating fictional types. "Sometimes," he told another visitor late at night. "I don't know whether I'm real or whether I'm a character in one of my own novels." His early success had made him feel like the hero of a fairy tale. In 1919 he was working in a New York advertising agency for thirty-five dollars a week. He was engaged, he told his friends in his flamboyant fashion, "to the most beautiful girl in Alabama *and* Georgia." He had met her at a dance in Montgomery, when he was serving in the Army as aide-de-camp to General J. A. Ryan. That spring she broke off their engagement because it seemed that they would never have money enough to marry. He gave up his job, stayed drunk for three weeks, and then went home to St. Paul, where he wrote *This Side of Paradise*. He also sold a few magazine stories and earned, during the year, eight hundred dollars as a writer. In 1920, when his novel was published, he made eighteen thousand dollars, spent all of it, and ended the year in debt. He married the girl and brought her to New York, where they wandered about, he wrote, "like children in a great bright unexplored barn." A few days later, he was "riding in a taxi one afternoon between very tall buildings under a mauve and rosy sky; I began to bawl because I had everything I wanted and knew I would never be so happy again." And, remembering that he had been penniless and jilted not long before, he also felt that he "would always cherish an abiding distrust, an animosity, toward the leisure class—not the conviction of a revolutionist but the smoldering hatred of a peasant. In the years since then I have never been able to stop wondering where my friends' money came from, nor to stop thinking that at one time a sort of *droit de seigneur* might have been exercised to give one of them my girl."

He cultivated a sort of double vision. He was continually trying to present the glitter of life in the Princeton eating clubs, on the Riviera, on the North Shore of Long Island, and in the Hollywood studios; he surrounded his characters with a mist of admiration and simultaneously he drove the mist away. He always liked to write about "where the milk is watered and the sugar is sanded, the rhinestone passed for diamond and the stucco for stone." It was as if all his novels described a big dance to which he had taken, as he once wrote, the prettiest girl:

> There was an orchestra—Bingo-Bango
> Playing for us to dance the tango
> And the people all clapped as we arose,
> For her sweet face and my new clothes—

and as if at the same time he stood outside the ballroom, a little Midwestern boy with his nose to the glass, wondering how much the tickets cost and who paid for the music. He regarded himself as a pauper living among millionaires, a Celt among Sassenachs, a sullen peasant among the nobility, and he said that his point of vantage "was the dividing line between two generations," prewar and postwar. It was this habit of keeping a double point of view that distinguished his work. There were popular and serious novelists in his time, but there was something of a gulf between them; Fitzgerald was one of the very few popular writers who were also serious artists. There were realists and romantics; Fitzgerald was among the wildest of the romantics, but he was also among the few Americans who tried, like Stendhal in France, to make the romance real by showing its causes and its consequences. It did not matter too much that the causes were trivial and the consequences often tragic or sordid. "After all," he wrote in one of his notebooks—or rather he copied into the notebook from a published story that he had decided not to preserve—"any given moment had its value; it can be questioned in the light of after-events, but the moment remains. The young prince in velvet gathered in lovely domesticity around the queen among the hush of rich draperies may presently grow up to be Pedro the Cruel or Charles the Mad, but the moment of beauty was there."

"I am probably one of the most expert liars in the world," he said in his notes, "and expect everyone to discount nine-tenths of what I say, but I have made two rules in attempting to be both an intellectual and a man of honor simultaneously—*that I do not tell lies that will be of value to myself,* and secondly, *that I do not lie to myself.*" It is a difficult technical problem to tell the truth in fiction; often a writer falls into

06649

conventional lies simply because he can't find the right words or turns of phrase to express what he is trying to say. Fitzgerald, who regarded himself primarily as a craftsman, had both the technique and the need for being honest. He said in a notebook at the time of his own crisis, "I have asked a lot of my emotions—one hundred and twenty stories. The price was high, right up with Kipling, because there was one little drop of something—not blood, not a tear, not my seed, but me more intimately than these, in every story, it was the extra I had. Now it is gone and I am just like you now."

His crisis, in 1935 and 1936, was caused by a series of big and little misfortunes: serious illness (a recurrence of tuberculosis, from which he had suffered briefly in college), family troubles, insomnia, gin and water, reduced earning power, debts he couldn't pay, and, worst of all, a feeling that he had used up and wasted his abilities. His mistake, he wrote, was "an over-extension of the flank, a burning of the candle at both ends; a call upon physical resources that I did not possess, like a man over-drawing at his bank. . . . Every act of life from the morning toothbrush to the friend at dinner had become an effort." Now that he couldn't sleep, his days and nights were jumbled together: "In the real dark night of the soul," he wrote, "it is always three o'clock in the morning, day after day." There was a moment when he felt suddenly that he had cracked, as an old plate cracks. He tried running away from himself; one day, having left his home in Baltimore, he arrived in a town in North Carolina with seventy cents in his pocket. He lived for two days on tinned meat and soda crackers, washed down with two cans of beer, while he wrote a story to pay his hotel bill; then he went home again to his problems. There was something in his character, a Midwestern toughness or an Irish Puritanism, that would not let him give in; he made the best of whatever was left to him. "Sometimes," he wrote, "the cracked plate has to be retained in the pantry, has to be kept in service as a household necessity. It can never again be warmed on the stove nor shuffled with the other plates in the dishpan; it will not be brought out for company, but it will do to hold crackers late at night or go into the icebox under leftovers."

"A man does not recover from such jolts," Fitzgerald said in an article written at the time—"he becomes a different person and, eventually, the new person finds new things to care about." In the summer of 1937 the new person was strong enough to make a trip to Hollywood; that was the epilogue to the play and on the whole it makes a more heartening story than I had expected to find. Fitzgerald had been given a six months' contract by Metro-Goldwyn-Mayer, and when the contract expired in January, 1938, it was renewed for a year at an increased salary. He was drinking very little and proved to be a capable screen craftsman, although his best scenarios were not produced in the form in which he wrote them. During his first eighteen months in Hollywood he earned $88,391—the figure comes from his literary agent, Harold Ober—while he lived frugally, paid off his big debts and put his insurance policies in order.

The story is not a simple one of moral redemption and success in a new field. At the beginning of February, 1939, a week after the M-G-M contract ran out, he was sent East by Walter Wanger; with the help of Budd Schulberg he was to write a film about the Dartmouth Winter Carnival. He started drinking on the eastbound plane, got into a violent dispute with Wanger and continued drinking at Dartmouth and in New York; it was his biggest, saddest, most desperate spree. Back in Hollywood he couldn't find another job and suspected that the producers had put his name on an informal blacklist. He took to his bed; for three months he was under the care of day and night nurses. It was a recurrence of tuberculosis, he told his friends (who suspected a recurrence of alcoholism), and it was complicated by "a nervous breakdown of such severity that for a long time it threatened to paralyze both arms—or to quote the doctor: 'The Good Lord tapped you on the shoulder.'" After a partial recovery in the summer he faced another crisis to which he referred obliquely in his letters; it was "that personally and publicly dreary month of Sept. last [when] about everything went to pieces all at once" —and still it wasn't the end of the story.

The will to survive wasn't dead in him and he still had personal and artistic obligations that he was determined to meet, even though he had fewer resources with which to meet them. In the past he had often exaggerated his physical troubles for dramatic effect, but it seems that he wasn't exaggerating when he said that all through the winter of 1939-40 he suffered from "the awful lapses and sudden reverses and apparent cures and thorough poisoning effect of lung trouble. Suffice to say there were months with a high of 99.8, months at 99.6 and then up and down and a stabilization of 99.2 every afternoon when I could write in bed." His Hollywood friends report that he was gray-faced and emaciated and seldom left his room, but he was writing again—if only for a few hours each day—and that was the important news. Although seven of his books were still in print, nobody was reading them and his name was almost forgotten; now he was setting out to regain his place in literature.

His record of production for the last year of his life would have been remarkable for a man in perfect health. He began the year by making plans for a novel and, simultaneously, by writing twenty stories for *Esquire,* including seventeen in the Pat Hobby series. Most of the Hobby stories weren't very good by his own standards, but they caught the Hollywood atmosphere and they also made fun of the author's weaknesses, thereby proving that Fitzgerald hadn't lost his ironic attitude toward himself or his gift of double vision. Suddenly he resumed his interrupted correspondence with his friends and he sent his daughter an extraordinary series of letters that continued all through the year; perhaps they were too urgent and too full of tired wisdom for a girl in college, but then Fitzgerald was writing them as a sort of personal and literary testament.

In the spring he wrote—and twice rewrote from the beginning—a scenario based on his story, "Babylon Revisited"; it was the best of his scenarios and, according to the producer who ordered it, the best he ever read. Shirley Temple wasn't available for the part of Honoria and the story has never been filmed. Again Fitzgerald began drinking, but then he sobered up and went to work for a studio in September, earning enough, he thought, to carry him through the writing of *The Last Tycoon*. Work on it was delayed by a serious heart attack in November, but for most of the month he was writing steadily. He had said in a letter to his daughter, "I wish now I'd *never* relaxed or looked back—but said at the end of *The Great Gatsby*: 'I've found my line—from now on this comes first. This is my immediate duty—without this I am nothing.'" In the year 1940 he had found his line again—and had found something more than that, since he now possessed a deeper sense of the complexities of life than he had when writing *Gatsby*. He was doing his best work of the year in December and it was some of the best he ever did. He had been sober for a long time and seemed to be less worried about illness, when suddenly, four days before Christmas, there was a second coronary attack and he died—not like a strayed reveler but like a partner of the elder J. P. Morgan, working too hard until his heart gave out.

Some Notes on
F. Scott Fitzgerald

by Leslie Fiedler

1. *Nothing succeeds like failure*

The case of F. Scott Fitzgerald belongs first of all to the history of taste in our time. It is immensely difficult at the present moment to distinguish our responses to Fitzgerald's achievement from our self-congratulatory feelings about certain recent changes in our own literary standards. We are likely to overestimate his books in excessive repentance of the critical errors of the 'thirties—for having preferred Steinbeck or James T. Farrell for reasons we would no longer defend. Fitzgerald has come to seem more and more poignantly the girl we left behind—dead, to boot, before we returned to the old homestead, and therefore particularly amenable to sentimental idealization.

And so a fictionist with a "second-rate sensitive mind" (the term is Tennyson's description of himself, and evokes the tradition of late Romanticism in which Fitzgerald worked) and a weak gift for construction is pushed into the very first rank of American novelists, where it becomes hard to tell his failures from his successes. Who cares as long as the confetti flies and the bands keep playing! It is all to the good, of course, that hundreds of thousands of us require the reprinting of his books, actually read him again along with the recent Mizener biography. He had threatened for too long to remain a "case" about whom everyone merely *talks*. If we were only content with reclaiming an imperfect good writer, who achieved just once a complete artistic success, but who in every book at some point breaks through his own intolerable resolve to be charming above all and touches the truth!

But, Lord have mercy on us, we want a "great" writer. It is at once the comedy and tragedy of twentieth-century American letters that we simply cannot keep a full stock of contemporary "great novelists." In the novel, unlike recent poetry in which certain reputations have grown slowly and steadily, we have had an erratic market: reputations fantas-

"Some Notes on F. Scott Fitzgerald." From *An End to Innocence* (Boston: Beacon Press, 1955) by Leslie Fiedler. Copyright © 1955 by the Beacon Press. Reprinted by permission of the author and Beacon Press.

tically overpriced are in an instant deflated, and new booms are launched. From moment to moment we have the feeling that certain claims, at least, are secure, but even as we name them they shudder and fall. Who now mentions James Branch Cabell? And who can think of Dos Passos and Steinbeck without a twinge of shame for dead enthusiasms? Dreiser and Farrell find a few surly defenders—but even their granted merits seem irrelevant to our current situation. Whom have we left? Faulkner and Hemingway, and even now the stock of the latter has begun to fall; a thousand imitators reveal the weaknesses we had not seen, and the younger critics begin, to the shrill screams of Hemingway's contemporaries, the drastic revision. Into our depopulated pantheon, therefore, we impress Fitzgerald.

Who else? There are several reasons that impel the choice: we have reached the point from which the 'twenties, Fitzgerald's 'twenties, can be regarded with the maximum nostalgia; we readopt the hairdos, the songs—and the authors. We see him now as one who refused to whore after strange Marxist gods, our lonely St. Anthony, faithful to literature in the sociological desert. The versions of Fitzgerald that these estimates imply are perhaps not quite true, but they are believed in and will do. And yet the *essential* appeal of Fitzgerald is elsewhere—astonishingly enough, in his *failure*.

Mr. Schulberg in his recent novel has remarked that in America nothing fails like success; but of course the obverse is also true: among us, nothing succeeds like failure. We are, behind a show of the grossest success-worship, a nation that dreams of failure as a fulfillment. The Christian paradox of the defeated as victor haunts our post-Christian world. None of us seems *really* to believe in the succeeding of success, though we do not know how to escape from its trap; and it has become one of the functions of our writers to supply us with vicarious failures for our second-hand redemption.

Edgar Allan Poe provides the prototype, of course: dope, whisky, the shadow of madness, poverty and early death—and Fitzgerald is the perfect modern avatar. It is the Fall not of a King, but of an Artist, the disaffected son of the middle class, of us all, that we demand to stir our pity and terror. For the great quasi-literate public, Fitzgerald is providing right now the *tragic experience:* creating, in the great amphitheater without walls of articles in *Life,* abridgments in the *Atlantic Monthly,* paragraphs in the papers, and 25-cent reprints, a debased equivalent of what the Athenian found in the *Oedipus Rex.* When any American writer refuses to live into the conventional public myth, the people remake him, as even Poe was retouched by Griswold, who invented in malice the American Writer, and as Stephen Crane was lied and vilified into the image necessary to us all.

But Fitzgerald *willed* his role as a failure, for all his paeans to success. Long before his own actual crack-up, he dreamed it, prophesied it in his stories and novels; and if one cannot read his true desire in the fictional projections, Mr. Mizener's account of the life more than confirms the intimations. Mr. Mizener's greatest merit as a biographer is that he does not cut the fabric of Fitzgerald's life to his own views, but by balancing a half-dozen partial readings of his career permits still others (including this one) that do not suggest themselves explicitly to him. Instinctively, Fitzgerald hoarded his defeats like his truest treasures: his rejection as a young man by Ginevra King, his expulsion from Princeton, the imagined attacks of tuberculosis and the real ones (a disease in which the will is all), the cutting to pieces of his prized movie script by Joe Mankiewicz— and above all, the drinking.

II. *Booze done it!*

From the beginnings of Western literature, there has been a tradition of the flaw as essential to the writer, but at various times there have been various notions of the ideal charismatic weakness: blindness in the most ancient days, incest in the Byronic period, homosexuality in the *fin de siècle*. But in America the flaw has been pre-eminently drunkenness, from Griswold's Poe dead in the gutters of Baltimore to Schulberg's Halliday-Fitzgerald dying among the undergraduates at Dartmouth. It was quite another sort of culture hero, the battered John L. Sullivan, who said mournfully, "Booze done it!"; but the words make an appropriate epitaph for our typical writer.

Every writer in Fitzgerald makes his first staggering entrance loaded: McKiscoe in *Tender Is the Night*, "Four-eyes" in *Gatsby*, Wylie in *The Last Tycoon;* the profession is inseparable from the vice. It is, I suppose, because the 'twenties were the time when drinking became quite simply the American Character, or at least its public face, that Fitzgerald was so much at home in that world, unalienated from the general binge. Mr. Mizener's book makes quite clear the pathetic hollowness of Fitzgerald's claim to be a spokesman for the 'twenties in the formal sense, a kind of higher John Held, Jr.; and a quick, embarrassed rereading of *This Side of Paradise,* with its queasy panegyrics of "kissing" and "petting," reveals a writer far too naïve and principled to speak for a time without principle. And yet Fitzgerald and his audience were, until the 'twenties died, at home with each other; the American citizen as lush and the American artist as lush cried into the same beer. It was not that only Americans, or American writers, drank (there was always James Joyce, as Hemingway reminded Fitzgerald between drinks), but that for Americans it so much *mattered;* and that in the United States, before drinking could become an overwhelming habit, it had first to be forbidden. It is surely no accident that the protagonist of Fitzgerald's best book has, like his author, grown wealthy on Prohibition, the sensitive bootlegger as the last Romantic—the "great" Gatsby, for whom only the drunken writer turns out to mourn after his inevitable defeat.

The greatest drunken writer whom Fitzgerald created, however, appeared in none of his books—being, of course, Fitzgerald himself. A part of the apparent waste of Fitzgerald's life stems from his having invested most of his energy in composing himself; and his Collected Works have not been finished until ten years after his death. One cannot claim to have read him without having read *The Far Side of Paradise* or the letters and reminiscences collected in *The Crack-Up*. It is the glory and the curse of the Romantic writer that his achievement cannot survive his legend without real loss. When the lives of Scott and Zelda are forgotten, or when they have become merely chronologies without the legendary distortions and pathos, his books will be less rewarding. Think of Byron, to whom his sins are as necessary as drunkenness and the madness of his wife are to Fitzgerald!

III. *Portrait of the artist as a young girl*

The obverse of the Romantic habit of living one's life as if it were a work of art is that of writing one's books as if they were autobiographies. Fitzgerald is wary in this respect, but his dodges are superficial and ineffective. In his later books, he resolutely refuses to use the writer or artist as protagonist or point-of-view character. Even in *The Last Tycoon*, where the writer Wylie is obviously the character through whom the story of Stahr *must* be told, Fitzgerald's resolve to keep the writer as character peripheral quite ruins any possibility of a coherent organization; and in the end Fitzgerald smuggles himself into the skin of Stahr and of the young girl through whom the events are seen. Nothing is gained, and a good deal is lost—organization, certainly, and consistency of characterization.

It is not by pretending that one's central character is a gangster or psychiatrist or producer that one avoids turning art into confession; it is a question of method and irony and detachment, the devices that made *Stephen Hero* into *Portrait of the Artist as a Young Man*, the devices that Fitzgerald never mastered.

Any one of Fitzgerald's novels will illustrate the point; but perhaps *Tender Is the Night* will serve best of all. Almost all the main characters (Nicole Diver, the female lead, is of course based on Zelda), whatever their outsides, turn out to be F. Scott Fitzgerald. Dick Diver, the protagonist, who seems from a distance the assured aristocrat, the obverse of the author, reveals on the first close-up the Irish lilt, the drunkenness, the tortured sensibility that are Fitzgerald's. The pretentious novelist (enter drunk, to be sure!), Albert McKiscoe, is Scott in caricature, his social insecurity, his pretenses, even the early success he feared and hated.

Abe North, faintly disguised as a musician, is Ring Lardner; but Ring
Lardner was Fitzgerald's favorite *alter ego,* in whom he liked to see the
image of his own doom (exit drunk, of course!). One could do a marvelous movie with all these parts played by the same actor—a different
stance, different costuming, and as the camera moves close: the same face.

Even the young moving-picture actress, Rosemary Hoyt, turns out to
be a version of the author. She is Irish (always a clue), full of embarrassment and guilty pride at a too-sudden success, and quite indeterminate
in her sex. Indeed, the book is shot through with a thematic playing
with the ambiguity of sex: Dick Diver makes his first entrance in a pair
of black lace panties, and homosexuals, male and female, haunt the
climaxes of the novel. "Economically," Rosemary's mother tells her at
one point, "you're a boy, not a girl." Economically! One recalls the
portrait of Fitzgerald as the most beautiful showgirl in the Triangle
Show.

I had felt all this before reading in Mr. Mizener's biography that in
The World's Fair, an abandoned book from whose fragments the first
part of *Tender Is the Night* is made, Rosemary was indeed a boy, who was
to kill his mother according to the original plot. It has been observed by
Malcolm Cowley that Fitzgerald has always a double vision of himself, as
outsider and insider at once, the man of the world and the bumpkin
gawking at him; but it has not been remarked that at the end of his
writing career the outsider had become defined as the Young Girl, a
kind of anima figure, desiring hopelessly the older man who is *also* Fitzgerald, himself double: in the eyes of the girl all power and glamor, in
his own view aging and corrupt or at the point of death.

In his last two novels, the same relationship appears, and the same
sort of character as narrator, a portrait of the artist as a breathless young
girl, still virgin though not without experience. Each time the affair ends
in a deflowering without love and an eventual desertion, Diver-Fitzgerald
abandoning Rosemary-Fitzgerald for Nicole-Zelda, and Stahr-Fitzgerald
leaving Cecilia-Fitzgerald for Kathleen; the protagonists choosing both
times that Other Woman by whom Fitzgerald symbolizes the lure of
death and destruction which is stronger even than self-love.

This constant impulse to confuse himself with his characters destroys
first of all the consistency of the people in his books; but, even worse, it
leads Fitzgerald into an indulgence in self-pity, which is the grossest
manifestation of his prevailing sentimentality. He is sentimental about
everything—Princeton, the First World War, sex (egregiously!), Skull
and Bones, Gold Star Mothers—but especially about his own plight.
Everywhere in his work there is a failure of irony and detachment that
amounts finally to a failure of intelligence, an indulgence of the "second-
rate sensitive mind."

Like most American writers, Fitzgerald had to work without an accepted tradition to sustain him or received standards against which to

measure himself. All his life, he moved uncertainly between the demands of his own erratic sensibility and a desire to please a great, undefined audience—to be loved by everybody. Like one of his own epicene coquettes, he postured and flirted with all comers, trying to cling meanwhile to a virginity which became more and more a technicality. To be wanted and admired, he was willing to seem to say less than he meant, to appear merely chic; so that it is still possible to read even his best books with no understanding and much pleasure. How could he ever find time to learn how to put a novel together with skill! All his life, point-of-view baffled him, and he was forced to make his transitions with such awkward links as: "To resume Rosemary's point of view, it should be said . . ." or "This is Cecilia taking up the story . . ."

iv. *What terrible and golden mystery . . .*

And yet . . . there is always the style of the details, the glow and motion of the close of *Gatsby* or the opening of *Tender Is the Night*, those wonderful approaches and fadeouts. There is always the naïve honesty of reminiscence, the embarrassing rightness of his adolescents. And there is the supreme negative virtue: Fitzgerald's refusal to swap his own lived sentimentalities for the mass sentimentalities of social protest that swamp the later Hemingway. Even the compulsive theme of the *femme fatale,* the All-American banality of woman as destroyer, is capable of subtleties forever beyond the "proletarian novel." When Fitzgerald treats social themes he is absurd; surely there appears in the overrated fragment, *The Last Tycoon,* the least convincing Communist in American fiction. But he resisted the temptation to end *Tender Is the Night* with Dick Diver sending his kids off to the Soviet Union, a close that might well have won him the plaudits he so needed in 1934.

But, beyond all this, one feels in his work a great theme, however elusive and imperfectly realized. It is not love, though love is superficially everywhere in his writing; nor is it Europe, though he lived there and set one book and many stories in the expatriate background. Though he was educated in Catholic schools, it is not religion. His books have no religious insights, only religious décor—the obsessive metaphor of the "ruined priest," a theatrical making of the cross to close a book, a belated Aubrey-Beardsley-ish priest. The sensibility of the Catholic in America becomes, like everything else, puritan: the devil, self-consciously introduced in *This Side of Paradise,* shrinks to an evil aura around a tart's head. There is in Fitzgerald no profound sense of evil or sin, only of guilt; and no gods except the Rich.

The Rich—there is the proper subject matter of Fitzgerald, as everyone has perceived: their difference from the rest of us, and the meanings of that difference. That "other woman" who is death is also wealth; the girl, like Daisy, with gold in her voice. Of course, the wealthy in Fitzgerald are not *real,* but that is precisely the point. Whether in declared fantasy like "A Diamond as Big as the Ritz" or in nominally realistic novels, they resemble veritable millionaires as little as Natty Bumppo resembles an actual frontiersman. But they are, at least—like that Cooper character and unlike the nasty rich in proletarian novels—myths rather than platitudes, viable to the imagination.

It is not just snobbishness that drew Fitzgerald to the rich, the boy from St. Paul dreaming his life long of an imagined Princeton. In all his writing, one senses Fitzgerald in search of an American equivalent to *les grands,* the aristocracy to whom the French writers were able to turn in their reversion from the grubby bourgeois world. Was there anywhere, in America or among Americans abroad, a native aristocracy to whom "style" was a goal and a dream? It is not money getters, but spenders, to whom Fitzgerald turned in his search for allies, out of a sense that the squandering of unearned money was an art, like writing, that squandering of an unearned talent; and that among the very rich there might be a perpetual area of freedom, like that in which the artist momentarily feels himself in the instant of creative outpouring.

The world where a penny saved is a penny earned is the world of anti-art. The lower middle class in particular, Fitzgerald felt, were the enemies of style. He wanted a class that knows how to *use* writers, or at least desires a kind of life in which the imagination would have a chance to live. It was a hopeless dream, and in the end Fitzgerald learned two things: first, that the rich, whatever the quality of their living, regard the artist not as an ally but as a somewhat amusing *arriviste;* and, second, that to live the life of high style is to remain a moral child, who destroys whatever does not suit his whim. To be "rich," in the sense he dreamed, is to refuse responsibility, to deny fate, to try (as in the terrible scene toward the close of "The Diamond as Big as the Ritz") to bribe God. There is implicit in such a life a doom as absolute as its splendor, and in this sense alone the career of the very rich is like that of the artist.

It is a vision atrocious and beautiful enough to be true, and it survives in Fitzgerald's work, despite the incoherence and sentimentality, with the force of truth. It is fitting that our chronicler of the rich be our prophet of failure. To those who plead that Fitzgerald could not face up to life and success, it can be said that at least he kept faith with death and defeat.

EARLY WORK

This Side of Paradise

by Charles E. Shain

The novel with which Fitzgerald won Zelda, *This Side of Paradise,* is usually praised for qualities that pin it closely to an exact moment in American life. Later readers are apt to come to it with the anticipation of an archeologist approaching an interesting ruin. Its publication is always considered to be the event that ushered in the Jazz Age. Glenway Wescott, writing for his and Fitzgerald's generation, said that it had "haunted the decade like a song, popular but perfect." Social historians have pointed out that the college boys of the early twenties really read it. There have been public arguments as to whether or not the petting party first occurred when Fitzgerald's novel said it did or two years earlier. Anyone reading the novel with such interests will not be entirely disappointed. One of the responsibilities it assumes, especially in its first half, is to make the hero, Amory Blaine, report like a cultural spy from inside his generation. "None of the Victorian mothers—and most of the mothers were Victorian—had any idea how casually their daughters were accustomed to be kissed." "The 'belle' had become the 'flirt,' the 'flirt' had become the 'baby vamp.' " "Amory saw girls doing things that even in his memory would have been impossible; eating three-o'clock, after-dance suppers in impossible cafés, talking of every side of life with an air half of earnestness, half of mockery, yet with a furtive excitement that Amory con-

"*This Side of Paradise,*" from *F. Scott Fitzgerald* (Minneapolis: University of Minnesota Pamphlets on American Writers, No. 15, 1961) by Charles Shain. Copyright © 1961 by the University of Minnesota. Reprinted by permission of the author and the University of Minnesota Press.

sidered stood for a real moral let-down." The "moral let-down" enjoyed
by the postwar generation has given the work its reputation for scandal
as well as for social realism.

Today, the novel's young libertines, both male and female, would not
shock a schoolgirl. Amory Blaine turns out to be a conspicuous moralist
who takes the responsibility of kissing very seriously and disapproves of
affairs with chorus girls. (He has no scruples, it must be said, against
going on a three-week drunk when his girl breaks off their engagement.)
At the end of the story he is ennobled by an act of self-sacrifice in an
Atlantic City hotel bedroom that no one would admire more than a
Victorian mother. For modern readers it is probably better to take for
granted the usefulness of *This Side of Paradise* for social historians and
to admire from the distance of another age the obviously wholesome
morality of the hero. Neither of these is the quality that saves the novel
for a later time. What Fitzgerald is really showing is how a young American of his generation discovers what sort of figure he wants to cut, what
modes of conduct, gotten out of books as well as out of a keen sense of
his contemporaries, he wants to imitate. The flapper and her boy friend
do not actually pet behind the closed doors of the smoking room. They
talk, and each one says to the other, unconvincingly, "Tell me about
yourself. What do you feel?" Meaning, "Tell me about myself. How do
I feel?" The real story of *This Side of Paradise* is a report on a young
man's emotional readiness for life.

The only interesting morality it presents is the implied morality that
comes as a part of his feelings when the hero distinguishes, or fails to
distinguish, between an honest and a dishonest emotion. The highly
self-conscious purpose of telling Amory Blaine's story was, one suspects,
to help Fitzgerald to discover who he really was by looking into the eyes
of a girl—there are four girls—or into the mirror of himself that his
college contemporaries made. And the wonder of it is that such a self-
conscious piece of autobiography could be imagined, presented, and
composed as a best-selling novel by a young man of twenty-three.

The novel is very uneven, and full of solemn attempts at abstract
thought on literature, war, and socialism. It has vitality and freshness
only in moments, and these are always moments of feeling. Fitzgerald
said of this first novel many years later, "A lot of people thought it was
a fake, and perhaps it was, and a lot of others thought it was a lie, which
it was not." It offers the first evidence of Fitzgerald's possession of the gift
necessary for a novelist who, like him, writes from so near his own bones,
the talent that John Peale Bishop has described as "the rare faculty of
being able to experience romantic and ingenuous emotions and a half
hour later regard them with satiric detachment." The ingenuous emotions
most necessary to the success of *This Side of Paradise* are vanity and all
the self-regarding sentiments experienced during first love and the first
trials of pride. The satire visited upon them is often as delicate and

humorous as in this picture of Amory at a moment of triumphant egoism: "As he put in his studs he realized that he was enjoying life as he would probably never enjoy it again. Everything was hallowed by the haze of his own youth. He had arrived, abreast of the best in his generation at Princeton. He was in love and his love was returned. Turning on all the lights, he looked at himself in the mirror, trying to find in his own face the qualities that made him see clearer than the great crowd of people, that made him decide firmly, and able to influence and follow his own will. There was little in his life now that he would have changed. . . . Oxford might have been a bigger field."

The ideas in the novel, unlike the tributes paid to a life of feeling, have the foreign country of origin and the importer's labels still on them. Edmund Wilson said *This Side of Paradise* was not really about anything. "Intellectually it amounts to little more than a gesture—a gesture of indefinite revolt." Toward the end of the novel Fitzgerald's normally graceful sentences begin to thicken and "sword-like pioneering personalities, Samuel Butler, Renan and Voltaire," are called in to add the weight of their names to Amory's reflections on the hypocrisy of his elders. The best pages of the novel come early, where Fitzgerald was remembering in marvelous detail the scenes at Newman School and Princeton. Later in his life he would always find it easy to return to those adolescent years, when feelings were all in all. Bishop once accused him of taking seventeen as his norm and believing that after that year life began to fall away from perfection. Fitzgerald replied, "If you make it fifteen I will agree with you."

The Fitzgerald novel, then, began in his acute awareness of a current American style of young life and in his complete willingness to use his own experience as if it were typical. The charm of his first stories and novels is simply the charm of shared vanity and enthusiasm for oneself as an exceptional person. Fitzgerald often persuades us that he was the one sensitive person there—on the country club porch or in a New York street—the first time something happened, or at the very height of the season. And when this ability to exploit his life began to succeed beyond his dreams, the only next step he could think of was to use it harder.

F. Scott Fitzgerald

by *Edmund Wilson*

It has been said by a celebrated person[1] that to meet F. Scott Fitzgerald is to think of a stupid old woman with whom someone has left a diamond; she is extremely proud of the diamond and shows it to everyone who comes by, and everyone is surprised that such an ignorant old woman should possess so valuable a jewel; for in nothing does she appear so inept as in the remarks she makes about the diamond.

The person who invented this simile did not know Fitzgerald very well and can only have seen him, I think, in his more diffident or uninspired moods. The reader must not suppose that there is any literal truth in the image. Scott Fitzgerald is, in fact, no old woman, but a very good-looking young man, nor is he in the least stupid, but, on the contrary, exhilaratingly clever. Yet there *is* a symbolic truth in the description quoted above: it is true that Fitzgerald has been left with a jewel which he doesn't know quite what to do with. For he has been given imagination without intellectual control of it; he has been given the desire for beauty without an aesthetic ideal; and he has been given a gift for expression without very many ideas to express.

Consider, for example, the novel—*This Side of Paradise*—with which he founded his reputation. It has almost every fault and deficiency that a novel can possibly have. It is not only highly imitative but it imitates an inferior model. Fitzgerald, when he wrote the book, was drunk with Compton Mackenzie, and it sounds like an American attempt to rewrite *Sinister Street.* Now, Mackenzie, in spite of his gift for picturesque and comic invention and the capacity for pretty writing that he says he learned from Keats, lacks both the intellectual force and the emotional imagination to give body and outline to the material which he secretes in such enormous abundance. With the seeds he took from Keats's garden, one of the best-arranged gardens in England, he exfloreated so profusely that he blotted out the path of his own. Michael Fane, the hero of *Sinister Street,* was swamped in the forest of description; he was smothered by creepers and columbine. From the time he went up to Oxford,

---

"F. Scott Fitzgerald." From *The Shores of Light* (New York: Vintage Books, 1961). Copyright © 1952 by Edmund Wilson. Reprinted by permission of the author.

[1] This was Edna St. Vincent Millay, who met Scott Fitzgerald in Paris in the spring of 1921.

his personality began to grow dimmer, and, when he last turned up (in Belgrade) he seemed quite to have lost his identity. As a consequence, Amory Blaine, the hero of *This Side of Paradise,* had a very poor chance of coherence: Fitzgerald did endow him, to be sure, with a certain emotional life which the phantom Michael Fane lacks; but he was quite as much a wavering quantity in a phantasmagoria of incident that had no dominating intention to endow it with unity and force. In short, one of the chief weaknesses of *This Side of Paradise* is that it is really not *about* anything: its intellectual and moral content amounts to little more than a gesture—a gesture of indefinite revolt. The story itself, furthermore, is very immaturely imagined: it is always just verging on the ludicrous. And, finally, *This Side of Paradise* is one of the most illiterate books of any merit ever published (a fault which the publisher's proofreader seems to have made no effort to remedy). Not only is it ornamented with bogus ideas and faked literary references, but it is full of literary words tossed about with the most reckless inaccuracy.

I have said that *This Side of Paradise* commits almost every sin that a novel can possibly commit: but it does not commit the unpardonable sin: it does not fail to live. The whole preposterous farrago is animated with life. It is rather a fluttering and mercurial life: its emotions do not move you profoundly; its drama does not make you hold your breath; but its gaiety and color and movement did make it come as something exciting after the realistic heaviness and dinginess of so much serious American fiction. If one recalls the sort of flavorless fodder of which Ernest Poole's *The Harbor* was an example, one can understand the wild enthusiasm with which *This Side of Paradise* was hailed. The novel was also well-written—well-written in spite of its illiteracies. It is true, as I have said above, that Fitzgerald mishandles words; his works are full of malapropisms of the most disconcerting kind. You will find: "Whatever your flare [sic] proves to be—religion, architecture, literature"; "the Juvenalia of my collected editions"; "There were nice things in it [the room] . . . offsprings of a vicarious [vagarious] impatient taste"; "a mind like his, lucrative in intelligence, intuition and lightning decision"; etc., etc. It reminds one rather of:

> Agib, who could readily, at sight,
> Strum a march upon the loud Theodolite.
> He would diligently play
> On the Zoetrope all day,
> And blow the gay Pantechnicon all night.

It is true that Scott Fitzgerald plays the language entirely by ear. But his instrument, for all that, is no mean one. He has an instinct for graceful and vivid prose that some of his more pretentious fellows might envy.

In regard to the man himself, there are perhaps two things worth knowing, for the influence they have had on his work. In the first place, he comes from the Middle West—from St. Paul, Minnesota. Fitzgerald is as much of the Middle West of large cities and country clubs as Sinclair Lewis is of the Middle West of the prairies and little towns. What we find in him is much what we find in the more prosperous strata of these cities: sensitivity and eagerness for life without a sound base of culture and taste; a structure of millionaire residences, brilliant expensive hotels and exhilarating social activities built not on the eighteenth century but simply on the flat Western land. And it seems to me rather a pity that he has not written more of the West: it is perhaps the only milieu that he thoroughly understands. When Fitzgerald approaches the East, he brings to it the standards of the wealthy West—the preoccupation with display, the appetite for visible magnificence and audible jamboree, the vigorous social atmosphere of amiable flappers and youths comparatively untainted as yet by the snobbery of the East. In *The Beautiful and Damned,* for example, we feel that he is moving in a vacuum; the characters have no real connection with the background to which they have been assigned; they are not part of the organism of New York as the characters, in, say, the short story *Bernice Bobs Her Hair* are a part of the organism of St. Paul. Surely F. Scott Fitzgerald should some day do for Summit Avenue what Lewis has done for Main Street.

But you are not to suppose from all this that the author of *This Side of Paradise* is merely a typical well-to-do Middle Westerner, with correct clothes and clear skin, who has been sent to the East for college. The second thing one should know about him is that Fitzgerald is partly Irish and that he brings both to life and to fiction certain qualities that are not Anglo-Saxon. For, like the Irish, Fitzgerald is romantic, but also cynical about romance; he is bitter as well as ecstatic; astringent as well as lyrical. He casts himself in the role of playboy, yet at the playboy he incessantly mocks. He is vain, a little malicious, of quick intelligence and wit, and has an Irish gift for turning language into something iridescent and surprising. He often reminds one, in fact, of the description that a great Irishman, Bernard Shaw, has written of the Irish: "An Irishman's imagination never lets him alone, never convinces him, never satisfies him; but it makes him that he can't face reality nor deal with it nor handle it nor conquer it: he can only sneer at them that do . . . and imagination's such a torture that you can't bear it without whisky. . . . And all the while there goes on a horrible, senseless, mischievous laughter."

For the rest, F. Scott Fitzgerald is a rather childlike fellow, very much wrapped up in his dream of himself and his projection of it on paper. For a person of his mental agility, he is extraordinarily little occupied with the general affairs of the world: like a woman, he is not much given to abstract or impersonal thought. Conversations about politics or general ideas have a way of snapping back to Fitzgerald. But this seldom becomes annoying; he is never pretentious or boring. He is quite devoid of affectation and takes the curse off his relentless egoism by his readiness to laugh at himself and his boyish uncertainty of his talent. And he exhibits, in his personality as well as in his writings, a quality rare today among even the youngest American writers: he is almost the only one among them who is capable of lighthearted high spirits. Where a satirist like Sinclair Lewis would stew "the Problem of Salesmanship" in acrid rancorous fumes, Fitzgerald, in *The Beautiful and Damned,* has made of it hilarious farce. His characters—and he—are actors in an elfin harlequinade; they are as nimble, as gay and as lovely—and as hard-hearted—as fairies: Columbine elopes with Harlequin on a rope ladder dropped from the Ritz and both go morris-dancing amuck on a case of bootleg liquor; Pantaloon is pinked with an epigram that withers him up like a leaf; the Policeman is tripped by Harlequin and falls into the Pulitzer Fountain. Just before the curtain falls, Harlequin puts on false whiskers and pretends to be Bernard Shaw; he gives reporters an elaborate interview on politics, religion and history; a hundred thousand readers see it and are more or less impressed; Columbine nearly dies laughing; Harlequin sends out for a case of gin.

Let me quote a characteristic incident in connection with *The Beautiful and Damned.* Since writing *This Side of Paradise*—on the inspiration of Wells and Mackenzie—Fitzgerald has become acquainted with a different school of fiction: the ironical-pessimistic. In college, he had supposed that the thing to do was to write biographical novels with a burst of ideas toward the close; since his advent in the literary world, he has discovered that another genre has recently come into favor: the kind which makes much of the tragedy and what Mencken has called "the meaninglessness of life." Fitzgerald had imagined, hitherto, that the thing to do in a novel was to bring out a meaning in life; but he now set bravely about it to contrive a shattering tragedy that should be, also, a hundred-percent meaningless. As a result of this determination, the first version of *The Beautiful and Damned* culminated in an orgy of horror for which the reader was imperfectly prepared. Fitzgerald destroyed his characters with a succession of catastrophes so arbitrary that, beside them, the perversities of Hardy seemed the working of natural laws. The heroine was to lose her beauty at a prematurely early age, and her character was to go to pieces with it; Richard Carmel, a writer of promise, was to lose his artistic ideals and prostitute himself to the popular taste; and the wealthy Anthony Patch was not only to lose his money but, finding himself unable to make a living, abjectly to succumb to drink and eventually to go insane. But the bitterest moment of the story was to come at the very end, when Anthony was to be wandering the streets of New York in an attempt to borrow some money. After several humiliating failures, he finally approaches an old friend whom he sees with an elegant lady just getting into a cab. This is the brilliant Maury Noble, a cynic, an intellectual and a man of genuine parts. Maury cuts Anthony dead and drives away in the taxi. "But," the author explains, "he really had not seen Anthony. For Maury had indulged his appetite for alcoholic beverage once too often: he was now stone-blind!" But the point of my story is this: though Fitzgerald had been perfectly serious in writing this bathetic passage, he did not hesitate, when he heard people laugh at it, to laugh about it himself, and with as much surprise and delight as if he had just come across it in Max Beerbohm. He at once improvised a burlesque: "It seemed to Anthony that Maury's eyes had a fixed glassy stare; his legs moved stiffly as he walked and when he spoke his voice was lifeless. When Anthony came nearer, he saw that Maury was dead."

To conclude, it would be quite unfair to subject Scott Fitzgerald, who is still in his twenties and has presumably most of his work before him, to a rigorous overhauling. His restless imagination may yet produce something durable. For the present, however, this imagination is certainly not seen to the best advantage: it suffers badly from lack of discipline and poverty of aesthetic ideas. Fitzgerald is a dazzling extemporizer, but his stories have a way of petering out: he seems never to have planned them completely or to have thought out his themes from the beginning. This is true even of some of his most successful fantasies, such as *The Diamond as Big as the Ritz* or his comedy, *The Vegetable.* On the other hand, *The Beautiful and Damned,* imperfect though it is, marks an advance over *This Side of Paradise:* the style is more nearly mature and the subject more solidly unified, and there are scenes that are more convincing than any in his previous fiction.

But, in any case, even the work that Fitzgerald has done up to date has a certain moral importance. In his very expression of the anarchy by which he finds himself bewildered, of his revolt which cannot fix on an object, he is typical of the war generation—the generation so memorably described on the last page of *This Side of Paradise* as "grown up to find all gods dead, all wars fought, all faiths in men shaken." [2] There is a moral in *The Beautiful and Damned* that the author did not perhaps intend to point. The hero and the heroine of this giddy book are creatures without method or purpose: they give themselves up to wild debaucheries and do not, from beginning to end, perform a single serious act; yet somehow you get the impression that, in spite of their fantastic behavior, Anthony and Gloria Patch are the most rational people in the book. Wherever they come in contact with institutions, with the serious life of their time, these are made to appear ridiculous, they are subjects for scorn or mirth. We see the army, finance and business successively and casually exposed as completely without point or

[2] ". . . grown up to find all Gods dead, all wars fought, all faiths in man shaken. . . ." *This Side of Paradise,* p. 304. [A.M.]

dignity. The inference we are led to draw is that, in such a civilization as this, the sanest and most honorable course is to escape from organized society and live for the excitement of the moment. It cannot be merely a special reaction to a personal situation which gives rise to the paradoxes of such a book. It may be that we cannot demand too high a degree of moral balance from young men, however able or brilliant, who write books in the year 1921: we must remember that they have had to grow up in, that they have had to derive their chief stimulus from the wars, the society and the commerce of the Age of Confusion itself.

A Gesture of Indefinite Revolt

by James E. Miller, Jr.

Fitzgerald once referred to an early version of *This Side of Paradise* as a "picaresque ramble" or a "prose, modernistic Childe Harolde," [1] terms which well describe the episodic nature of his novel. There is no continuous line of action but rather a series of episodes related one to the other by Amory Blaine, the central character. The story is the biography of Amory Blaine during the formative years of his life. The episodes are related in that they constitute collectively the education of the hero, but there is no single plot-line to unify the novel. Such a loose structure lends itself well to documentation: an abundance of detailed incidents may be included so long as they revolve around the hero. As the reviewer for the *Publisher's Weekly* said—"It isn't a story in the regular sense: there's no beginning, except the beginning of Amory Blaine, born healthy, wealthy and extraordinarily good-looking, and by way of being spoiled by a restless mother whom he quaintly calls by her first name, Beatrice. There's no middle to the story, except the eager fumbling at life of this same handsome boy, proud, clean-minded, born to conquer yet fumbling, at college and in love with Isabelle, then Clara, then Rosalind, then Eleanor. No end to the story except the closing picture of this same boy in his early twenties, a bit less confident about life, with no God in his heart . . . his ideas still in riot." [2] With no central action, the book can have no beginning, middle, or end in the conventional sense.

Henry James's great demand for the novel was a center of interest or a motivating idea. Taking his cue from James, Percy Lubbock asserted that a novel "cannot begin to take shape" until it has "a subject, one and whole and irreducible . . . for its support." The question the critic must pose is "what the novel in his hand is about. What was the novelist's intention, in a phrase?" If the novel's "subject" cannot be stated in a phrase, if it is not "expressible in ten words that reveal its

---

"A Gesture of Indefinite Revolt." From *The Fictional Technique of Scott Fitzgerald* (The Hague: Martinus Nijhoff, 1957). Copyright © 1957 by James E. Miller, Jr. Reprinted by permission of the author and Martinus Nijhoff.
[1] Fitzgerald, "Letters to Friends," *The Crack-Up*, p. 252.
[2] R. S. S., "Ernest Poole and Tarkington at their best," *Publisher's Weekly* XCVII (April 17, 1920), 1289.

unity," then the critic can proceed no further. "The form of the book depends on it, and until it is known there is nothing to be said of the form." [3] It was with a note of contempt that Wells had said of James, "The thing his novel is *about* is always there." [4] This *relevance,* thought Wells, deprived the novel of "life."

What, we may well ask, is *This Side of Paradise* about? Edmund Wilson asserted that, as a consequence of its deriving so much from *Sinister Street,* "Amory Blaine . . . had a very poor chance for coherence . . . he was . . . an uncertain quantity in a phantasmagoria of incident which had no dominating intention to endow it with unity and force." Wilson concluded, "In short, *This Side of Paradise* is really not *about* anything; intellectually it amounts to little more than a gesture—a gesture of indefinite revolt." [5] By definition the saturation novel is not about any one thing: it is about "life" and must, therefore, include those irrelevancies which prevent life itself from coming to a focus and being *about* something.

But, as James said, even the *slice* of life must have been *cut;* it cannot exist in an amorphous state. Even the *saturation* novel has technique of some kind, though the author may not have been conscious of its use. Contrary to Lubbock, therefore, one *can* talk about the form or technique of a novel whose subject is not reducible to a brief statement. The question is whether or not one can reduce the subject or theme of *This Side of Paradise* to some general terms on which to base a discussion of technique. Referring to a previous version of his novel (when it was entitled *The Romantic Egotist*), Fitzgerald once remarked, "I really believe that no one else could have written so searchingly the story of the youth of our generation." [6] It would seem safe to assume that much of the same intention of method and theme implicit in this remark carried over into the published work. To this "story of the youth of our generation" might be added Wilson's phrase, "a gesture of indefinite revolt." If we acknowledge that *This Side of Paradise* is *about* the obscurely motivated and vaguely directed rebellion of the youth of Fitzgerald's generation, we may not have discovered a precise and lucid "pointed intention," but we do have a basis for analysis and evaluation.

Granting *This Side of Paradise* its method of *saturation* we can still critically examine its technique. Indeed, most critics have agreed that the crucial failure in the book was the failure of Fitzgerald to see his material objectively—that is, a failure in point of view. Fitzgerald has adopted no machinery as an integral part of his story whose function it is to evaluate the characters and the incidents. The story is told from

[3] Lubbock, *The Craft of Fiction,* p. 41.
[4] Wells, *Boon,* p. 109.
[5] Wilson, "The Literary Spotlight: F. Scott Fitzgerald," *The Bookman* LV (March, 1922), pp. 21-22.
[6] Fitzgerald, "Letters to Friends," *The Crack-Up,* p. 252.

the point of view of the hero, Amory Blaine, and the reader is left with Blaine's judgment unless Fitzgerald, by implication or by direct intervention, indicates otherwise. The general impression left with the reader, after he has finished the book, is as Paul Rosenfeld put it, that Fitzgerald "does not sustainedly perceive his girls and men for what they are, and tends to invest them with precisely the glamour with which they in pathetic assurance rather childishly invest themselves." [7]

Fitzgerald was, of course, young and immature when he wrote his novel, and, in writing about himself, was frequently unable to see his material objectively. The critical problem, however, is to discover what, in the book, betrays Fitzgerald's moral position. Some of the most revealing passages as to the author's attitude appear in the stage directions of the scenes done in play form, in which the author, because of his choice of method, is forced to speak in his own person. Fitzgerald does not confine himself to mere description; he seizes the opportunity for little chats with and asides to the reader. He betrays something of his whole position and attitude in the opening stage directions for the Amory-Rosalind meeting scene. In setting the scene, he first describes Rosalind's excessively pink and luxurious bedroom and enumerates the items laid out for Rosalind's debut. He then says confidentially to the reader: "One would enjoy seeing the bill called forth by the finery displayed and one is possessed by a desire to see the princess for whose benefit— Look! There's some one! Disappointment!" (179) It turns out to be only the maid. Fitzgerald obviously expects the reader to be as awed as he by the expensive scene which he has painted. He seems to expect the material wealth displayed to suffice for the reader to invest the characters, not even introduced yet, with intense interest and glamour. He does indeed seem blinded by the glitter of his own costly creation.

When Rosalind does enter, Fitzgerald asserts on her behalf: "In the true sense she is not spoiled. Her fresh enthusiasm, her will to grow and learn, her endless faith in the inexhaustibility of romance, her courage and fundamental honesty—these things are not spoiled." (183) One might question Fitzgerald's emphasis of her romantic rather than realistic nature when, in fact, she turns down Amory, whom she presumably loves, because he has no money, and exclaims, "I can't be shut away from the trees and flowers, cooped up in a little flat, waiting for you." Her "endless faith" in romance turns out to be a horror of household duties and an egocentric craving for luxury: "I don't want to think about pots and kitchens and brooms. I want to worry whether my legs will get slick and brown when I swim in the summer." (209-10) Fitzgerald is so entranced by the beauty and riches he has portrayed that he seems unable to comprehend Rosalind's fundamental selfishness and superficiality. The portrayal of Rosalind is, technically, a failure in characterization. For Fitzgerald attributes qualities to her which are

<hr>

[7] Paul Rosenfeld, "F. Scott Fitzgerald," *The Crack-Up*, p. 319.

mutually exclusive. His assertion that Rosalind is not spoiled is in conflict with the way he portrays her as acting. Fitzgerald closes the meeting scene: "And deep under the aching sadness that will pass in time, Rosalind feels that she has lost something, she knows not what, she knows not why." (211) The tone is all wrong, for it assumes a depth for Rosalind which, by this time, the reader knows she is incapable of achieving; these closing pretentious if somewhat lyrical phrases seem to be an attempt to surround her with a poetry which she does not deserve.

Because Rosalind rejects him, Amory goes on a drunken spree, and during one of his brief moments of sobriety, bewails his great loss:

> "My own girl—my own— Oh—"
> He clinched his teeth so that the tears streamed in a flood from his eyes.
> "Oh . . . my baby girl, all I had, all I wanted! . . . Oh, my girl, come back, come back! I need you . . . need you . . . We're so pitiful . . . just misery we brought each other . . . She'll be shut away from me . . . I can't see her; I can't be her friend. It's got to be that way—it's got to be—"
> And then again:
> "We've been so happy, so very happy . . ." (216)

Perhaps Amory is so affected by his broken love affair that he could talk in this sophomoric fashion. The effect of this speech on the reader, contrary to what Fitzgerald seems to expect, is one of embarrassment— embarrassment for the novelist. And when he says that there had been "so much dramatic tragedy" for Amory, one is convinced that Fitzgerald has attempted and expected an effect which he does not get. What the reader has seen is certainly not tragedy and not very good drama.

Again, in preparing the scene for the meeting of Eleanor and Amory, Fitzgerald's diction and imagery suggest an attempt at dramatic profundity which does not succeed:

> But Eleanor—did Amory dream her? Afterward their ghosts played, yet both of them hoped from their souls never to meet. Was it the infinite sadness of her eyes that drew him or the mirror of himself that he found in the gorgeous clarity of her mind? She will have no other adventure like Amory, and if she reads this she will say:
> "And Amory will have no other adventure like me." (238)

The tone created by Fitzgerald's language is struggling for a far more serious effect than is actually achieved in the scene. And when Eleanor and Amory take their final parting, Fitzgerald writes:

> Their poses were strewn about the pale dawn like broken glass. The stars were long gone and there were left only the little sighing gusts of wind and the silences between . . . but naked souls are poor things ever, and soon he turned homeward and let new lights come in with the sun. (258)

The dramatic details and images, like those of the beginning of this scene, betray the romantic haze through which Fitzgerald conceived his characters and their struggles.

Fitzgerald's inability to remain detached and uninvolved interfered, naturally, with the development of the theme of *This Side of Paradise*. In order that the revolt of his generation be made comprehensible and convincing, it was imperative that Fitzgerald present his youth objectively. The precise nature of the revolt undertaken by the youth never clearly emerges. There is, presumably, a "questioning aloud the institutions" (131) of all phases of American life, including educational, religious, political, and moral. But the questioning remains submerged, only half articulated, lost in a multitude of cross purposes.

Much of the "revolt" seems on the periphery rather than at the center of the novel. There is Burne Holiday's objection to the social system represented by the clubs at Princeton. But this "did not seem such a vital subject as it had in the two years before" (134) to Amory. There is Amory's periodic religious questioning. In a letter to Tom D'Invilliers after the war he says, "I confess that the war instead of making me orthodox, which is the correct reaction, has made me a passionate agnostic. . . . This crisis-inspired religion is rather valueless and fleeting at best." (176) And at the end of the book, the reader is told that "there was no God in his [Amory's] heart." (304) Even in the long monologue in which Amory presents the case for socialism to the Capitalist and his Sycophant (Mr. Ferrenby and Garvin are more symbols than characters), it is all on the spur of the moment and the theories which Amory expresses are mixed up in his mind with "the richest man [getting] the most beautiful girl if he wants her." (299)

But the aspect of the revolt best remembered is the "questioning of moral codes." (66) Fitzgerald wrote of his generation: "None of the Victorian mothers—and most of the mothers were Victorians—had any idea how casually their daughters were accustomed to be kissed." (64) The "revolt" seldom goes much beyond the kiss. When Amory goes on his trip with the Princeton musical comedy, he sees "girls doing things that even in his memory would have been impossible." (65) And what are these acts that seem so shocking? "Eating three-o'clock, after-dance suppers in impossible cafés, talking of every side of life with an air half of earnestness, half of mockery, yet with a furtive excitement that Amory considered stood for a real moral let-down." (65)

Yet, in Amory's own case, there seems to be an ambivalent attitude developed toward sex. There is in him an extreme daring (for the year 1920), but also a recurring aversion. As his first love affair just reaches a climax in a kiss, "sudden revulsion seized Amory, disgust, loathing for the whole incident. He desired frantically to be away, never to see Myra again, never to kiss any one." (15) Amory is given "a puzzled, furtive interest in everything concerning sex" (20) but his repugnance of sex seems to be a fixed and uncontrollable part of his reaction. When he and Fred Sloane are spending what was meant to be a wild evening out with a couple of girls, Amory thinks he sees a pale man watching him. Up in the girls' apartment, just as "temptation [is creeping] over him like a warm wind," (122) he sees the vision again, whereupon he abruptly leaves and runs into an alley, where "before his eyes a face flashed . . . a face pale and distorted with a sort of infinite evil that twisted it like flame in the wind; *but he knew, for the half instant that the gong tanged and hummed, that it was the face of Dick Humbird.*" (126) Dick Humbird was Amory's friend at Princeton who had been killed in an automobile accident; Amory had been riding in another car and had seen the wreck and Dick's body shortly after the accident. In this ambiguous fashion Amory connects sex not only with evil but also with death. The terrifying evil which surrounds sex for Amory is extended to encompass beauty also: "Eleanor was, say, the last time that evil crept close to Amory under the mask of beauty." (238) Yet Eleanor is treated as a pure, poetic influence on Amory. And when Amory, near the end of the book, attempts to assess the meaning of his experience, he discovers that sex and beauty have become inextricably mixed with evil: "The problem of evil had solidified for Amory into the problem of sex. . . . Inseparably linked with evil was beauty. . . . Amory knew that every time he had reached toward it longingly it had leered out at him with the grotesque face of evil." (302) Although this development in Amory of a puritan-like sensibility does not let him serve well as a symbol of revolt, the novel perhaps gains in value from the increased complexity and subtlety in the presentation of his character.

At one point in his story, Amory cries out, "My whole generation is restless." (299) The novel is more a representation of that restlessness than it is a coherent assertion of revolt. Perhaps that is why Edmund Wilson characterized the novel as a "gesture of indefinite revolt." Just what constitutes the revolt is not readily apparent; what is being revolted *against* does not clearly emerge. But it is because of the vague rebelliousness or "restlessness" in it that *This Side of Paradise* retains importance in literary history. It stands at the beginning of a decade famed for its literature of revolt. It is the first of the post-war novels by the then new generation of authors, the generation which had "grown up to find all Gods dead, all wars fought, all faiths in man shaken." (304) As Alfred Kazin has said, *This Side of Paradise* "announced the lost generation." [8] In spite of the apparently blurred and mixed purposes in the novel, the sexual, social, and literary restlessness of the younger generation came through clear enough to capture the imagination of a decade.

[8] Alfred Kazin, *On Native Grounds* (New York: Reynal & Hitchcock, 1942), p. 316.

The Courtship of Miles Standish

by Donald Ogden Stewart

In the Manner of F. Scott Fitzgerald

This story occurs under the blue skies and bluer laws of Puritan
New England, in the days when religion was still taken seriously by
a great many people, and in the town of Plymouth where the "Mayflower," having ploughed its platitudinous way from Holland, had
landed its precious cargo of pious Right Thinkers, moral Gentlemen
of God, and—Priscilla.

Priscilla was—well, Priscilla had yellow hair. In a later generation,
in a 1921 June, if she had toddled by at a country club dance you
would have noticed first of all that glorious mass of bobbed corn-colored
locks. You would, then, perhaps, have glanced idly at her face, and suddenly said "Oh my gosh!" The next moment you would have clutched
the nearest stag and hissed, "Quick—yellow hair—silver dress—oh Ju-
das!" You would then have been introduced, and after dancing nine
feet you would have been cut in on by another panting stag. In those
nine delirious feet you would have become completely dazed by one
of the smoothest lines since the building of the Southern Pacific. You
would then have borrowed somebody's flask, gone into the locker room
and gotten an edge—not a bachelor-dinner edge but just enough to
give you the proper amount of confidence. You would have returned
to the ballroom, cut in on this twentieth century Priscilla, and taken
her and your edge out to a convenient limousine, or the first tee.

It was of some such yellow-haired Priscilla that Homer dreamed
when he smote his lyre and chanted, "I sing of arms and the man";
it was at the sight of such as she that rare Ben Jonson's Dr. Faustus
cried, "Was this the face that launched a thousand ships?" In all ages
has such beauty enchanted the minds of men, calling forth in one
century the Fiesolian terza rima of "Paradise Lost," in another the
passionate arias of a dozen Beethoven symphonies. In 1620 the pagan

"The Courtship of Miles Standish." From *The Parody Outline of History* (New
York: Doubleday & Company, Inc., 1921) by Donald Ogden Stewart. Copyright © 1921
by George H. Doran. Reprinted by permission of the author and Doubleday & Company, Inc.

daughter of Helen of Troy and Cleopatra of the Nile happened, by a characteristic jest of the great Ironist, to embark with her aunt on the "Mayflower."

Like all girls of eighteen Priscilla had learned to kiss and be kissed on every possible occasion; in the exotic and not at all uncommon pleasure of "petting" she had acquired infinite wisdom and complete disillusionment. But in all her "petting parties" on the "Mayflower" and in Plymouth she had found no Puritan who held her interest beyond the first kiss, and she had lately reverted in sheer boredom to her boarding school habit of drinking gin in large quantities—a habit which was not entirely approved of by her old-fashioned aunt, although Mrs. Brewster was glad to have her niece stay at home in the evenings "instead," as she told Mrs. Bradford, "of running around with those boys, and really, my dear, Priscilla says some the *funniest* things when she gets a little—er—'boiled,' as she calls it—you must come over some evening, and bring the governor."

Mrs. Brewster, Priscilla's aunt, is the ancestor of all New England aunts. She may be seen today walking down Tremont Street, Boston, in her Educator shoes on her way to S. S. Pierce's which she pronounces to rhyme with *hearse*. The twentieth century Mrs. Brewster wears a highnecked black silk waist with a chatelaine watch pinned over her left breast and a spot of Gordon's codfish (no bones) over her right. When a little girl she was taken to see Longfellow, Lowell, and Ralph Waldo Emerson; she speaks familiarly of the James boys, but this has no reference to the well-known Missouri outlaws. She was brought up on blueberry cake, Postum, and "The Atlantic Monthly"; she loves the Boston "Transcript," God, and her relatives in Newton Centre. Her idea of a daring joke is the remark Susan Hale made to Edward Everett Hale about sending underwear to the heathen. She once asked Donald Ogden Stewart to dinner with her niece; she didn't think his story about the lady mind reader who read the man's mind and then slapped his face, was very funny; she never asked him again.

The action of this story all takes place in Mrs. Brewster's *Plymouth home on two successive June evenings. As the figurative curtain rises* Mrs. Brewster *is sitting at a desk reading the latest instalment of Foxe's "Book of Martyrs."*

The sound of a clanking sword is heard outside. Mrs. Brewster *looks up, smiles to herself, and goes on reading. A knock—a timid knock.*

Mrs. Brewster: Come in.

(*Enter* Captain Miles Standish, *whiskered and forty. In a later generation, with that imposing mustache and his hatred of Indians, Miles would undoubtedly have been a bank president. At present he seems somewhat ill at ease, and obviously relieved to find only* Priscilla's *aunt at home.*)

MRS. BREWSTER: Good evening, Captain Standish.

MILES: Good evening, Mrs. Brewster. It's—it's cool for June, isn't it?

MRS. BREWSTER: Yes. I suppose we'll pay for it with a hot July, though.

MILES (*nervously*): Yes, but it—it is cool for June, isn't it?

MRS. BREWSTER: So you said, Captain.

MILES: Yes. So I said, didn't I?

(*Silence.*)

MILES: Mistress Priscilla isn't home, then?

MRS. BREWSTER: Why, I don't think so, Captain. But I never can be sure where Priscilla is.

MILES (*eagerly*): She's a—a fine girl, isn't she? A fine girl.

MRS. BREWSTER: Why, yes. Of course, Priscilla has her faults—but she'd make some man a fine wife—some man who knew how to handle her—an older man, with experience.

MILES: Do you really think so, Mrs. Brewster? (*After a minute.*) Do you think Priscilla is thinking about marrying anybody in particular?

MRS. BREWSTER: Well, I can't say, Captain. You know—she's a little wild. Her mother was wild, too, you know—that is, before the Lord spoke to her. They say she used to be seen at the Mermaid Tavern in London with all those play-acting people. She always used to say that Priscilla would marry a military man.

MILES: A military man? Well, now tell me Mrs. Brewster, do you think that a sweet delicate creature like Priscilla—

A VOICE (*in the next room*): Oh DAMN!

MRS. BREWSTER: That must be Priscilla now.

THE VOICE: Auntie!

MRS. BREWSTER: Yes, Priscilla dear.

THE VOICE: Where in hell did you put the vermouth?

MRS. BREWSTER: In the cupboard, dear. I do hope you aren't going to get—er—"boiled" again tonight, Priscilla.

(*Enter* PRISCILLA, *infinitely radiant, infinitely beautiful, with a bottle of vermouth in one hand and a jug of gin in the other.*)

PRISCILLA: Auntie, that was a dirty trick to hide the vermouth. Hello Miles—shoot many Indians today?

MILES: Why—er—er—no, Mistress Priscilla.

PRISCILLA: Wish you'd take me with you next time, Miles. I'd love to shoot an Indian, wouldn't you, auntie?

MRS. BREWSTER: Priscilla! What an idea! And please dear, give Auntie Brewster the gin. I—er—promised to take some to the church social tonight and it's almost all gone now.

MILES: I didn't see you at church last night, Mistress Priscilla.

PRISCILLA: Well I'll tell you, Miles. I started to go to church—really felt awfully religious. But just as I was leaving I thought, "Priscilla, how about a drink—just one little drink?" You know, Miles, church goes so much better when you're just a little boiled—the lights and everything just kind of—oh, its glorious. Well last night, after I'd had a little liquor, the funniest thing happened. I felt awfully good, not like church at all—so I just thought I'd take a walk in the woods. And I came to a pool—a wonderful honest-to-God pool—with the moon shining right into the middle of it. So I just undressed and dove in and it was the most marvelous thing in the world. And then I danced on the bank in the grass and the moonlight—oh, Lordy, Miles, you ought to have seen me.

MRS. BREWSTER: Priscilla!

PRISCILLA: 'Scuse me, Auntie Brewster. And then I just lay in the grass and sang and laughed.

MRS. BREWSTER: Dear, you'll catch your death of cold one of these nights. I hope you'll excuse me, Captain Standish; it's time I was going to our social. I'll leave Priscilla to entertain you. Now be a good girl, Priscilla, and please dear don't drink straight vermouth—remember what happened last time. Good night, Captain—good night, dear.

(*Exit* MRS. BREWSTER *with gin.*)

PRISCILLA: Oh damn! What'll we do, Miles—I'm getting awfully sleepy.

MILES: Why—we might—er—pet a bit.

PRISCILLA (*yawning*): No. I'm too tired—besides, I hate whiskers.

MILES: Yes, that's so, I remember.

(*Ten minutes' silence, with* MILES *looking sentimentally into the fireplace,* PRISCILLA *curled up in a chair on the other side.*)

MILES: I was—your aunt and I—we were talking about you before you came in. It was a talk that meant a lot to me.

PRISCILLA: Miles, would you mind closing that window?

(MILES *closes the window and returns to his chair by the fireplace.*)

MILES: And your aunt told me that your mother said you would some day marry a military man.

PRISCILLA: Miles, would you mind passing me that pillow over there?

(MILES *gets up, takes the pillow to* PRISCILLA *and again sits down.*)

MILES: And I thought that if you wanted a military man why—well, I've always thought a great deal of you, Mistress Priscilla—and since my Rose died I've been pretty lonely, and while I'm nothing but a rough old soldier yet—well, what I'm driving at is—you see, maybe you and I could sort of—well, I'm not much of a hand at fancy love speeches and all that—but—

(*He is interrupted by a snore. He glances up and sees that* PRISCILLA *has fallen fast asleep. He sits looking hopelessly into the fireplace for a long time, then gets up, puts on his hat and tiptoes out of the door.*)

THE NEXT EVENING

PRISCILLA *is sitting alone, lost in revery, before the fireplace. It is almost as if she had not moved since the evening before.*
A knock, and the door opens to admit JOHN ALDEN, *nonchalant, disillusioned, and twenty-one.*

JOHN: Good evening. Hope I don't bother you.

PRISCILLA: The only people who bother me are women who tell me I'm beautiful and men who don't.

JOHN: Not a very brilliant epigram—but still—yes, you *are* beautiful.

PRISCILLA: Of course, if it's an effort for you to say—

JOHN: Nothing is worthwhile without effort.

PRISCILLA: Sounds like Miles Standish; many things I do without effort are worthwhile; I am beautiful without the slightest effort.

JOHN: Yes, you're right. I could kiss you without any effort—and that would be worthwhile—perhaps.

PRISCILLA: Kissing me would prove nothing. I kiss as casually as I breathe.

JOHN: And if you didn't breathe—or kiss—you would die.

PRISCILLA: Any woman would.

JOHN: Then you are like other women. How unfortunate.

PRISCILLA: I am like no woman you ever knew.

JOHN: You arouse my curiosity.

PRISCILLA: Curiosity killed a cat.

JOHN: A cat may look at a—Queen.

PRISCILLA: And a Queen keeps cats for her amusement. They purr so delightfully when she pets them.

JOHN: I never learned to purr; it must be amusing—for the Queen.

PRISCILLA: Let me teach you. I'm starting a new class tonight.

JOHN: I'm afraid I couldn't afford to pay the tuition.

PRISCILLA: For a few exceptionally meritorious pupils, various scholarships and fellowships have been provided.

JOHN: By whom? Old graduates?

PRISCILLA: No—the institution has been endowed by God—

JOHN: With exceptional beauty—I'm afraid I'm going to kiss you. Now.

(They kiss.)

(Ten minutes pass.)

PRISCILLA: Stop smiling in that inane way.

JOHN: I just happened to think of something awfully funny. You know the reason why I came over here tonight?

PRISCILLA: To see me. I wondered why you hadn't come months ago.

JOHN: No. It's really awfully funny—but I came here tonight because Miles Standish made me promise this morning to ask you to marry him. Miles is an awfully good egg, really Priscilla.

PRISCILLA: Speak for yourself, John.

(They kiss.)

PRISCILLA: Again.

JOHN: Again—and again. Oh Lord, I'm gone.

(An hour later JOHN leaves. As the door closes behind him PRISCILLA sinks back into her chair before the fireplace; an hour passes, and she does not move; her aunt returns from the Bradfords' and after a few ineffectual attempts at conversation goes to bed alone; the candles gutter, flicker, and die out; the room is filled with moonlight, softly stealing through the silken skein of sacred silence. Once more the clock chimes forth the hour—the hour of fluted peace, of dead desire and epic love. Oh not for aye, Endymion, mayst thou unfold the purple panoply of priceless years. She sleeps—PRISCILLA sleeps— and down the palimpsest of age-old passion the lyres of night breathe forth their poignant praise. She sleeps—eternal Helen—in the moonlight of a thousand years; immortal symbol of immortal aeons, flower of the gods transplanted on a foreign shore, infinitely rare, infinitely erotic.*)

* For the further adventures of Priscilla, see F. Scott Fitzgerald's stories in the "Girl With the Yellow Hair" series, notably "This Side of Paradise," "The Offshore Pirate," "The Ice Palace," "Head and Shoulders," "Bernice Bobs Her Hair," "Benediction" and "The Beautiful and Damned."

THE GREAT GATSBY

F. Scott Fitzgerald's
The Great Gatsby

Legendary Bases and Allegorical Significances

by John Henry Raleigh

F. Scott Fitzgerald's character Gatsby, as has often been said, represents the irony of American history and the corruption of the American
dream. While this certainly is true, yet even here, with this general
legend, Fitzgerald has rung in his own characteristic changes, doubling
and redoubling ironies. At the center of the legend proper there is the
relationship between Europe and America and the ambiguous inter-
action between the contradictory impulses of Europe that led to the
original settling of America and its subsequent development: mercantil-
ism and idealism. At either end of American history, and all the way
through, the two impulses have a way of being both radically exclusive
and mutually confusing, the one melting into the other: the human
faculty of wonder, on the one hand, and the power and beauty of things,
on the other.

The Great Gatsby dramatizes this continuing ambiguity directly in the

"F. Scott Fitzgerald's *The Great Gatsby*," by John H. Raleigh. From *The University of Kansas City Review*, 24 (Autumn 1957). Copyright © 1957 by John H. Raleigh. Reprinted by permission of the author and *The University of Kansas City Review*.

life of Gatsby and retrospectively by a glance at history at the end of the novel. Especially does it do so in the two passages in the novel of what might be called the ecstatic moment, the moment when the human imagination seems to be on the verge of entering the earthly paradise. The two passages are (1) the real Gatsby looking on the real Daisy, and (2) the imaginary Dutchmen, whom Nick conjures up at the end of the novel, looking on the "green breast" of Long Island.

Here is the description of Gatsby and Daisy:

> Out of the corner of his eye Gatsby saw that the blocks of the sidewalks really formed a ladder and mounted to a secret place above the trees—he could climb to it, if he climbed alone, and once there he could suck on the pap of life, gulp down the incomparable milk of wonder.
>
> His heart beat faster and faster as Daisy's white face came up to his own. He knew that when he kissed this girl, and forever wed his unutterable visions to her perishable breath, his mind would never romp again like the mind of God. So he waited, listening for a moment longer to the tuning-fork that had been struck upon a star. Then he kissed her. At his lips' touch she blossomed for him like a flower and the incarnation was complete.

And below is Nick's imaginative reconstruction of the legendary Dutchman. He is sprawled on the sand at night, with Gatsby's mansion behind him and Long Island Sound in front of him:

> And as the moon rose higher the inessential houses began to melt away until gradually I became aware of the old Island that flowered once for Dutch eyes—a fresh green breast of the new world. Its vanished trees, the trees that had made way for Gatsby's house, had once pandered in whispers to the last and greatest of all human dreams; for a transitory enchanted moment man must have held his breath in the presence of this continent, compelled into an aesthetic contemplation he neither understood nor desired, face to face for the last time in history with something commensurate to his capacity for wonder.[1]

The repetition in the two passages of the words "wonder" and "flower" hardly need comment, or the sexuality, illicit in the Dutchmen's and both infantile and mature in Gatsby's—or the star-lit, moon-lit setting in both. For these are the central symbols in the book: the boundless imagination trying to transfigure under the stars the endlessly beautiful object. Now, of course, the Dutchmen and Gatsby are utterly different types of being and going in different directions. The Dutchmen are pure matter, momentarily and unwillingly raised into the realms of the

---

[1] Fitzgerald wrote: ". . . until gradually I became aware of the old island here that flowered once for the Dutch sailors' eyes—a fresh, green breast of the new world." *The Great Gatsby*, pp. 217-218. [A.M.]

spirit, while Gatsby is pure spirit coming down to earth. They pass one another, so to speak, at the moment when ideal and reality seem about to converge. Historically, the Dutch, legendarily stolid, pursued their mercantile ways and produced finally a Tom Buchanan but also, it should be remembered, a Nick Carraway. But their ecstatic moment hung on in the air, like an aroma, intoxicating prophets, sages, poets, even poor farm boys in twentieth-century Dakota. The heady insubstantiability of the dream and the heavy intractability of the reality were expressed by Van Wyck Brooks (who could well have been Fitzgerald's philosopher in these matters) in his *The Wine of the Puritans* as follows:

> You put the old wine [Europeans] into new bottles [American continent] . . . and when the explosion results, one may say, the aroma passes into the air and the wine spills on the floor. The aroma or the ideal, turns into transcendentalism and the wine or the real, becomes commercialism.

No one knew better than Gatsby that nothing could finally match the splendors of his own imagination, and the novel would suggest finally that not only had the American dream been corrupted but that it was, in part anyway, necessarily corrupted, for it asked too much. Nothing of this earth, even the most beautiful of earthly objects, could be anything but a perversion of it.

The Great Gatsby, then, begins in a dramatization, as suggested, of the basic thesis of the early Van Wyck Brooks: that America had produced an idealism so impalpable that it had lost touch with reality (Gatsby) and a materialism so heavy that it was inhuman (Tom Buchanan). The novel as a whole is another turn of the screw on this legend, with the impossible idealism trying to realize itself, to its utter destruction, in the gross materiality. As Nick says of Gatsby at the end of the novel:

> . . . his dream must have seemed so close that he could hardly fail to grasp it. He did not know that it was already behind him somewhere back in that vast obscurity beyond the city, where the dark fields of the republic rolled on under the night.

Yet he imagines too that Gatsby, before his moment of death, must have had his "realization" of the intractable brutishness of matter:

> . . . he must have felt that he had lost the old warm world, paid a high price for living too long with a single dream. He must have looked up at an unfamiliar sky through frightening leaves and shivered as he found what a grotesque thing a rose is and how raw the sunlight was upon the scarcely created grass.

Thus Fitzgerald multiplies the ironies of the whole legend: that the mercantile Dutchmen should have been seduced into the esthetic; that Gatsby's wondrous aspirations should attach themselves to a Southern belle and that in pursuit of her he should become a gangster's lieutenant; that young Englishmen ("agonizingly aware of the easy money in the vicinity") should scramble for crumbs at Gatsby's grandiose parties (the Dutchmen once more); that idealism, beauty, power, money should get all mixed up; that history should be a kind of parody of itself, as with the case of the early Dutch and the contemporary English explorers.

Still *The Great Gatsby* would finally suggest, at a level beyond all its legends and in the realm of the properly tragic, that it is right and fitting that the Jay Gatzes of the world should ask for the impossible, even when they do so as pathetically and ludicrously as does Gatsby himself. Writing to Fitzgerald about his novel, Maxwell Perkins, after enumerating some specific virtues, said:

> . . . these are such things as make a man famous. And all the things, the whole pathetic episode, you have given a place in time and space, for with the help of T. J. Eckleburg, and by an occasional glance at the sky, or the city, you have imparted a sort of sense of eternity.

A "sense of eternity"—this is indeed high praise, but I think that Perkins, as he often was, was right.

For at its highest level *The Great Gatsby* does not deal with local customs or even national and international legends but with the permanent realities of existence. On this level nothing or nobody is to blame, and people are what they are and life is what it is, just as, in Bishop Butler's words, "things are what they are." At this level, too, most people don't count; they are merely a higher form of animality living out its mundane existence: the Tom Buchanans, the Jordan Bakers, the Daisy Fays. Only Nick and Gatsby count. For Gatsby, with all his absurdities and his short, sad, pathetic life, is still valuable; in Nick's parting words to him: "You're worth the whole damn bunch put together." Nick, who in his way is as much of this world as Daisy is in hers, still sees, obscurely, the significance of Gatsby. And although he knows that the content of Gatsby's dream is corrupt, he senses that its form is pristine. For, in his own fumbling, often gross way, Gatsby was obsessed with the wonder of human life and driven by the search to make that wonder actual. It is the same urge that motivates visionaries and prophets, the urge to make the facts of life measure up to the splendors of the human imagination, but it is utterly pathetic in Gatsby's case because he is trying to do it so subjectively and so uncouthly, and with dollar bills. Still Nick's obscure instinct that Gatsby is essentially all right is sound. It often seems as if the novel is about the contrast between the two, but the bond between them reveals that they are not opposites but rather complements, opposed together, to all the other characters in the novel.

Taken together they contain most of the essential polarities that go to make up the human mind and its existence. Allegorically considered, Nick is reason, experience, waking, reality, and history, while Gatsby is imagination, innocence, sleeping, dream, and eternity. Nick is like Wordsworth listening to "the still sad music of humanity," while Gatsby is like Blake seeing hosts of angels in the sun. The one can only look at the facts and see them as tragic; the other tries to transform the facts by an act of the imagination. Nick's mind is conservative and historical, as is his lineage; Gatsby's is radical and apocalyptic—as rootless as his heritage. Nick is too much immersed in time and in reality; Gatsby is hopelessly out of it. Nick is always withdrawing, while Gatsby pursues the green light. Nick can't be hurt, but neither can he be happy. Gatsby can experience ecstasy, but his fate is necessarily tragic. They are generically two of the best types of humanity: the moralist and the radical.

One may well ask why, if their mental horizons are so lofty, is one a bond salesman and the other a gangster's lieutenant, whose whole existence is devoted to a love affair that has about it the unmistakable stamp of adolescence? The answer is, I think, that Fitzgerald did not know enough of what a philosopher or revolutionary might really be like, that at this point in his life he must have always thought of love in terms of a Princeton Prom, and that, writing in the twenties, a bond salesman and a gangster's functionary would seem more representative anyway. Van Wyck Brooks might have said, at one time, that his culture gave him nothing more to work with. A lesser writer might have attempted to make Nick a literal sage and Gatsby a literal prophet. But it is certain that such a thought would never have entered Fitzgerald's head, as he was only dramatizing the morals and manners of the life he knew. The genius of the novel consists precisely in the fact that, while using only the stuff, one might better say the froth and flotsam of its own limited time and place, it has managed to suggest, as Perkins said, a sense of eternity.

The Eyes of Dr. Eckleburg:
A Re-examination of *The Great Gatsby*

by Tom Burnam

F. Scott Fitzgerald's *The Great Gatsby* seems, deceptively, to be a simple work, and the plot can be summarized in a paragraph or two. In the spring of 1922 Nick Carraway rents a house on Long Island Sound. Near by live Nick's cousin Daisy Buchanan and her rich, burly, racist, congenitally unfaithful husband Tom, whose current mistress is Myrtle Wilson. Next door to Nick in an enormous mansion is Jay Gatsby, rich too but rootless as air, mysterious as his rare smile "with a quality of eternal reassurance in it." While visiting the Buchanans, Nick meets Jordan Baker, a petulant charming girl flawed by an incurable dishonesty; from her he learns (truthfully) that Gatsby, as a young officer about to go overseas, had been in love with Daisy in 1917 before her marriage to Buchanan.

At Gatsby's request, Nick arranges a meeting between Gatsby and Daisy, the first of several. But Daisy cannot break away from Tom, particularly after she learns that Gatsby's wealth comes from racketeering. As Daisy and Gatsby are driving back to Long Island from a party in New York, they run down Myrtle Wilson and do not stop. Though Gatsby unintentionally reveals to Nick that it was Daisy at the wheel, Daisy allows Tom to tell Myrtle Wilson's husband George (who already thinks that Gatsby was his wife's lover) that Gatsby is responsible for Myrtle's death. George Wilson shoots Gatsby and then himself, and that is that.

It is even possible to read *The Great Gatsby* and remain content with a single symbol: the green light (which, as a student once informed me, ought legally to be red) at the end of Daisy's dock. To those who do not feel a need to inquire further, the light obviously stands for what Nick Carraway says it stands for: "the orgiastic future that year by year recedes before us." True, even the most pragmatic reader may wish to add that the green light might also represent to Gatsby a projection of

"The Eyes of Dr. Eckleburg: A Re-examination of *The Great Gatsby*" by Tom Burnam. From *College English* (October 1952). Copyright © 1952 by Tom Burnam. Reprinted by permission of the author and the National Council of Teachers of English.

his wishes: a signal to go ahead, to "beat on . . . against the current," to attempt so desperately with his "unbroken series of successful gestures" the recapturing of that past which he can never attain.

But there is still more in *The Great Gatsby* than a protagonist, a plot, and a green light. Many elements in the story, perhaps, will puzzle the practical-minded, for on the level of simple narrative they cannot be accounted for. What does one make, for example, of the faded blue eyes of Dr. T. J. Eckleburg, those staring, vacant, yet somewhat terrible eyes so much more than an abandoned signboard; of the ash heap and its "ash-gray men, who move dimly and already crumbling through the powdery air" over which the eyes brood changelessly; of George Wilson's despairing mutter as he gazes at the eyes, "You may fool me, but you can't fool God!" [1]

And there is the matter, too, of the odd scene in which Nick and Jordan Baker discuss Jordan's carelessness with automobiles. One could easily find structural reasons for such a conversation between Nick and Daisy, or Gatsby and Daisy, for it is Daisy who runs down Myrtle Wilson. But why emphasize *Jordan's* inability to handle an automobile safely? [2] I believe the answers to this question and the others I have posed are concerned with a more complex organization than is commonly assumed, an organization of symbols the whole meaning of which was not entirely clear to Fitzgerald himself. For Fitzgerald-as-Fitzgerald and Fitzgerald-as-Carraway, the gleeman of the Gatsby saga, are not the same, though both appear alternately throughout the novel, intertwining like the threads in a fabric whose sheen depends not only on the materials out of which it is made but on the light in which it is viewed.

It seems to me a very interesting fact that the overt theme of *The Great Gatsby* has little to do, actually, with the novel's use of symbol. It is indeed likely, as a matter of fact, that the subdominant motif— which I hope soon to expose—very often overshadows what Fitzgerald apparently intended to be his principal theme. Of course, it is true that in making its point about the paradoxical futility of an attempt to recapture the past, *The Great Gatsby* obviously also says much more; one measure of its greatness is the complex and ironic quality of Gatsby's attempt to beat against the current. For he—and he alone, barring Carraway—survives sound and whole in character, uncorrupted by the corruption which surrounded him, which was indeed responsible for him; from his attempt at the childishly impossible he emerges with dignity and maturity. Yet no major work of fiction with which I am

---

[1] It is interesting, though not so relevant as might at first glance be supposed, that the eyes were written into the book after Fitzgerald saw what Arthur Mizener accurately calls a "very bad picture" on the dust jacket, a picture originally intended to represent Daisy's face.

[2] The scene does serve partly to foreshadow Nick's final breaking-off with Jordan; but only partly.

acquainted reserves its symbols for the subtheme; the more one thinks about *The Great Gatsby*, the more one comes to believe that F. Scott Fitzgerald may not have entirely realized what he was doing.

I think it is evident that not even the most skilful novelist could make us quite accept a young bond salesman of Nick Carraway's background and experience (even one who was "rather literary in college") as capable of composing the wonderful description in chapter iii of Gatsby's parties, or the passage later on in the same chapter beginning "I began to like New York," or managing to contrive that unique and poignant apostrophe to the "hundred pairs of golden and silver slippers" which "shuffled the shining dust . . . while fresh faces drifted here and there like rose petals blown by the sad horns around the floor." In other words, Nick as Nick is one thing and Fitzgerald as himself is another—something, incidentally, which Fitzgerald tacitly admits in a letter presently to be quoted. Thus the novel may very well involve not merely the theme which Nick presents in his own character, but also another which may be called, for lack of a better name, the "Fitzgerald theme." And it is toward the latter, I believe, that almost all the symbolism in *The Great Gatsby* is directed.

Nick Carraway, as Nick, could very well point everything he said toward the magnificent and at the same time sordid spectacle, Gatsby; could praise in Gatsby "something gorgeous . . . some heightened sensitivity to the promises of life" and rub out the obscene word some prowling urchin has scrawled on the white steps of the dead Gatsby's deserted mansion. But F. Scott Fitzgerald is the one who introduces, I think unconsciously, a fascinating examination of certain values only peripherally related to Gatsby's rise, his dream, and his physical downfall. And, if we turn to this other area, this non-Carraway thematic possibility, we see at once that *The Great Gatsby* is not, like *Lord Jim*, a study of illusion and integrity, but of carelessness. Our "second" theme—perhaps the more important regardless of Fitzgerald's original intention—becomes a commentary on the nature and values, or lack of them, of the reckless ones.

We know that the critics were not alone in sensing a certain lack in *The Great Gatsby*. Fitzgerald himself felt it, was uncomfortable about it, tried to explain it away even though there is evidence that he always regarded *Gatsby* as his greatest piece of work.[3] No one agreed, however, about what the lack was. Fitzgerald could not define it consistently; in a letter to John Peale Bishop postmarked August 9, 1925, he calls *The Great Gatsby* "blurred and patchy" and adds: "I never at any one time

---

[3] See, for example, the letter to his daughter dated June 12, 1940, in which he says: ". . . I wish now I'd *never* relaxed or looked back—but said at the end of *The Great Gatsby*: 'I've found my line—from now on this comes first. This is my immediate duty —without this I am nothing'" (*The Crack-Up*, p. 294).

saw him clear myself—for he started out as one man I knew and then changed into myself [n.b.!]—the amalgam was never complete in my mind." [4] In a letter written the same year to Edmund Wilson, however, he shifts his ground: "The worst fault in [*The Great Gatsby*] I think is a BIG FAULT: I gave no account (and had no feeling about or knowledge of) the emotional relations between Gatsby and Daisy from the time of their reunion to the catastrophe." And then he goes on to make a particularly significant remark if we keep in mind the distinction between Nick Carraway and Scott Fitzgerald: "However the lack is so astutely concealed by the retrospect of Gatsby's past *and by blankets of excellent prose* [my italics] that no one has noticed it—though everyone has felt the lack and called it by another name." Later in the same letter Fitzgerald calls this "BIG FAULT" by a still different, though cognate, term: ". . . the lack of any emotional backbone at the very height of it [i.e., the Gatsby story]." [5]

Now, all of this self-analysis, it seems to me, misses the point. The "lack" is there, all right, and Fitzgerald strikes at least a glancing blow when he speaks of the "blankets of excellent prose"—Fitzgerald prose, please note, not Nick Carraway prose; for in the letter to Wilson, Fitzgerald is clearly speaking as author and craftsman. But, still, he misses; for it is doubtful that the "emotional relations" between Gatsby and Daisy *need* any more explaining than they get in the novel. In spite of Peter Quennel's description of Daisy as "delightful," [6] one feels that neither her character nor the quality of her emotional resources justifies any very exhaustive analysis. Certainly one must assume that, if the novel means anything, it cannot concern itself with the love of Jay Gatsby, boy financier, for the pretty wife of Tom Buchanan, football hero. In other words, the point of the Carraway theme, at least, has everything to do with precisely the emptiness of the Gatsby-Daisy "emotional relations"—those same emotional relations which Fitzgerald seemed to feel, I think quite wrongly, it was a "BIG FAULT" not to elaborate upon. That Daisy exists both in, and as, an emotional vacuum into which Gatsby, being Gatsby, could attempt to pour only the most obvious and contrived cheap-novel sentimentalism has everything to do with the ironic quality of his final defeat at her hands. And the novel would be the worse, I believe, for the very thing the author says it needs: an exegesis of this vacuum and Gatsby's response to it. Fitzgerald's instinct for craftsmanship, we may be thankful, operated before his analysis as critic.

---

[4] *Ibid.*, p. 271.
[5] *Ibid.*, p. 270.
[6] *New Statesman and Nation*, XXI, No. 519 (February 1, 1941), 112. Apparently no irony is intended. It might be added that Quennel transforms Gatsby into "the son of a poverty-stricken Long Island farmer."

No, it is not the details of Gatsby's later love for Daisy; nor is it that Gatsby turns into Fitzgerald, though this is closer; nor yet is it (as, says Fitzgerald,[7] Mencken thought) that the central story is "a sort of anecdote"—none of these things is responsible for that feeling of something missing which many readers have experienced but that none seems able to account for. As a matter of fact, what is really "missing" in *The Great Gatsby* is not so much a specific element in plot or even theme; the *sense* of something missing comes, rather, from the inherent confusion of themes, the duality of symbol-structure of which Fitzgerald seems to have been unaware. The book, great as it is, still falls short of its possibilities because its energies are spent in two directions. If *The Great Gatsby* revealed to us only its protagonist, it would be incomparable. Revealing, as it does, perhaps a little too much of the person who created it, it becomes somewhat less sharp, less pointed, more diffused in its effect.

In the last chapter of the novel, you may recall, Carraway describes the "schedule" which Gatsby, as a boy, had written in the flyleaf of a cheap western novel.[8] The "schedule" starts, "Rise from bed . . . 6.00 A.M.," and ends, "Study needed inventions . . . 7.00-9.00 P.M.," with all the hours and half-hours between thoroughly accounted for. Carraway finds the reaction of Gatsby's father to the schedule somewhat amusing: "He was reluctant to close the book, reading each item aloud and then looking eagerly at me. I think he rather expected me to copy down the list for my own use." It is, however, important to recognize that not the dream of progress, but rather the fact of such scheduling of one's resources to the quarter of an hour, is exactly the sort of thing by which F. Scott Fitzgerald was both repelled and fascinated. As Arthur Mizener makes plain in his excellent biography,[9] Fitzgerald was always haunted by the theory that one's physical and emotional "capital" was a fixed and ordered quantity, to be carefully parceled out along the years of one's life and overdrawn only at one's peril. The Nick Carraway who earlier in the novel had wanted the world to be "at a sort of moral attention forever" is closer to Fitzgerald's heart, we may be sure, than the Nick Carraway who, back in his own fictional character, stands ironically detached from a young boy's effort to reduce his small world to a pattern.

It is commonplace to cite chapter, verse, and semicolon to support the view that Fitzgerald's tragedy was that he had not been born to wealth. His famous remark to Hemingway, and Hemingway's wisecrack-

[7] In the letter to Edmund Wilson (*The Crack-Up*, p. 270).

[8] *Hopalong Cassidy*, for the benefit of those who might wish to speculate on the co-incidence of a revival of literary interest in more than one direction

[9] *The Far Side of Paradise* (Boston, 1951).

ing reply;[10] the story of his extravagances and debts (towards the latter of which, however, he was never careless)[11] and his seeking for whatever he thought he saw in the possession of money; his marriage to the belle of Montgomery, Zelda Sayre—all these are to buttress a critical edifice which seems to go no higher than an assumption that Fitzgerald might have been happier if richer. True, anyone who can define happiness as "a slowly rising scale of gratification of the normal appetites" [12] does lay himself open to certain accusations. Yet to say that Fitzgerald wanted money, and to stop there, seems to me to say nothing. What did he seek that money could, he thought, provide? Or, perhaps more accurately, what did he think the rich possessed, because of their money, that he wanted so badly?

The answer, I believe, is that he wanted order. Fitzgerald, like Mark Twain, saw around him only chaos. And, again like Mark Twain, he tried to find an ordered cosmos in his own terms. Twain plunged himself into a machine-world where *B* always follows *A*, as a lever on a typesetter always responds to the cam which actuates it. Fitzgerald seemed to think he could discover in that magic world of the rich "safe and proud above the hot struggles of the poor" the sanctuary he seems always to have sought. Like "Manley Halliday" in Budd Schulberg's *The Disenchanted,* Fitzgerald had "a strong sense of pattern." The list which Gatsby's father shows to Nick Carraway is not so important for what the old man thinks it represents, that his son "was bound to get ahead," though this is a part of the Carraway theme. Rather, in its boyish effort to reduce the world to terms in the Chaucerian sense of "boundaries," the "schedule" imposes on the haphazard circumstances of life a purpose and a discipline, just as Fitzgerald the man attempts in his novel the same sort of thing.

Many elements now seem to fall into place. The conversation about carelessness between Jordan Baker and Nick assumes a different stature, and in the thin red circle which Gatsby's blood traces in his swimming pool "like the leg of transit" we can see a meaning: the end-and-begin-

---

[10] Fitzgerald is supposed to have said that the rich are different from the rest of us (a remark expanded by Fitzgerald in "The Rich Boy" and referred to by Hemingway in "The Snows of Kilimanjaro"), to which Hemingway is supposed to have answered, "Yes, they have more money." Mizener seems to treat the exchange with a rather heavy hand when he remarks that Hemingway's reply is "clever enough" as a "casual joke" but that as a reply to a serious observation it is "remarkably stupid." Mizener's comment is on p. 86 of "Scott Fitzgerald and the Imaginative Possession of American Life," *Sewanee Review,* LIV, No. 1 (January-March, 1946), 66; I do not find it repeated, however, in *The Far Side of Paradise.* The anecdote itself, as a matter of fact, is referred to only obliquely in the book (on pp. 270-71).

[11] On this point, see Mizener's comment on p. 23 of his article, "Fitzgerald in the Twenties," *Partisan Review,* XVII, No. 1 (January, 1950), 7; also see *The Far Side of Paradise,* pp. 90, 131, 144, 180, 253, 272.

[12] As Fitzgerald did in a story called "Dalyrimple Goes Wrong."

ling within which lies, at least, something else than *khaos,* the mother of all disaster. "It is not what Gatsby was," a student of mine once wrote, "but what had hold of him that was his downfall." "What had hold of him"—and of F. Scott Fitzgerald himself—was the dream that all share who seek to impose some kind of order on a cluttered universe. The meaning Gatsby sought—the "order," if you will—was Daisy; when the betrayal came, his dream disintegrated, and Fitzgerald interposes the most remarkable and terrible "blanket of prose" of all:

> . . . he must have felt that he had lost the old warm world, paid a high price for living too long with a single dream. He must have looked up at an unfamiliar sky through frightening leaves and shivered as he found what a grotesque thing a rose is and how raw the sunlight was upon the scarcely created grass. A new world, material without being real, where poor ghosts, breathing dreams like air, drifted fortuitously about . . . like that ashen, fantastic figure gliding toward him through the amorphous trees.

That "old, warm world," we feel, was not Gatsby's vision alone. Certainly by 1925, when *The Great Gatsby* appeared, Fitzgerald must have long since begun to suspect that not even the wealth of Croesus could really keep one "safe," though that might be a dream as hard of dying as Gatsby's.

Lionel Trilling thinks that Jay Gatsby "is to be thought of as standing for America itself." [13] Perhaps; everyone is Everyman, in a sense, and Gatsby can stand for America as conveniently as he can stand for himself. But it seems to me that the true significance of *The Great Gatsby* is both more personal and more specific. The "spiritual horror" which Mr. Trilling finds in the novel he ascribes to "the evocation of New York in the heat of summer, the party in the Washington Heights flat, the terrible 'valley of ashes' seen like a corner of the Inferno from the Long Island Railroad . . . Gatsby's tremendous, incoherent parties . . . the huge, sordid and ever-observant eyes of the oculist's advertising sign." [14] This we may accept; but summer heat and ashes and oculists' signs are horrible not per se but *per causam.* The cause of the horror is, in *The Great Gatsby,* the terrifying contrast between the Buchanans, Jordan Baker, the obscene barflies who descend in formless swarms on Gatsby's house, all symbolized by the gritty disorganized ash heaps with their crumbling men, and the solid ordered structure so paradoxically built on sand (or ashes) which Gatsby's great dream lends to his life. And over it all brood the eyes of Dr. Eckleburg, symbols—of what? Of the eyes of God, as Wilson, whose own world disintegrates with the death of Myrtle, calls them? As a symbol of Gatsby's dream, which like the eyes is pretty shabby after all and scarcely founded on the "hard rocks"

[13] P. viii, Introduction to undated "New Classics" edition of *Gatsby.*
[14] *Ibid.,* p. xii.

Carraway admires? Or—and I think this most likely—do not the eyes in spite of everything they survey, perhaps even because of it, serve both as a focus and an undeviating base, a single point of reference in the midst of monstrous disorder?

> It was all very careless and confused [says Nick]. They were careless people, Tom and Daisy—they smashed up things and creatures and then retreated back into their money or their vast carelessness, or whatever it was that kept them together, and let other people clean up the mess they had made.

Here Fitzgerald nearly calls his turn—yet he misses again. For Tom and Daisy retreat "back into their money *or* their vast carelessness." And in the implication of the phrase we see that Fitzgerald was himself unready to give up his old, warm world; that Jay Gatsby was not the only one to pay a high price for living too long with a single dream.

The Great Gatsby:
Thirty-Six Years After

by A. E. Dyson

In 1925 T. S. Eliot found himself as moved and interested by *The Great Gatsby* as he had been by any novel for a very long time. Since then the novel has attracted praise from a great many discriminating critics on both sides of the Atlantic, and the deep interest of first generation readers has been shared by others coming at a later time, and from different backgrounds. My own first reading of *Gatsby* is an experience I still recall vividly, and it has remained for me one of the few novels in any language (*Tender Is the Night* is another) for which the appetite regularly and pleasurably returns. Amazing enough, one reflects each time, that so short a work should contain so much, and its impact remain so fresh. Thirty-six years after its appearance I would say with confidence, then, that *Gatsby* has not only outlived its period and its author, but that it is one of the books that will endure.

Any new consideration must now, if this is so, be concerned with it as a work which belongs not only to American but to world literature; not only to the immediate soil from which it sprang (prohibition, big business, gangsters, jazz, uprootedness, and the rest) but to the tragic predicament of humanity as a whole. This is worth stating at the start, if only because an English critic might otherwise feel diffident about approaching a masterpiece which in many ways is so obviously American, and which has been cited so often in definitions of the peculiarly American experience of the twentieth century. An Englishman will miss, no doubt, many important nuances that to an American will be instantly obvious, and he will be less sure of himself in discussing ways in which Fitzgerald does, or does not, look forward to Salinger, Bellow, and other writers of our present Affluent Society. He might, however, hope to see other things (and I am relieved to find Leo Marx lending his support to this hope) which will prove no less important in a final assessment, and which might be *less* easily perceptible at home than abroad.

"The Great Gatsby: Thirty-Six Years After" by A. E. Dyson. From *Modern Fiction Studies* VII (Spring 1961). Copyright © 1961 by the Purdue Research Foundation. Reprinted by permission of the author and the Purdue Research Foundation.

This, at any rate, must be my excuse for venturing, in what follows, to bypass the type of sociological interest usually and rightly displayed, and to consider *Gatsby* as something even bigger than the demythologising of the American Myth. The squalor and splendour of Gatsby's dreams belong, I shall suggest, to the story of humanity itself; as also does the irony, and judgment, of his awakening.

I

The action takes place in "the waste land" (this phrase is actually used), and is, at one level, the study of a broken society. The "valley of ashes" in which Myrtle and Wilson live symbolizes the human situation in an age of chaos. It is "a certain desolate area of land" in which "ash-gray men" swarm dimly, stirring up "an impenetrable cloud, which screens their obscure operations from your sight." This devitalized limbo is presided over by the eyes of Dr. T. J. Eckleburg.

> The eyes of Doctor T. J. Eckleburg are blue and gigantic—their retinas are one yard high. They look out of no face, but, instead, from a pair of enormous yellow spectacles which pass over a non-existent nose.

Dr. Eckleburg is an advertisement for spectacles, now faded and irrelevant: put there by some "wild wag of an oculist" who has himself, by this time, either sunk down "into eternal blindness, or forgot them and moved away." As a simple but haunting symbol of the *deus absconditus* who might once have set the waste land in motion Dr. Eckleburg recurs at certain crucial moments in the novel. He is the only religious reference, but his sightless gaze precludes the possibility of judging the "ash-gray men" against traditional religious norms, and confers upon them the right to pity as well as to scorn. It ensures, too, that though the actual setting of the valley is American, and urban, and working-class (I intend to use the word "class" in this account again, without further apology), the relevance, as in Eliot's own *Waste Land,* is to a universal human plight.

Beneath Dr. Eckleburg's unseeing eyes the ash-gray men drift. "Drift" is a word used many times, and with the exception of Gatsby himself, who at least thinks he knows where he is going, it applies to all the main characters, including Carraway, the narrator.

Tom and Daisy, the "moneyed" class, have for years "drifted here and there unrestfully wherever people played polo and were rich together." Tom's restlessness is an arrogant assertiveness seeking to evade in bluster the deep uneasiness of self-knowledge. His hypocrisy and lack of human feeling make him the most unpleasant character in the book, but he is also, when it comes to the point, one of the sanest. In the battle with

Gatsby he has the nature of things on his side, so that his victory is as inevitable as it is unadmirable. The discovery that his sanity is even less worthwhile in human terms than Gatsby's self-centred fantasy is not the least of the novel's ironies.

Daisy is more complex than Tom, and far less real. Her manner has in it, as Carraway notes, all the promise of the world. Her eyes, "looking up into my face, promis[ed] that there was no one in the world she so much wanted to see"; her voice held "a promise that she had done gay, exciting things just a while since and that there were gay, exciting things hovering in the next hour." But this is all yesterday and tomorrow. Today, there is only emptiness. " 'What'll we do with ourselves this afternoon?' cried Daisy, 'and the day after that, and the next thirty years?' "

When Gatsby arrives with his "romantic readiness," his unqualified faith in Daisy's ideal and absolute reality, he is broken against her sheer non-existence. She turns out to be literally nothing, and vanishes from the novel at the very point when, if she existed at all, she would have to start being really there. Her romantic facade, so adequate in appearance to the dreams Gatsby has built around it, is without reality. She has no belief in it herself, and so it means nothing. It is no more than an attempt to alchemize the dreariness of an unsuccessful life into some esoteric privilege of the sophisticated. The account she gives of her "cynicism" is not without genuine pain. But the pain is transmuted in the telling into a pleasure—the only genuine pleasure, one feels, of which she would be capable.

> The instant her voice broke off, ceasing to compel my attention, my belief, I felt the basic insincerity of what she had said. . . . I waited, and sure enough, in a moment she looked at me with an absolute smirk on her lovely face, as if she had asserted her membership in a rather distinguished secret society to which she and Tom belonged.

Behind the facade of the rich, the "rather distinguished secret society" to which they belong, is money and carelessness—the two protections upon which, in moments of crisis, they fall back, leaving those outside to sink or swim as best they can.

The social break-up at this level is paralleled in the working class. Myrtle, Tom's mistress, is the quintessence of vulgarity. Her "class" is no strong, peasant culture, but a drifting wreckage of the spiritless and defeated. Her only hope is to escape—and it is her one positive quality, her vitality, which leads her to seek happiness in a role other than that to which she is born. With Tom's prestige and money behind her she sets up a town establishment, throws parties, apes the rich, outgrows her husband ("I thought he knew something about breeding, but he wasn't fit to lick my shoe"), looks down on her own class with aloof disdain

("Myrtle raised her eyebrows at the shiftlessness of the lower orders. 'These people! You have to keep after them all the time.'") In playing this moneyed role, she achieves most of its actual corruptions whilst adding the new ingredient of vulgarity. One minute she avoids the word "bitch" when buying a dog (" 'Is it a boy or a girl?' she asked delicately"), the next takes for granted that a total stranger will want to sleep with her sister.

And yet, in a universe of ash-gray men represented by her husband and presided over by the eyes of Dr. Eckleburg, it is difficult to feel she is very obviously to blame. Fitzgerald's ironic awareness of life's perversities is symbolized in the fact that her one positive quality, her vitality, should find expression in the waste land only as vulgarity and disloyalty, and that it should become the instrument of her death. In the same way, Gatsby's great positive quality—his faith, and the loyalty to Daisy that goes with it—finds expression only as a tawdry self-centredness, and it, too, contributes to his death.

II

Among these rootless people Carraway comes to live: implicated to a certain extent in the action which he records, and controlling the tone of the narrative. His implication is impersonal, in that his own emotions and destiny are not centrally involved: personal, in that his humanity forces him, even against his will, to understand and pity Gatsby, and that this amounts to a not uncostly selflessness which turns out to be the most important moral positive the novel has to offer.

Carraway is the one middle-class character in the novel—vaguely at home in the worlds both of Daisy and of Myrtle, but belonging to neither, and so able to see and judge both very clearly. He is conscious of "advantages" of moral education that enable him to see through false romanticisms to their underlying insincerity, and savour their bitter ironies. Yet he, too, has his restlessness, as uprooted as everyone else in truth, though more determined than the rest to preserve some "decencies," to cling to some principle of order and sanity in the wreckage.

His family comes from the Middle West. It is proud of having a Duke somewhere in the family tree, but relies in practice for its safety and self-respect on big-business—the "wholesale hardware business" which Carraway never wholly loses sight of as his birthright. He has been made restless by the war, and is now looking for some sort of armour against life in detachment and moral alertness. The "intimate revelations of young men" bore him. He is tolerant of other people, but would escape from the sloughs of emotional despond into some simple pattern of control and acceptance.

Conduct may be founded on the hard rock or the wet marshes, but after a certain point I don't care what it's founded on. When I came back from the East last autumn I felt that I wanted the world to be in uniform and at a sort of moral attention forever; I wanted no more riotous excursions with privileged glimpses into the human heart.

Cast into the situation which is the subject of the novel, his attitude is from the first ambivalent. "I was within and without, simultaneously enchanted and repelled by the inexhaustible variety of life." He sees the sordidness, the unreality of the New York "rich," and his ironic observation upon it is habitually devastating. But he is able to hope, even while seeing as clearly as he does, that the vitality, the variety, the promise of excitement, may not be wholly false. Infected with the restlessness that he records in others, he is half convinced that some rewarding experience might lie behind the world of throbbing taxis, rich perfumes, gay parties, if one could only find a way through to it. "I began to like New York, the racy, adventurous feel of it at night, and the satisfaction that the constant flicker of men and women and machines gives to the restless eye." He responds almost equally to the haunting loneliness of it, and the unceasing promise. His imagination is willing to entertain what his intellect and experience of life rejects: "Imagining that I, too, was hurrying towards gayety and sharing their intimate excitement, I wished them well."

Carraway's attitude towards Gatsby is, from the first, typical. He recognises in Gatsby the epitome of his society, and is accordingly enchanted and repelled by him in the highest degree. His conscious moral instinct is to disapprove: but his imagination is fascinated since perhaps here, in this extraordinary man, the romantic promise is at last fulfilled. He wavers, therefore, between almost complete contempt for Gatsby, and almost complete faith in him; and this ambivalent attitude persists until Gatsby's collapse, after which it gives way to a deeper, and costlier, attitude of pity, towards which the whole novel moves. The eventual shattering of Gatsby's high romantic hopes against an inexorably unromantic reality turns him, for Carraway, into a tragic figure. The quality of the ironic observation reflects this change, and Carraway's closing meditation, rising above the particular events, finds a universal, and tragic, significance in Gatsby's fate.

III

Carraway's first mention of the hero, some time before he actually appears, is a clear statement of his own judgment upon him: "Gatsby, who represented everything for which I have an unaffected scorn." But it is an acknowledgment also of the fascination which Gatsby exerts over him. "If personality is an unbroken series of successful gestures, then there was something gorgeous about him, some heightened sensitivity to the promises of life."

In one sense Gatsby is the apotheosis of his rootless society. His background is cosmopolitan, his past a mystery, his temperament that of an opportunist entirely oblivious to the claims of people or the world outside. His threadbare self-dramatisation, unremitting selfishness, and attempts to make something out of nothing are the same in kind as those of the waste-land society, and different only in intensity. Yet this intensity springs from a quality which he alone has: and this we might call "faith." He really believes in himself and his illusions: and this quality of faith, however grotesque it must seem with such an object, sets him apart from the cynically armoured midgets whom he epitomizes. It makes him bigger than they are, and more vulnerable. It is, also, a quality which commands respect from Carraway: since at the very least, "faith" protects Gatsby from the evasiveness, the conscious hypocrisy of the Toms and Daisies of the world, conferring something of the heroic on what he does; and at the best it might still turn out to be the "way in" to some kind of reality beyond the romantic facade, the romantic alchemy which, despite his cynicism, Carraway still half hopes one day to find.

Gatsby's first appearance is in his garden at night looking out at the single green light which is the symbol of his dreams. He is content to "be alone": and isolation is an essential part of his make-up, a necessary part of his god-like self-sufficiency. He is next heard of as a mystery: the man whom nobody knows, but whose hospitality everybody accepts.

> There was music from my neighbor's house through the summer nights. In his blue gardens men and girls came and went like moths among the whisperings and the champagne and the stars.

When Carraway meets him as a host, and first hears that "old sport" which becomes so moving at the end, he does not even know that it *is* Gatsby. This social gaffe is an occasion for the sublime courtesy and forgiveness that Gatsby has to dispense, the "charm" which is too deeply a part of his act for any accusation of insincerity to be even remotely appropriate.

> He smiled understandingly—much more than understandingly. It was one of those rare smiles with a quality of eternal reassurance in it, that you may come across four or five times in life. It faced—or seemed to face— the whole external world for an instant, and then concentrated on *you* with an irresistible prejudice in your favor. It understood you just so far as you wanted to be understood, believed in you as you would like to be-

lieve in yourself, and assured you that it had precisely the impression of you that, at your best, you hoped to convey. Precisely at that point it vanished. . . .

As Gatsby's guests become more hilarious, his own "correctness" grows. He is apart from the chaos which his money has mysteriously called into being, presiding over it with benevolent detachment: considerate to his fellows when they are careless, decorous when they are disorderly. As the party finishes, he remains alone on the steps of his mansion—his formality and his solitude an intriguing enigma, that has still to be explored.

A sudden emptiness seemed to flow now from the windows and the great doors, endowing with complete isolation the figure of the host, who stood on the porch, his hand up in a formal gesture of farewell.

IV

This, then, is the setting. The novel is concerned with Gatsby's reasons for appearing out of the blue and becoming host to half the rich "moths" of New York. He is, it turns out, in love with Daisy. The whole elaborate decor has been constructed for the sole purpose of staging a dramatic reunion with her: a reunion which will impress her with Gatsby's "greatness," and eradicate, at a stroke, the five years of married life which she has drifted through since seeing him last.

As we soon learn, his affair with Daisy had been a youthful romance, one among many, and nurtured in an atmosphere of cynicism, deceit, purposelessness. But it had, unlike Gatsby's other affairs, been complicated first by Daisy's casualness, and then by their unavoidable separation: and somehow, during the muddle, Gatsby had fallen in love, and the affair had become the "greatest thing in his life." The romantic promise which in Daisy herself was the merest facade became, for him, an ideal, an absolute reality. He built around her the dreams and fervors of his youth: adolescent, self-centred, fantastic, yet also untroubled by doubt, and therefore strong; attracting to themselves the best as well as the worst of his qualities, and eventually becoming an obsession of the most intractable kind.

As Carraway comes to know Gatsby, he wavers between scepticism and faith. He sees, clearly, in Gatsby the faults which he scorns in others—"charm" that is simply a technique for success, self-centredness masquerading as heroic vision, romantic pretensions based on economic corruption and a total disregard for humanity—yet he is impressed, despite himself, by the faith which transmutes all this into another pattern. Gatsby is different from the others in that he means every word he says, really believes in the uniqueness of his destiny. His romantic clichés, unlike those of Tom or Daisy, are used with simple belief that they are his own discovery, his own prerogative, his own guarantee of Olympian apartness and election. He is "trying to forget something very sad that happened . . . long ago." He has "tried very hard to die, but . . . seemed to bear an enchanted life." To listen to him is like "skimming hastily through a dozen magazines"—and yet is not like that at all, since Gatsby's faith really has brought the dead clichés back to life again, or at any rate to some semblance of life. So much in his account that might have been empty boasting turns out to be true. He has been to Oxford—after a fashion. His credentials from the commissioner of police for whom he was "able to do . . . a favor once" are genuine—they prevent him from being arrested for breaking a traffic law. His love for Daisy, too, is real, up to a point: there is a moment when it seems that he has achieved the impossible, and actually realized his fantastic programme for returning to the past.

The tragedy—for it is a tragic novel, though of an unorthodox kind— lies in the fact that Gatsby can go only so far and no further. Faith can still remove sizeable molehills, but is absolutely powerless when it comes to mountains. The ultimate romantic affirmation, "I'll always love you alone" cannot be brought to life: certainly not in the waste land; not when people like Daisy, and Gatsby himself, are involved. Gatsby's faith has to break, in the end, against a reality radically incompatible with it. But in so breaking, it makes him a tragic figure: and unites him symbolically with many men more worthy than himself—with, indeed, the general lot of mankind.

V

Gatsby's whole project is characterized by that mingling of the fantastic and the scrupulously correct which is his settled attitude to life (the phrase "old sport" is itself a masterly fusion of the two extremes). He approaches Carraway with his all-important request not directly, but by way of Jordan Baker. And why? Because "Miss Baker's a great sports-woman, you know, and she'd never do anything that wasn't all right." His "correctness," like most of his other qualities, is peculiarly inverted, but not wholly a sham. He uses it exclusively to get his own way, and yet he is so wholly taken-in himself that he cannot be accused, as anyone else might be, of hypocrisy.

And what *does* Gatsby want of Carraway? " 'He wants to know,' continued Jordan, 'if you'll invite Daisy to your house some afternoon and then let him come over.' "

He wants Carraway, to put this bluntly, to help him capture a friend's wife—and this simply because Carraway happens to be the man living next door, from which a spectacular view of the Gatsby mansion is to be enjoyed. "The modesty of the demand shook me," Carraway comments: and it is part of the greatness of the novel that though Carraway sees the whole situation very clearly, and has no bias in favor either of emotional extravagance or of Gatsby himself, his comment is not wholly ironical. It is not even primarily ironical, since Carraway is already beginning to see also, in all its tawdry splendor, the nature of Gatsby's vision: and given that, the demand really *is* modest.

He had waited five years and bought a mansion where he dispensed starlight to casual moths—so that he could "come over" some afternoon to a stranger's garden.

Carraway's comment to Jordan ("Did I have to know all this before he could ask such a little thing?") is again only marginally ironic. The situation is too unanchored for simple moral judgments—partly because, given Gatsby's faith among the ashes, it is difficult to find norms against which to judge; partly because Gatsby is, after all, "big," so that nothing he does can be simply contemptible; and partly because Carraway himself is not given to conventional attitudes towards human relationships, so that his judgment rises out of a growing awareness of a complex situation and is in no sense imported from outside. He readily agrees, in any event, to Gatsby's request, his "unaffected scorn" of the man wholly overcome, now, by fascinated interest in the unfolding events.

The actual meeting of Gatsby and Daisy is the central episode of the novel. Everything leads up to it, and what follows is a working out of implications which are in the meeting itself. There is the tension as Gatsby waits, and the embarrassing absurdity of the first few minutes together—the irony here highly comic, and very much at Gatsby's expense. Then comes the moment of happiness, when the ideal seems to have been actualized. Daisy herself is carried away by the elation of the moment. " 'I'm so glad Jay.' Her throat 'full of' . . . aching, grieving beauty, told only of her unexpected joy." [1] And Gatsby is transfigured: he "literally glowed; without a word or a gesture of exultation a new well-being radiated from him and filled the little room."

This is followed by the slow hint, in the next hour or so, that the dream has already started to shatter against reality. Now, the irony becomes tragic rather than comic in tone, as Carraway's sympathy veers round towards Gatsby, and starts to become engaged. No reality, how-

[1] "'I'm glad, Jay. Her throat, full of aching, grieving beauty, told only of her unexpected joy." *The Great Gatsby*, p. 108. [A.M.]

ever great or vital, could have stood up to an illusion on the scale that
Gatsby has constructed.

> Almost five years! There must have been moments even that afternoon
> when Daisy tumbled short of his dreams—not through her own fault, but
> because of the colossal vitality of his illusion. It had gone beyond her,
> beyond everything. . . . No amount of fire and freshness can challenge
> what a man can store up in his ghostly heart.

And Daisy, far from having "fire and freshness," has only her pale
imitation of it. She has grown up in her world of money and carelessness, where "all night the saxophones wailed the hopeless comment of
the Beale Street Blues," and dawn was always an hour of disenchantment. What Gatsby demands of her is that she should go to Tom and
say, in all sincerity, "I never loved you." This is the unadmirable im-
possibility upon which his faith is staked: and Carraway's warning to
him, as soon as the full extent of the "rather harrowing" intention becomes clear, is a striking example of the way in which the most elemen-
tary commonsense can sometimes knock a man's private world to pieces.

> "I wouldn't ask too much of her," I ventured. "You can't repeat the past."
> "Can't repeat the past?" he cried incredulously. "Why, of course you can!"

Gatsby has ignored, and disbelieved in, such depressing commonplaces
as Carraway's—the depressing commonplaces which are at the heart of
Daisy's cynicism, and of the grayness of the ash-gray men. In his own
private world past and future can be held captive in the present. His
faith allows almost boundless possibilities to be contemplated: and if the
"universe" which has "spun itself out in his brain" does happen to be
one of "ineffable gaudiness," this does not alter the fact that it is more
remarkable, and colorful, than the realities against which it breaks. Like
Tamburlaine, Gatsby has made a "Platonic conception of himself" out
of the extravagant emotions and aspirations of an adolescent. Like
Tamburlaine, too, he has made himself vulnerable by acknowledging
the power of a Zenocrate. It is only poetic justice, perhaps, that his own
Zenocrate should turn out to be Daisy. But whoever it had been, the
result would have been the same.

The battle between Gatsby and Tom is at one level the battle between
illusion and reality. Tom has the nature of things on his side, and it is
part of the nature of things that he and Daisy belong together. Daisy
has to say to Gatsby not "I loved you alone," but "I loved you too." This
"too" is Tom's victory, and he can follow it up by equating Gatsby's
romance with his own hole-in-the-corner affair with Myrtle—calling it
a "presumptuous little flirtation" and announcing that it is now at an

end. After this Gatsby has no weapons left for the fight. He goes on watching over Daisy to the end, but half aware himself, now, of the annihilating fact that he is watching over nothing. "So I walked away and left him standing there in the moonlight—watching over nothing."

He has "broken up like glass against Tom's hard malice": and for this reason he can now be pitied, since Tom's attitude, though conclusively realistic, is also hard, and inhuman, and smaller than Gatsby's own. The reality turns out to be less admirable, less human than the fantasy. The events leading to Gatsby's death symbolize, very powerfully, that his downfall, though inevitable, is by no means an unambiguous triumph of moral powers. His death is brought about by Daisy, who first lets him shield her and then deserts him: by Tom, who directs the demented Wilson to the place where he is to be found; and by Wilson himself—a representative of the ash-gray men who comes to Gatsby, in his disillusionment, as a terrible embodiment of the realities which have killed his dream.

[Gatsby] must have looked up at an unfamiliar sky through frightening leaves and shivered as he found what a grotesque thing a rose is and how raw the sunlight was upon the scarcely created grass. A new world, material without being real, where poor ghosts, breathing dreams like air, drifted fortuitously about . . . like that ashen, fantastic figure gliding toward him through the amorphous trees.

A nightmare of this kind demands some sympathy: and if Dr. Eckleburg is unable to provide it, as he looks down unseeingly upon the drama, then there is all the more call for humanity to supply the need. But Gatsby's "friends" fade away in the hour of death: and Gatsby, whose contribution to his own death has been loyalty to Daisy (the one real and valuable emotion bound up with his fantasy), is left alone at the end.

VI

But not completely alone. His father turns up, with pathetic evidences of Gatsby's youthful aspirations and his generosity as a son; one of the guests who has attended Gatsby's parties attends the funeral; and Carraway himself remains, determined to act in a decently human way. ". . . it grew upon me that I was responsible, because no one else was interested—interested, I mean, with that intense personal interest to which every one has some vague right at the end."

Carraway is also, by now, converted to Gatsby: "I found myself on Gatsby's side, and alone." His final compliment to Gatsby, "They're a rotten crowd. . . . You're worth the whole damn bunch put together" may not add up to much, but it is at least true, and a statement to which everything has been moving. At the very least, it is a recognition that being right about the nature of things is no excuse for being inhuman. In its broader implications, it is part of the larger meaning of the novel: which is that in a tragic and imperfect world scorn and condemnation can often come too easily as attitudes. Human warmth and pity may not be able to set everything to rights: but they are costlier and more decent attitudes than mere judgment; and in the waste land, perhaps juster than judgment itself.

Carraway's befriending of Gatsby is certainly not easy for himself. The cost is symbolized in the ending of his short affair with Jordan Baker. He had been attracted to Jordan in the first place by her self-sufficiency ("Almost any exhibition of complete self-sufficiency draws a stunned tribute from me"), partly by her appearance of "moral attention." ("She was a slender, small-breasted girl, with an erect carriage, which she accentuated by throwing her body backward at the shoulders like a young cadet.") and partly by the needs of his own loneliness. But Jordan turns out, in the end, to be as worthless as the rest: "moral attention" may be necessary at times in self-defense, but as a total attitude to life it has its limits. Carraway's desire for emotional detachment had, from the start, a certain pessimism underlying it—an acceptance of disenchantment which finds expression in some of the most characteristic of his reflections.

> I was thirty. Before me stretched the portentous, menacing road of a new decade. . . . Thirty—the promise of a decade of loneliness, a thinning list of single men to know, a thinning brief-case of enthusiasm, thinning hair.

He cannot make reality more acceptable than it is, or find a way out of the waste land, or suggest a cure for the cynicism which is eating out the heart of society. He can, however, prize the highest human values that he sees, and respond to the misfortunes of others with a pity which has in it a feeling for human suffering as a whole. It is characteristic that in the closing sentences he should find in Gatsby's tragic awakening a symbol of the disenchantment of mankind as a whole—and end on a note which, transcending both Gatsby's personal fate, and the *folie-de-grandeur* of the America which he also represents, achieves a universal tragic vision as haunting as any I can think of in a novel.

> And as I sat there brooding on the old, unknown world, I thought of Gatsby's wonder when he first picked out the green light at the end of Daisy's dock. He had come a long way to this blue lawn, and his dream must have seemed so close that he could hardly fail to grasp it. He did not know that it was already behind him, somewhere back in that vast obscurity

beyond the city, where the dark fields of the republic rolled on under the night.

Gatsby believed in the green light, the orgiastic future that year by year recedes before us. It eluded us then, but that's no matter—to-morrow we will run faster, stretch out our arms farther . . . And one fine morning—

So we beat on, boats against the current, borne back ceaselessly into the past.

Scott Fitzgerald's
Criticism of America

by Marius Bewley

Critics of Scott Fitzgerald tend to agree that *The Great Gatsby* is somehow a commentary on that elusive phrase, the American dream. The assumption seems to be that Fitzgerald approved. On the contrary, it can be shown that *The Great Gatsby* offers some of the severest and closest criticism of the American dream that our literature affords. Read in this way, Fitzgerald's masterpiece ceases to be a pastoral documentary of the Jazz Age and takes its distinguished place among those great national novels whose profound corrective insights into the nature of American experience are not separable from the artistic form of the novel itself. That is to say, Fitzgerald—at least in this one book—is in a line with the greatest masters of American prose. *The Great Gatsby* embodies a criticism of American experience—not of manners, but of a basic historic attitude to life—more radical than anything in James's own assessment of the deficiencies of his country. The theme of *Gatsby* is the withering of the American dream.

Essentially, this phrase represents the romantic enlargement of the possibilities of life on a level at which the material and the spiritual have become inextricably confused. As such, it led inevitably toward the problem that has always confronted American artists dealing with American experience—the problem of determining the hidden boundary in the American vision of life at which the reality ends and the illusion begins. Historically, the American dream is anti-Calvinistic, and believes in the goodness of nature and man. It is accordingly a product of the frontier and the West rather than of the Puritan Tradition. The simultaneous operation of two such attitudes in American life created a tension

"Scott Fitzgerald's Criticism of America," by Marius Bewley. From *The Sewanee Review*, LXII (Spring 1954). Copyright © 1954 by The University of the South. Appeared in an expanded form in *The Eccentric Design Form in the Classic American Novel* (New York: Columbia University Press, 1959; London: Chatto & Windus Ltd., 1959) by Marius Bewley. Reprinted by permission of *The Sewanee Review* and the author. *This essay was slightly changed and enlarged in* The Eccentric Design (*Columbia University Press, 1959), pp. 259-87. Since the added material is not concerned with* The Great Gatsby, *I am using the earlier version as the text here.*

out of which much of our greatest art has sprung. Youth of the spirit—
perhaps of the body as well—is a requirement of its existence; limit and
deprivation are its blackest devils. But it shows an astonishing incapacity
to believe in them:

> I join you . . . in branding as cowardly the idea that the human mind
> is incapable of further advances. This is precisely the doctrine which the
> present despots of the earth are inculcating, and their friends here re-
> echoing; and applying especially to religion and politics; "that it is not
> probable that anything better will be discovered than what was known
> to our fathers." . . . But thank heaven the American mind is already too
> much opened to listen to these impostures, and while the art of printing
> is left to us, science can never be retrograde. . . . To preserve the freedom
> of the human mind . . . every spirit should be ready to devote itself to
> martyrdom. . . . But that the enthusiasm which characterizes youth should
> lift its parricide hands against freedom and science would be such a mon-
> strous phenomenon as I could not place among the possible things in this
> age and country.

That is the hard kernel, the seed from which the American dream
would grow into unpruned luxuriance. Jefferson's voice is not remote
from many European voices of his time, but it stands in unique relation
to the country to whom he spoke. That attitude was bred into the bone
of America, and in various, often distorted, ways, it has lasted. Perhaps
that is where the trouble begins, for if these virtues of the American
imagination have the elements of greatness in them, they call immediately
for discriminating and practical correctives. The reality in such an attitude lies in its faith in life; the illusion lies in the undiscriminating
multiplication of its material possibilities.

The Great Gatsby is an exploration of the American dream as it exists
in a corrupt period, and it is an attempt to determine that concealed
boundary that divides the reality from the illusions. The illusions seem
more real than the reality itself. Embodied in the subordinate characters
in the novel, they threaten to invade the whole of the picture. On the
other hand, the reality is embodied in Gatsby; and as opposed to the
hard, tangible illusions, the reality is a thing of the spirit, a promise
rather than the possession of a vision, a faith in the half-glimpsed, but
hardly understood, possibilities of life. In Gatsby's America, the reality
is undefined to itself. It is inarticulate and frustrated. Nick Carraway,
Gatsby's friend and Fitzgerald's narrator, says of Gatsby:

> Through all he said, even through his appalling sentimentality, I was
> reminded of something—an elusive rhythm, a fragment of lost words, that
> I had heard somewhere a long time ago. For a moment a phrase tried to
> take shape in my mouth and my lips parted like a dumb man's, as though
> there was more struggling upon them than a wisp of startled air. But they

made no sound, and what I had almost remembered was incommunicable forever.

This is not pretentious phrase-making performing a vague gesture towards some artificial significance. It is both an evocative and an exact description of that unholy cruel paradox by which the conditions of American history have condemned the grandeur of the aspiration and vision to expend itself in a waste of shame and silence. But the reality is not entirely lost. It ends by redeeming the human spirit, even though it live in a wilderness of illusions, from the cheapness and vulgarity that encompass it. In this novel, the illusions are known and condemned at last simply by the rank complacency with which they are content to be themselves. On the other hand, the reality is in the energy of the spirit's resistance, which may not recognize itself as resistance at all, but which can neither stoop to the illusions nor abide with them when they are at last recognized. Perhaps it is really nothing more than ultimate immunity from the final contamination, but it encompasses the difference between life and death. Gatsby never succeeds in seeing through the sham of his world or his acquaintances very clearly. It is of the essence of his romantic American vision that it should lack the seasoned powers of discrimination. But it invests those illusions with its own faith, and thus it discovers its projected goodness in the frauds of its crippled world. *The Great Gatsby* becomes the acting out of the tragedy of the American vision. It is a vision totally untouched by the scales of values that order life in a society governed by traditional manners; and Fitzgerald knows that although it would be easy to condemn and "place" the illusions by invoking these outside values, to do so would be to kill the reality that lies beyond them, but which can sometimes only be reached through them.

For example, Fitzgerald perfectly understood the inadequacy of Gatsby's romantic view of wealth. But that is not the point. He presents it in Gatsby as a romantic baptism of desire for a reality that stubbornly remains out of his sight. It is as if a savage islander, suddenly touched with Grace, transcended in his prayers and aspirations the grotesque little fetish in which he imagined he discovered the object of his longing. The scene in which Gatsby shows his piles of beautiful imported shirts to Daisy and Nick has been mentioned as a failure of Gatsby's, and so of Fitzgerald's, critical control of values. Actually, the shirts are sacramentals, and it is clear that Gatsby shows them, neither in vanity nor in pride, but with a reverential humility in the presence of some inner vision he cannot consciously grasp, but toward which he desperately struggles in the only way he knows.

In an essay called "Myths for Materialists" Mr. Jacques Barzun once wrote that figures, whether of fact or fiction, insofar as they express destinies, aspirations, attitudes typical of man or particular groups, are invested with a mythical character. In this sense Gatsby is a "mythic" character, and no other word will define him. Not only is he an embodiment (as Fitzgerald makes clear at the outset) of that conflict between illusion and reality at the heart of American life; he is an heroic personification of the American romantic hero, the true heir of the American dream. "There was something gorgeous about him," Nick Carraway says, and although "gorgeous" was a favorite word with the 'twenties, Gatsby wears it with an archetypal American elegance.

One need not look far in earlier American literature to find his forebears. Here is the description of a young bee hunter from *Col. David Crockett's Exploits and Adventures in Texas,* published in 1836:

> I thought myself alone in the street, where the hush of morning was suddenly broken by a clear, joyful, and musical voice, which sang. . . .
> I turned toward the spot whence the sounds proceeded, and discovered a tall figure leaning against the sign post. His eyes were fixed on the streaks of light in the east, his mind was absorbed, and he was clearly unconscious of anyone being near him. He continued his song in so full and clear a tone, that the street re-echoed. . . .
> I now drew nigh enough to see him distinctly. He was a young man, not more than twenty-two. His figure was light and graceful at the same time that it indicated strength and activity. He was dressed in a hunting shirt, which was made with uncommon neatness, and ornamented tastily with fringe. He held a highly finished rifle in his right hand, and a hunting pouch, covered with Indian ornaments, was slung across his shoulders. His clean shirt collar was open, secured only by a black riband around his neck. His boots were polished, without a soil upon them; and on his head was a neat fur cap, tossed on in a manner which said, "I don't give a d—n," just as plainly as any cap could speak it. I thought it must be some popinjay on a lark, until I took a look at his countenance. It was handsome, bright, and manly. There was no mistake in that face. From the eyes down to the breast he was sunburnt as dark as mahogany while the upper part of his high forehead was as white and polished as marble. Thick clusters of black hair curled from under his cap. I passed on unperceived, and he continued his song. . . .

This young dandy of the frontier, dreaming in the dawn and singing to the morning, is a progenitor of Gatsby. It is because of such a traditional American ancestry that Gatsby's romanticism transcends the limiting glamor of the Jazz Age.

But such a romanticism is not enough to "mythicize" Gatsby. Gatsby, for all his shimmer of representative surfaces, is never allowed to become soiled by the touch of realism. In creating him, Fitzgerald observed as high a decorum of character as a Renaissance playwright: for Gatsby's parents were shiftless and unsuccessful farm people, Gatsby really "sprang from his Platonic conception of himself. He was a son of God—a phrase which, if it means anything, means just that—and he must be about His

Father's business, the service of a vast, vulgar, and meretricious beauty."

Fitzgerald created Gatsby with a sense of his own election; but the beauty it was in his nature to serve had already been betrayed by history. Even in the midst of the blighted earthly paradise of West Egg, Long Island, Gatsby bore about him the marks of his birth. He is a kind of exiled Duke in disguise. We know him by his bearing, the decorous pattern of his speech. Even his dress invariably touches the imagination: "Gatsby, in a white flannel suit, silver shirt, and gold-colored tie. . . ." There is something dogmatically Olympic about the combination. After Gatsby's death when his pathetic old father journeys east for the funeral, one feels that he is only the kindly shepherd who once found a baby on the cold hillside.

But so far I have been talking in general terms. This beautiful control of conventions can be studied more closely in the description of Gatsby's party at which (if we except that distant glimpse of him at the end of Chapter I, of which I shall speak later) we encounter him for the first time. We are told later that Gatsby was gifted with a "hint of the unreality of reality, a promise that the rock of the world was founded securely on a fairy's wing." Fitzgerald does not actually let us meet Gatsby face to face until he has concretely created this fantastic world of Gatsby's vision, for it is the element in which we must meet Gatsby if we are to understand his impersonal significance:

> There was music from my neighbor's house through the summer nights. In his blue gardens men and girls came and went like moths among the whisperings and the champagne and the stars. At high tide in the afternoon I watched his guests diving from the tower of his raft, or taking the sun on the hot sand of his beach while his two motor-boats slit the waters of the Sound, drawing aquaplanes over cataracts of foam. On week-ends his Rolls-Royce became an omnibus, bearing parties from the city between nine in the morning and long past midnight, while his station wagon scampered like a brisk yellow bug to meet all trains. And on Mondays eight servants, including an extra gardener, toiled all day with mops and scrubbing-brushes and hammers and garden-shears, repairing the ravages of the night before.

The nostalgic poetic quality, which tends to leave one longing for sterner stuff, is, in fact, deceptive. It is Gatsby's ordeal that he must separate the foul dust that floated in the wake of his dreams from the reality of the dream itself: that he must find some vantage point from which he can bring the responsibilities and the possibilities of life into a single focus. But the "ineffable gaudiness" of the world to which Gatsby is committed is a fatal deterrent. Even within the compass of this paragraph we see how the focus has become blurred: how the possibilities of life are conceived of in material terms. But in that heroic list of the vaster luxury items—motor-boats, aquaplanes, private beaches, Rolls-

Royces, diving towers—Gatsby's vision maintains its gigantic unreal stature. It imposes a rhythm on his guests which they accept in terms of their own tawdry illusions, having no conception of the compulsion that drives him to offer them the hospitality of his fabulous wealth. They come for their weekends as George Dane in Henry James's *The Great Good Place* went into his dream retreat. But the result is not the same: "on Mondays eight servants, including an extra gardener, toiled all day with mops and scrubbing-brushes and hammers and garden-shears, repairing the ravages of the night before." That is the most important sentence in the paragraph, and despite the fairy-story overtone, it possesses an ironic nuance that rises toward the tragic. And how fine that touch of the extra gardener is—as if Gatsby's guests had made a breach in nature. It completely qualifies the over-fragility of the moths and champagne and blue gardens in the opening sentences.

This theme of the relation of his guests to Gatsby is still further pursued in Chapter IV. The cataloging of American proper names with poetic intention has been an ineffectual cliché in American writing for many generations. But Fitzgerald uses the convention magnificently:

> Once I wrote down on the empty spaces of a time-table the names of those who came to Gatsby's house that summer. It is an old time-table now, disintegrating at its folds, and headed "This schedule in effect July 5th, 1922." But I can still read the gray names, and they will give you a better impression than my generalities of those who accepted Gatsby's hospitality and paid him the subtle tribute of knowing nothing whatever about him.

The names of these guests could have been recorded nowhere else as appropriately as in the margins of a faded timetable. The embodiments of illusions, they are as ephemeral as time itself; but because their illusions represent the distortions and shards of some shattered American dream, the timetable they adorn is "in effect July 5th"—the day following the great national festival when the exhausted holiday crowds, as spent as exploded firecrackers, return to their homes. The list of names which Fitzgerald proceeds to enumerate conjures up with remarkable precision an atmosphere of vulgar American fortunes and vulgar American destinies. Those who are familiar with the social registers, business men's directories, and movie magazines of the 'twenties might be able to analyze the exact way in which Fitzgerald achieves his effect, but it is enough to say here that he shares with Eliot a remarkable clairvoyance in seizing the cultural implications of proper names. After two pages and more, the list ends with the dreamily elegiac close: "All these people came to Gatsby's house in the summer."

Why did they come? There is the answer of the plotted story—the free party, the motor-boats, the private beach, the endless flow of cocktails. But in the completed pattern of the novel one knows that they came for another reason—came blindly and instinctively—illusions in pursuit of a reality from which they have become historically separated, but by which they might alone be completed or fulfilled. And why did Gatsby invite them? As contrasted with them, he alone has a sense of the reality that hovers somewhere out of sight in this nearly ruined American dream; but the reality is unintelligible until he can invest it again with the tangible forms of his world, and relate it to the logic of history. Gatsby and his guests feel a mutual need for each other, but the division in American experience has widened too far, and no party, no hospitality however lavish, can heal the breach. The illusions and the reality go their separate ways. Gatsby stands at the door of his mansion, in one of the most deeply moving and significant paragraphs of the novel, to wish his guests good-bye:

> The caterwauling horns had reached a crescendo and I turned away and cut across the lawn toward home. I glanced back once. A wafer of a moon was shining over Gatsby's house, making the night fine as before, and surviving the laughter and the sound of his still glowing garden. A sudden emptiness seemed to flow now from the windows and the great doors, endowing with complete isolation the figure of the host, who stood on the porch, his hand up in a formal gesture of farewell.

If one turns back to Davy Crockett's description of the elegant young bee hunter, singing while the dawn breaks in the east, and thinks of it in relation with this midnight picture of Gatsby, "his hand up in a formal gesture of farewell," while the last guests depart through the debris of the finished party, the quality of the romanticism seems much the same, but the situation is exactly reversed; and from the latter scene there opens a perspective of profound meaning. Suddenly Gatsby is not merely a likable, romantic hero; he is a creature of myth in whom is incarnated the aspiration and the ordeal of his race.

"Mythic" characters are impersonal. There is no distinction between their public and their private lives. Because they share their meaning with everyone, they have no secrets and no hidden corners into which they can retire for a moment, unobserved. An intimacy so universal stands revealed in a ritual pattern for the inspection and instruction of the race. The "mythic" character can never withdraw from that air which is his existence—that is to say, from that area of consciousness (and hence of publicity) which every individual shares with the members, both living and dead, of his group or race. Gatsby is a "mythic" character in this sense—he has no private life, no meaning or significance that depends on the fulfillment of his merely private destiny, his happiness as an individual in a society of individuals. In a transcendent sense he touches our imaginations, but in this smaller sense—which is the world of the realistic novel—he even fails to arouse our curiosity. At this level, his love affair with Daisy is too easily "placed," a tawdry epic "crush" of no depth or interest in itself. But Gatsby not only remains undiminished by what is essentially the meanness of the affair: his stature grows, as we watch, to the proportions of a hero. We must inquire how Fitzgerald managed this extraordinary achievement.

Daisy Buchanan exists at two well-defined levels in the novel. She is what she is—but she exists also at the level of Gatsby's vision of her. The intelligence of no other important novelist has been as consistently undervalued as Fitzgerald's, and it is hardly surprising that no critic has ever given Fitzgerald credit for his superb understanding of Daisy's vicious emptiness. Even Fitzgerald's admirers regard Daisy as rather a good, if somewhat silly, little thing; but Fitzgerald knew that at its most depraved levels the American dream merges with the American debutante's dream—a thing of deathly hollowness. Fitzgerald faces up squarely to the problem of telling us what Daisy has to offer in a human relationship. At one of Gatsby's fabulous parties—the one to which Daisy brings her husband, Tom Buchanan—Gatsby points out to Daisy and Tom, among the celebrated guests, one particular couple:

> "Perhaps you know that lady," Gatsby indicated a gorgeous, scarcely human orchid of a woman who sat in state under a white-plum tree. Tom and Daisy stared, with that peculiarly unreal feeling that accompanies the recognition of a hitherto ghostly celebrity of the movies.
> "She's lovely," said Daisy.
> "The man bending over her is her director."

Superficially, the scene is highly civilized. One fancies one has seen it in Manet. But in the context we know that it has no reality whatever—the star and her director can get no nearer reality than by rehearsing a scene. Our attention is then taken up by other scenes at the party, but by suddenly returning to this couple after an interval of two pages to make his point, Fitzgerald achieves a curious impression of static or arrested action. We have the feeling that if we walked behind the white-plum tree we should only see the back of a canvas screen:

> Almost the last thing I remember was standing with Daisy and watching the moving-picture director and his Star. They were still under the white-plum tree and their faces were touching except for a pale, thin ray of moonlight between. It occurred to me that he had been very slowly bending toward her all evening to attain this proximity, and even while I watched I saw him stoop one ultimate degree and kiss at her cheek.
> "I like her," said Daisy, "I think she's lovely."
> But the rest offended her—and inarguably, because it wasn't a gesture but an emotion.

Daisy likes the moving-picture actress because she has no substance. She is a gesture that is committed to nothing more real than her own image on the silver screen. She has become a gesture divorced forever from the tiresomeness of human reality. In effect, this passage is Daisy's confession of faith. She virtually announces here what her criteria of human emotions and conduct are. Fitzgerald's illustration of the emptiness of Daisy's character—an emptiness that we see curdling into the viciousness of a monstrous moral indifference as the story unfolds—is drawn with a fineness and depth of critical understanding, and communicated with a force of imagery so rare in modern American writing, that it is almost astonishing that he is often credited with giving in to those very qualities which *The Great Gatsby* so effectively excoriates.

But what is the basis for the mutual attraction between Daisy and Gatsby? In Daisy's case the answer is simple. We remember that Nick Carraway has described Gatsby's personality as an "unbroken series of successful gestures." Superficially, Daisy finds in Gatsby, or thinks she finds, that safety from human reality which the empty gesture implies. What she fails to realize is that Gatsby's gorgeous gesturings are the reflex of an aspiration toward the possibilities of life, and this is something entirely different from those vacant images of romance and sophistication that fade so easily into the nothingness from which they came. But in a sense, Daisy is safe enough from the reality she dreads. The true question is not what Gatsby sees in Daisy, but the direction he takes from her, what he sees *beyond* her; and that has, despite the immaturity intrinsic in Gatsby's vision, an element of grandeur in it. For Gatsby, Daisy does not exist in herself. She is the green light that signals him into the heart of his ultimate vision. *Why* she should have this evocative power over Gatsby is a question Fitzgerald faces beautifully and successfully as he recreates that milieu of uncritical snobbishness and frustrated idealism—monstrous fusion—which is the world in which Gatsby is compelled to live.

Fitzgerald, then, has a sure control when he defines the quality of this love affair. He shows it in itself as vulgar and specious. It has no possible interest in its own right, and if it did have the pattern of the novel would be ruined. Our imaginations would be fettered in those details and interests which would detain us on the narrative level where the affair works itself out as human history, and Gatsby would lose his "mythic" quality. But the economy with which Gatsby is presented, the formal and boldly drawn structural lines of his imagination lead us at once to a level where it is obvious that Daisy's significance in the story lies in her failure to represent the objective correlative of Gatsby's vision. And at the same time, Daisy's wonderfully representative quality as a creature of the Jazz Age relates her personal failure to the larger failure of Gatsby's society to satisfy his need. In fact, Fitzgerald never allows

Daisy's failure to become a human or personal one. He maintains it with sureness on a symbolic level where it is identified with and reflects the failure of Gatsby's decadent American world. There is a famous passage in which Gatsby sees Daisy as an embodiment of the glamor of wealth. Nick Carraway is speaking first to Gatsby:

> "She's got an indiscreet voice," I remarked. "It's full of—" I hesitated. "Her voice is full of money," he said suddenly.
> That was it. I'd never understood before. It was full of money—that was the inexhaustible charm that rose and fell in it, the jingle of it, the cymbals' song of it. . . . High in a white palace the king's daughter, the golden girl . . .

Gatsby tries to build up the inadequacy of each value by the support of the other; but united they fall as wretchedly short of what he is seeking as each does singly. Gatsby's gold and Gatsby's girl belong to the fairy story in which the Princess spins whole rooms of money from skeins of wool. In the fairy story, the value never lies in the gold but in something beyond. And so it is in this story. For Gatsby, Daisy is only the promise of fulfillment that lies beyond the green light that burns all night on her dock.

This green light that is visible at night across the bay from the windows and lawn of Gatsby's house is the central symbol in the book. Significantly, our first glimpse of Gatsby at the end of Chapter I is related to it. Nick Carraway, whose modest bungalow in West Egg stands next to Gatsby's mansion, returning from an evening at the Buchanans', while lingering on the lawn for a final moment under the stars, becomes aware that he is not alone:

> . . . fifty feet away a figure had emerged from the shadow of my neighbor's mansion and was standing with his hands in his pockets regarding the silver pepper of the stars. Something in his leisurely movements and the secure position of his feet upon the lawn suggested that it was Mr. Gatsby himself, come out to determine what share was his of our local heavens.
> I decided to call to him. . . . But I didn't . . . for he gave a sudden intimation that he was content to be alone—he stretched out his arms toward the dark water in a curious way, and, as far as I was from him, I could have sworn he was trembling. Involuntarily I glanced seaward—and distinguished nothing except a single green light, minute and far away, that might have been the end of a dock. When I looked once more for Gatsby he had vanished, and I was alone again in the unquiet darkness.

It is hardly too much to say that the whole being of Gatsby exists only in relation to what the green light symbolizes. This first sight we have of Gatsby is a ritualistic tableau that literally contains the meaning of the completed book, although the full meaning of what is implicit in the symbol reveals itself slowly, and is only finally rounded out on the last page. We have a fuller definition of what the green light means in its particular, as opposed to its universal, signification in Chapter V. Gatsby is speaking to Daisy as they stand at one of the windows of his mansion:

> "If it wasn't for the mist we could see your home across the bay," said Gatsby. "You always have a green light that burns all night at the end of your dock."
>
> Daisy put her arm through his abruptly, but he seemed absorbed in what he had just said. Possibly it had occurred to him that the colossal significance of that light had now vanished forever. Compared to the great distance that had separated him from Daisy it had seemed very near to her, almost touching her. It had seemed as close as a star to the moon. Now it was again a green light on a dock. His count of enchanted objects had diminished by one.

Some might object to this symbolism on the grounds that it is easily vulgarized—as A. J. Cronin has proved. But if studied carefully in its full context it represents a convincing achievement. The tone or pitch of the symbol is exactly adequate to the problem it dramatizes. Its immediate function is that it signals Gatsby into his future, away from the cheapness of his affair with Daisy which he has vainly tried (and desperately continues trying) to create in the image of his vision. The green light is successful because, apart from its visual effectiveness as it gleams across the bay, it embodies the profound naiveté of Gatsby's sense of the future, while simultaneously suggesting the historicity of his hope. This note of historicity is not fully apparent at this point, of course. The symbol occurs several times, and most notably at the end:

> Gatsby believed in the green light, the orgiastic future that year by year recedes before us. It eluded us then, but that's no matter—to-morrow we will run faster, stretch out our arms farther. . . . And one fine morning—
> So we beat on, boats against the current, borne back ceaselessly into the past.

Thus the American dream, whose superstitious valuation of the future began in the past, gives the green light through which alone the American returns to his traditional roots, paradoxically retreating into the pattern of history while endeavoring to exploit the possibilities of the future. There is a suggestive echo of the past in Gatsby's sense of Daisy. He had known her, and fallen in love with her, five years before the novel opens. During that long interval while they had disappeared from each other's sight, Daisy has become a legend in Gatsby's memory, a part of his private past through which (as a "mythic" character) he

assimilates into the pattern of that historic past through which he would
move into the historic future. But the legendary Daisy, meeting her
after five years, has dimmed a little in luster:

> "And she doesn't understand," he said. "She used to be able to under-
> stand. We'd sit for hours—"
> He broke off and began to walk up and down a desolate path of fruit
> rinds and discarded favors and crushed flowers.
> "I wouldn't ask too much of her," I ventured. "You can't repeat the past."
> "Can't repeat the past?" he cried incredulously. "Why of course you can!"
> He looked around him wildly, as if the past were lurking here in the
> shadow of his house, just out of reach of his hand.

By such passages Fitzgerald dramatizes Gatsby's symbolic role. The
American dream, stretched between a golden past and a golden future,
is always betrayed by a desolate present—a moment of fruit rinds and
discarded favors and crushed flowers. Imprisoned in his present, Gatsby
belongs even more to the past than to the future. His aspirations have
been rehearsed, and his tragedy suffered, by all the generations of
Americans who have gone before. His sense of the future, of the possibilities of life, he has learned from the dead.

If we return to the passage in which, linked arm in arm, Gatsby and
Daisy stand at the window looking toward the green light across the bay,
it may be possible to follow a little more sympathetically that quality of
disillusion which begins to creep into Gatsby's response to life. It does
not happen because of the impoverished elements of his practical romance: it happens because Gatsby is incapable of compromising with his
inner vision. The imagery of this particular passage, as I suggested, is
gauged to meet the requirements of Gatsby's young romantic dream. But
two pages later Fitzgerald takes up the theme of Gatsby's struggle
against disenchantment once again, and this time in an imagery that
suggests how much he had learned from *The Waste Land*:

> When Klipspringer had played "The Love Nest" he turned around on
> the bench and searched unhappily for Gatsby in the gloom.
> "I'm all out of practice, you see. I told you I couldn't play. I'm all out
> of prac—"
> "Don't talk so much, old sport," commanded Gatsby. "Play!"
>
> > "In the morning,
> > In the evening,
> > Ain't we got fun—"
>
> Outside the wind was loud and there was a faint flow of thunder along the
> Sound. All the lights were going on in West Egg now; the electric trains,
> men carrying, were plunging home through the rain from New York. It was
> the hour of a profound human change, and excitement was generating on the
> air.

> "One thing's sure and nothing's surer
> The rich get richer and the poor get—children.
> In the meantime,
> In between time—"

As I went over to say good-by I saw that the expression of bewilderment had come back into Gatsby's face, as though a faint doubt had occurred to him as to the quality of his present happiness. Almost five years! There must have been moments even that afternoon when Daisy tumbled short of his dreams—not through her own fault, but because of the colossal vitality of his illusion. It had gone beyond her, beyond everything. He had thrown himself into it with a creative passion, adding to it all the time, decking it out with every bright feather that drifted his way. No amount of fire or freshness can challenge what a man can store up in his ghostly heart.

In view of such writing it is absurd to argue that Fitzgerald's art was a victim of his own attraction to the Jazz Age. The snatches of song that Klipspringer sings evoke the period with an immediacy that is necessary if we are to understand the peculiar poignancy of Gatsby's ordeal. But the songs are more than evocative. They provide the ironic musical prothalamion for Gatsby's romance, and as Gatsby listens to them an intimation of the practical truth presses in on him. The recognition is heightened poetically by that sense of the elements, the faint flow of thunder along the Sound, which forms the background of those artificial little tunes. And it is not odd that this evocation of the outdoor scene, while Klipspringer pounds at the piano inside, sustains in the imagination the image of that green light, symbol of Gatsby's faith, which is burning across the bay. This scene draws on the "violet hour" passage from "The Fire Sermon" in which "the human engine waits/Like a taxi throbbing waiting. . . ." It is the hour of a profound human change, and in the faint stirrings of Gatsby's recognition there is for a moment, perhaps, a possibility of his escape. But the essence of the American dream whose tragedy Gatsby is enacting is that it lives in a past and a future that never existed, and is helpless in the present that does.

Gatsby's opposite number in the story is Daisy's husband, Tom Buchanan, and Gatsby's stature—his touch of doomed but imperishable spiritual beauty, if I may call it so—is defined by his contrast with Tom. In many ways they are analogous in their characteristics—just sufficiently, so to point up the differences. For example, their youth is an essential quality of them both. But Tom Buchanan was "one of those men who reach such an acute limited excellence at twenty-one that everything afterward savors of anti-climax." Even his body—"a body capable of enormous leverage"—was "a cruel body." In the description of Tom we are left physically face to face with a scion of those ruthless generations who raised up the great American fortunes, and who now live in uneasy arrogant leisure on their brutal acquisitions. But Gatsby's youth leaves an impression of interminability. Its climax is always in the future, and it gives rather than demands. Its energy is not in its body, but in its spirit, and meeting Gatsby for the first time, one seizes, as Nick Carraway did, this impression in his smile:

> It was one of those rare smiles with a quality of eternal reassurance in it, that you may come across four or five times in life. It faced—or seemed to face—the whole external world for an instant, and then concentrated on *you* with an irresistible prejudice in your favor. It understood you just so far as you wanted to be understood, believed in you as you would like to believe in yourself, and assured you that it had precisely the impression of you that, at your best, you hoped to convey. Precisely at that point it vanished—and I was looking at an elegant young rough-neck, a year or two over thirty, whose elaborate formality of speech just missed being absurd.

This passage is masterly in the way in which it presents Gatsby to us less as an individual than as a projection, or mirror, of our ideal selves. To do that is the function of all "mythic" characters. Gatsby's youth is not simply a matter of three decades that will quickly multiply themselves into four or five. It is a quality of faith and hope that may be betrayed by history, may be killed by society, but that no exposure to the cynical turns of time can reduce to the compromises of age.

Again, Gatsby and Tom are alike in the possession of a certain sentimentality, but Tom Buchanan's is based on depraved self-pity. He is never more typical than when coaxing himself to tears over a half-finished box of dog biscuits that recalls a drunken and illicit day from his past, associated in memory with his dead mistress. His self-pity is functional. It is sufficient to condone his most criminal acts in his own eyes as long as the crimes are not imputable. But Gatsby's sentimentality exists in the difficulty of expressing, in the phrases and symbols provided by his decadent society, the reality that lies at the heart of his aspiration. "So he waited, listening for a moment longer to the tuning-fork that had been struck upon a star"—Gatsby's sentimentality (if it *is* sentimentality, and I rather doubt it) is as innocent as that. It has nothing of self-pity or indulgence in it—it is all aspiration and goodness; and it must be remembered that Fitzgerald himself is *outside* Gatsby's vocabulary, using it with great mastery to convey the poignancy of the situation.

Tom Buchanan and Gatsby represent antagonistic but historically related aspects of America. They are related as the body and the soul when a mortal barrier has risen up between them. Tom Buchanan is virtually Gatsby's murderer in the end, but the crime that he commits by proxy is only a symbol of his deeper spiritual crime against Gatsby's inner vision. Gatsby's guilt, insofar as it exists, is radical failure—a failure of the critical faculty that seems to be an inherent part of the American dream—to understand that Daisy is as fully immersed in the destructive element of the American world as Tom himself. After Daisy, while driving Gatsby's white automobile, has killed Mrs. Wilson and, implicitly at least, left Gatsby to shoulder the blame, Nick Carraway gives us a crucial insight into the spiritual affinity of the Buchanan couple, drawing together in their callous selfishness in a moment of guilt and crisis:

> Daisy and Tom were sitting opposite each other at the kitchen table, with a plate of cold fried chicken between them, and two bottles of ale. He was talking intently across the table at her, and in his earnestness his hand had fallen upon and covered her own. Once in a while she looked up at him and nodded in agreement.
>
> They weren't happy, and neither of them had touched the chicken or the ale—and yet they weren't unhappy either. There was an unmistakable air of natural intimacy about the picture, and anybody would have said that they were conspiring together.

They instinctively seek out each other because each recognizes the other's strength in the corrupt spiritual element they inhabit.

There is little point in tracing out in detail the implications of the action any further, although it could be done with an exactness approaching allegory. That it is not allegory is owing to the fact that the pattern emerges from the fullness of Fitzgerald's living experience of his own society and time. In the end the most that can be said is that *The Great Gatsby* is a dramatic affirmation in fictional terms of the American spirit in the midst of an American world that denies the soul. Gatsby exists in, and for, that affirmation alone.

When, at the end, not even Gatsby can hide his recognition of the speciousness of his dream any longer, the discovery is made in universalizing terms that dissolve Daisy into the larger world she has stood for in Gatsby's imagination:

> He must have looked up at an unfamiliar sky through frightening leaves and shivered as he found what a grotesque thing a rose is and how raw the sunlight was upon the scarcely created grass. A new world, material without being real, where poor ghosts, breathing dreams like air, drifted fortuitously about. . . .

"A new world, material without being real." Paradoxically, it was Gatsby's dream that conferred reality upon the world. The reality was in his faith in the goodness of creation, and in the possibilities of life. That these possibilities were intrinsically related to such romantic components limited and distorted his dream, and finally left it helpless in the face of the Buchanans, but it did not corrupt it. When the dream melted, it knocked the prop of reality from under the universe, and face to face with the physical substance at last, Gatsby realized that the illusion was *there*—there where Tom and Daisy, and generations of small-minded, ruthless Americans had found it—in the dreamless, visionless complacency of mere matter, substance without form. After this recognition, Gatsby's death is only a symbolic formality, for the world into which his mere body had been born rejected the gift he had been created to embody—the traditional dream from which alone it could awaken into life.

As the novel closes, the experience of Gatsby and his broken dream explicitly becomes the focus of that historic dream for which he stands. Nick Carraway is speaking:

> Most of the big shore places were closed now and there were hardly any lights except the shadowy, moving glow of a ferryboat across the Sound. And as the moon rose higher the inessential houses began to melt away until gradually I became aware of the old island here that flowered once for Dutch sailors' eyes—a fresh, green breast of the new world. Its vanished trees, the trees that had made way for Gatsby's house, had once pandered in whispers to the last and greatest of all human dreams; for a transitory enchanted moment man must have held his breath in the presence of this continent, compelled into an aesthetic contemplation he neither understood nor desired, face to face for the last time in history with something commensurate to his capacity for wonder.

It is fitting that this, like so many of the others in *Gatsby,* should be a moonlight scene, for the history and the romance are one. Gatsby fades into the past forever to take his place with the Dutch sailors who had chosen their moment in time so much more happily than he.

We recognize that the great achievement of this novel is that it manages, while poetically evoking a sense of the goodness of that early dream, to offer the most damaging criticism of it in American literature. The astonishing thing is that the criticism—if indictment wouldn't be the better word—manages to be part of the tribute. Gatsby, the "mythic" embodiment of the American dream, is shown to us in all his immature romanticism. His insecure grasp of social and human values, his lack of critical intelligence and self-knowledge, his blindness to the pitfalls that surround him in American society, his compulsive optimism, are realized in the text with rare assurance and understanding. And yet the very grounding of these deficiencies is Gatsby's goodness and faith in life, his compelling desire to realize all the possibilities of existence, his belief that we can have an Earthly Paradise populated by Buchanans. A great part of Fitzgerald's achievement is that he suggests effectively that these terrifying deficiencies are not so much the private deficiencies of Gatsby, but are deficiencies inherent in contemporary manifestations of the

American vision itself—a vision no doubt admirable, but stupidly defenseless before the equally American world of Tom and Daisy. Gatsby's deficiencies of intelligence and judgment bring him to his tragic death —a death that is spiritual as well as physical. But the more important question that faces us through our sense of the immediate tragedy is where they have brought America.

LATE WORK

Mechanisms of Misery

by D. W. Harding

Many of the features that go to making *The Great Gatsby* as fine as it is are also present in this latest novel of Scott Fitzgerald's.[1] There is still his power of seeming to lose himself in incident and letting the theme emerge by itself, there is his sensitiveness (occasionally touching sentimentality) and his awareness of the brutalities in civilized people's behavior, and there is simultaneously his keen appreciation, not entirely ironic, of the superficies of the same people's lives. This last is the feature that is most nearly lost in the new book. Here there is no more gusto, but right from the start an undercurrent of misery which draws away even the superficial vitality of the Euramerican life he depicts.

The story is the acutely unhappy one of a young psychiatrist, brilliant in every way, who gradually deteriorates. In place of plot there is a fine string of carefully graduated incidents to illustrate the stages of the descent. Rather than tragedy, however, the book appears to me to be one variety of the harrowing, if this can be taken to mean that as we read it our feelings are of misery and protest, and that, unlike tragedy, it can give no satisfactions to those who wish to go on living. On the other hand, it is so effectively and sincerely harrowing that its mechanisms deserve close examination.

In the first place the doomed hero is offered as the most admirable kind of modern man we can reasonably ask for, and throughout the

"The Mechanisms of Failure," by Dennis Harding. From *Scrutiny* III (December 1934). Copyright © 1934 by Dennis Harding. Reprinted by permission of the author.
[1] *Tender Is the Night.*

novel he is made to stand out as superior to all the other personæ.
This being so we look for some explanation of his collapse, and the
first mechanism of misery appears in the ambiguity here. Various possible explanations are hinted at but none is allowed to stand. His wife's
wealth, with its heavy burden of smart leisure, Dick deals with like a
disciplined artist; he shows himself heroically adequate to the strain of
her recurrent mental trouble; and he has as full an insight into himself
and the strains his work imposes as he has into his patients. Everything
that we could hope to do he is shown doing better, and—apparently as
a consequence—he cracks up. The gloomy generalization is made by
Dick himself in commenting on a man who precedes him to ruin: "Smart
men play close to the line because they have to—some of them can't
stand it, so they quit." But the pessimistic conviction of the book goes
deeper than that, and its puritan roots are suggested by Dick's misgivings
over his good fortunes and achievements in his heigh-day. He soliloquises:
"—And Lucky Dick can't be one of these clever men; he must be less
intact, even faintly destroyed. If life won't do it for him it's not a sub-
stitute to get a disease, or a broken heart, or an inferiority complex,
though it'd be nice to build out some broken side till it was better than
the original structure." Scott Fitzgerald sees to it that life *will* do it for
him.

But in addition to the puritan conviction, there is also present a curious mingling of a childish fantasy with an adult's attempt to correct
it, and much of the harrowing effect of the book depends on this. On the
one hand, Dick is the tragic fantasy hero who is so great and fine that
everyone else expects to go on taking and taking from him and never
give back; and so he gets tired, so tired; and he breaks under the strain
with no one big enough to help him, and it's terribly pathetic and admirable. The vital point of this childish fantasy is that he should remain
admirable and (posthumously) win everyone's remorseful respect. But
the story is too obviously sentimental in those terms. To try ruthlessly
to tear out the sentimentality, Scott Fitzgerald brings in a much more
mature bit of knowledge: that people who disintegrate in the adult
world don't at all win our respect and can hardly retain even our pity.
He gets his intense painfulness by inviting our hearts to go out to the
hero of the childish fantasy and then checking them with the embarrassment which everyone nearest him in the story, especially Nicole his wife,
feels for the failure.

The question is whether the situation could in fact occur. Not whether
the main events could be paralleled in real life, but whether all the
elements of action and feeling could co-exist in the way they are presented here, whether we are not being trapped into incompatible attitudes towards the same events. In short, is an emotional trick being
played on us?

There seem to me to be several tricks, though without extensive quotation they are hard to demonstrate. Chief among them is the social isolation of the hero, isolation in the sense that no one gives him any help and he has no genuinely reciprocal social relationships; he remains the tragic child hero whom no one is great enough to help. Even towards the end he is made to seem superior to the others so that they are inhibited from approaching him with help. That this should be so is made plausible by the continual returns of his old self amongst the wreckage, returns of self-discipline and willingness to shoulder responsibility that amount almost to alternations of personality. He explains it himself: "The manner remains intact for some time after the morale cracks." But it seems highly doubtful whether anyone could remain so formidable spiritually during a process of spiritual disintegration, especially to someone who had been as close to him as Nicole had been. But here another trick appears in the interests of plausibility: the patient-physician relationship between the two of them is now emphasized, and Nicole's abandonment of Dick is interpreted as an emergence from fixation, whereas much of the misery of the collapse springs from its wrecking what has earlier been made to seem a genuine and complete marriage.

Once achieved, Dick's isolation permits of the further device of making his suffering dumb. Reading the aquaplane episode in particular is like watching a rabbit in a trap. The story begins to become less harrowing and more like tragedy when, once or twice, Dick is articulate about himself. This happens momentarily when he comments on the manner remaining intact after the morale has cracked: but no other persona is allowed to be big enough to hear more, and " 'Do you practise on the Riviera?' Rosemary demanded hastily." At one point the cloud of dumb misery lifts again for a moment, when he thinks he is unobserved and Nicole sees from his face that he is going back over his whole story, and actually feels sympathy for him; but this episode only introduces the final harrowing isolation. His position at the end is the apotheosis of the hurt child saying "Nobody loves me," but the child's self-pity and reproaches against the grown-ups have largely been rooted out and in their place is a fluctuation between self-disgust and a fatalistic conviction that this is bound to happen to the nicest children.

The difficulty of making a convincing analysis of the painful quality of this novel, and the conviction that it was worth while trying to, are evidence of Scott Fitzgerald's skill and effectiveness. Personal peculiarities may of course make one reader react more intensely than another to a book of this kind, and I am prepared to be told that this attempt at analysis is itself childish—an attempt to assure myself that the magician didn't really cut the lady's head off, did he? I still believe there was a trick in it.

The Significance
of F. Scott Fitzgerald

by D. S. Savage

For literary history, the career of F. Scott Fitzgerald begins with an exuberantly immature best-selling novel entitled *This Side of Paradise* and concludes with the posthumous valedictory and confessional volume entitled *The Crack-Up*. The implied antithesis is neat, and not insignificant, and it is more than literary. There was, throughout, the closest correspondence between Fitzgerald's life and his writing, and yet the widest disparity between the man and the artist.

From this side of paradise, then, to the crack-up. Between the strenuously gay social adventure of the young Scott and Zelda in the New York of the Jazz Age and the anguished, shattered existence of the later years, the disparity seems complete. Yet in fact, as Mr. Arthur Mizener's biography[1] puts beyond question, it was but the furthest extension of a duality which was always there: the rift in the lute widened slowly to a chasm, but it is already evident in the frantic oscillations between misery and bliss, poverty and affluence, failure and success which characterized the young man from Princeton in 1919.

What happened then is of crucial importance in Fitzgerald's life. In an article in *The Crack-Up* called "Early Success" he tells how he gave up his job in an advertising office, retiring "not on my profits, but on my liabilities, which included debts, despair, and a broken engagement" and crept home to finish a novel.

That novel, begun in a training camp late in the war, was my ace in the hole. I had put it aside when I got a job in New York, but I was as constantly aware of it as of the shoe with cardboard in the sole, during all one desolate spring. It was like the fox and goose and the bag of beans. If I stopped working to finish the novel, I lost the girl. . . .

My friends who were not in love or who had waiting arrangements with

"The Significance of F. Scott Fitzgerald," by D. S. Savage. From the *Arizona Quarterly*, 8 (Autumn 1952) Copyright © 1952 by D. S. Savage. Reprinted by permission of the author and *Arizona Quarterly*.

[1] *The Far Side of Paradise:* A Biography of F. Scott Fitzgerald, by Arthur Mizener. Boston: Houghton Mifflin Company, 1951.

"sensible" girls, braced themselves patiently for a long pull. Not I—I was in love with a whirlwind and I must spin a net big enough to catch it out of my head, a head full of trickling nickels and sliding dimes, the incessant music box of the poor. It couldn't be done like that, so when the girl threw me over I went home and finished my novel. And then, suddenly, everything changed, and this article is about that first wild wind of success and the delicious mist it brings with it. . . .

The compensation of a very early success is a conviction that life is a romantic matter. In the best sense one stays young. When the primary objects of love and money could be taken for granted and a shaky eminence had lost its fascination, I had fair years to waste, years that I can't honestly regret, in seeking the eternal Carnival by the Sea.

That final paragraph says nearly everything. Fitzgerald was indeed a romantic who wished time to stand still forever at the hour of youth so that an aesthetic paradise might be superimposed upon life's harsh actuality. This could only be done, it seemed, by the power of money, and accordingly Fitzgerald wrote for money—magazine stories at two or three thousand dollars a time. This money brought him among the rich, to share, as he put it, "their mobility and the grace that some of them brought into their lives." His wider significance, which should always be borne in mind, is indicated by the coincidence of this temper with the prevalent mood of the time. That first novel fell into the hands of a ready world—"a whole race going hedonistic, deciding on pleasure." But the crack-up too was a particular incident in a general calamity. His early happiness, Fitzgerald wrote, often approached ecstasy, but "my happiness, or talent for self-delusion or what you will, was an exception. It was not the natural thing but the unnatural—unnatural as the Boom; and my recent experience parallels the wave of despair that swept the nation when the Boom was over."

Despair. In Kierkegaard's definition, *despair,* the contrary of *faith,* is the Sickness unto Death arising from an impotence in the self to choose and to become itself. In this precise sense, Fitzgerald was a man in despair. For two years previous to his eventual collapse, he tells us, his life had been a drawing on resources that he did not possess: "I had been mortgaging myself physically and spiritually up to the hilt." In a poignant passage he describes the sickness of despair as an *inability to love.*

I realized that in those two years in order to preserve something—an inner hush maybe, maybe not—I had weaned myself from all the things I used to love—that every act of life from the morning tooth-brush to the friend at dinner had become an effort. I saw that for a long time I had not liked people and things, but only followed the rickety old pretence of liking. I saw that even my love for those closest to me was become only an attempt to love, that my casual relations—with an editor, a tobacco seller, the child of a friend, were only what I remembered I *should* do, from other days.

All in the same month I became bitter about such things as the sound of the radio, the advertisements in the magazines, the screech of tracks, the dead silence of the country—contemptuous at human softness, immediately (if secretively) quarrelsome toward hardness—hating the night when I couldn't sleep and hating the day because it went toward night. I slept on the heart side now because I knew that the sooner I could tire that out, even a little, the sooner would come that blessed hour of nightmare which, like a catharsis, would enable me to better meet the new day.

Fears shall be in the way, and the almond tree shall flourish, and the grasshopper shall be a burden, and desire shall fail. . . . In this condition, for the first time "forced to think," he concluded that, essentially, he had never lived—that the essential business of his life he had left to this and that admired figure among his contemporaries.

So there was not an "I" any more—not a basis on which I could organize my self-respect. . . . It was strange to have no self—to be like a little boy left alone in a big house, who knew that now he could do anything he wanted to do, but found that there was nothing that he wanted to do. . . .

But was there in reality ever an "I"—would it not be more exact to say that he had parted finally with a fictive personality-image and come to a *realization* that he had no self and was in despair? Considering those of his contemporaries who somehow managed not to commit suicide or to become insane, he wrote mordantly that it led him to the idea that they had made some sort of irretrievable break with their past selves. "So, since I could no longer fulfill the obligations that life had set for me or that I had set for myself, why not slay the empty shell who had been posturing at it for four years?"

. . . I must continue to be a writer because that was my only way of life, but I would cease any attempts to be a person—to be kind, just or generous. There were plenty of counterfeit coins around that would pass instead of these and I knew where I could get them at a nickel on the dollar. . . . There was to be no more giving of myself—all giving was to be outlawed henceforth under a new name, and that name was Waste.

How characteristic of the man it was that after glancing bitterly in these articles at the novel's increasing subordination to the mechanical and communal art of the film, he should have gone to Hollywood to end his life as a patcher-up of film scripts. And how utterly in keeping with the pathos of his life that he should have collapsed and died in the middle of writing the novel which was to have comprehended his Hollywood experience and vindicated his name as an artist.

II

The more closely one looks into Fitzgerald the more clearly one perceives the crucial importance of that *disconcerting* early experience with Zelda. It confirmed him in his belief in the sovereign power of wealth, while arousing in him a moral revulsion against that power, thus accentuating the division which expressed itself most completely in the disparity between the man and the artist. Of the early success which gave him the money which brought him back his girl, Fitzgerald retrospectively insisted:

> The man with the jingle of money in his pocket who married the girl a year later would always cherish an abiding distrust, an animosity, toward the leisure class . . . since then I have never been able to stop wondering where my friends' money came from, nor to stop thinking that at one time a sort of *droit de seigneur* might have been exercised to give one of them my girl.

That early experience is the model for Gatsby's relations to Daisy in *The Great Gatsby,* while its later consequences are reflected in the relations of Dick and Nicole in *Tender Is the Night.*

Both these novels portray the shining world of the rich, and in each there is a critical exposure of the corrupting influence of money upon human values. Let us compare their plots. In the former, Jay Gatsby, a poor farm boy, amasses a fortune in order to be able to win back the rich girl he had fallen irrevocably in love with five years earlier, but who in his absence overseas in the army had married Tom Buchanan, a man of established social position but a coarse-grained brute. Nick Carraway, the narrator, arranges a meeting of the former lovers, but the romantic idealism proves to be all on one side, and Gatsby fails in the issue to win back Daisy from the faithless and self-assured Tom. Tom and Daisy extricate themselves from a sordid scrape by conspiring to pin the guilt of the manslaughter of Tom's disreputable mistress on to Gatsby, as a result of which he is murdered by the dead woman's husband. Gatsby's fortune is revealed to have been built on crime. Of the crowds who had swarmed to his parties only one man presents himself at the funeral; Nick returns to his home in the West, and Tom and Daisy are left to the self-enclosed enjoyment of their careless, glittering lives. "It was all very careless and confused. They were careless people, Tom and Daisy—they smashed up things and creatures and then retreated back into their money or their vast carelessness, or whatever it was that kept them together, and let other people clean up the mess they had made. . . ."

In *Tender Is the Night,* written after a nine-years silence during which he and Zelda had been ruinously dissipating their resources in the playgrounds of Europe and America, Dick Diver, an able and promising psychiatrist from the Middle West, undertakes the treatment in Europe of a Chicago millionaire's neurotic daughter, Nicole Warren. Treatment succeeds, but complications arise when the rich girl "falls in love" with the poor doctor, and against all advice he marries her, turning a professional responsibility into a personal commitment, and slowly finding all his energies diverted to the emotional needs of a wife who is simultaneously a patient. When Nicole has used him to the limit she abandons the exhausted man for a lover of the Tom Buchanan caste. The irony is that to Nicole's family his relation to her *is* nothing but a professional one—Dick's *services* have been *bought;* so that when Nicole has "cut the cord" he is no longer needed and can be casually returned to the poor parishes of his origin—"That's what he was educated for." Thus both Gatsby and Dick Diver, fascinated by wealth (and a woman) venture romantically into the world of the established rich and are destroyed.

This could be a variation on the edifying theme of the corrupting power of riches upon human values, but the matter goes deeper than that. Money is valued, not for itself, but for the entry it purchases to an earthly paradise of leisure far removed from the stresses of real life: an illusory region of eternal youth. In *Tender Is the Night,* a retrospective appraisal of the degenerative effects of "seven years of waste and tragedy," the mirage-paradise is shown in diffuse form as the search for the Carnival by the Sea: in *Gatsby,* however, written at the early peak of Fitzgerald's career—the summit from which, afterwards, all was decline—it is presented with contemporaneous immediacy and cast into unitary shape. The one is clinically more explicit, and offers a key with which to unlock the cryptic message of the other—for although *Gatsby* remains the most complete and concentrated statement of Fitzgerald's situation, its symbols are veiled.

We must look closer at this paradise which is bought by money. In doing so it will be well to follow a pregnant hint dropped by Mr. Mizener—"Somewhere very deep in [Fitzgerald's] imagination that complicated tangle of feelings he had about the rich interlocked with his feelings about the delight of vitality and the horror of its exhaustion." There is a very early story entitled *Absolution,* which not only reminds us that Fitzgerald was raised a Roman Catholic, and that the earthly paradise is an inverted theological conception, but serves to show the connection between Carnival—a fleshy word—and vitality. It opens: "There was once a priest with cold, watery eyes, who, in the still of the night, wept cold tears. . . . Sometimes, near four o'clock, there was a rustle of Swede girls along the path by his window, and in their shrill laughter he found a terrible dissonance that made him pray aloud for the twilight to come." The priest is confronted with an eager little boy on the exciting threshold of experience, and before his bright innocent gaze he breaks down and raves crazily about—an amusement park.

> Did you ever see an amusement park? . . . Well, go and see an amusement park. . . . It's a thing like a fair, only much more glittering. Go to one at night and stand a little way off from it in a dark place—under d rk trees. You'll see a big wheel made of lights turning in the air, and a long slide shooting boats down into the water. A band playing somewhere, a rd a smell of peanuts—and everything will twinkle. But it won't remind yc u of anything, you see. It will all just hang out there in the night like colored balloon—like a big yellow lantern on a pole.

But, he warns the boy, don't get up close, "because if you do you'll only feel the heat and the sweat and the life." When the priest collapses precipitously (and symbolically) to the floor, the boy rushes in panic from the room. "But underneath his terror he felt that his own inner convictions were confirmed. There was something ineffably gorgeous somewhere that had nothing to do with God." There could hardly be a more appropriate symbol for the earthly paradise than an amusement park with its sensational, circular mechanisms: while the heat, the sweat and the life associated with it form a link with the Swede girls invoked at the beginning of the story and again at its close.

It is exactly this profane vision which is the theme both of *The Great Gatsby* and of *Tender Is the Night*. At their pristine encounter it is first of all Daisy's heavenly house that captivates Gatsby. "Her porch was bright with the bought luxury of star-shine. . . . Gatsby was overwhelmingly aware of the youth and mystery that wealth imprisons and preserves, of the freshness of many clothes, and of Daisy, gleaming like silver, safe and proud above the hot struggles of the poor." It is such a stellar paradise that he must provide, five years later, if he is to turn back time and regain the lover who had forsaken him for a richer man. In both novels the paradisal condition is to be attained by a three-fold legerdemain comprising the transformation of space, the suspension of time and the negation of Experience with its distinctions of good-and-evil. In *Tender Is the Night* this last is accomplished by a conspiracy of manners—Dick Diver's perfect courtesy establishes a charmed circle within which all are released from the bondage of their actual imperfections. "To be included in Dick Diver's world for a while was a remarkable experience; people believed he made special reservations about them, recognizing the proud uniqueness of their destinies, buried under the compromises of how many years. He won everyone quickly with an exquisite consideration and a politeness that moved so fast and intuitively that it could be examined only in its effect." Here the negation of time is determined by the imperative necessity to stay young. Dick and Nicole experience time differently. "For him time stood still and then every few years accelerated in a rush, like the quick re-wind of a film, but for Nicole the years slipped away by clock and calendar and birthday, with the added poignance of her perishable beauty." The ruined Abe North negates time with alcohol, for "The drink made past happy things contemporary with the present as if they were still going on, contemporary even with the future as if they were about to happen again." Dick's inner collapse shows itself as a breakdown of manners, running significantly parallel to a physical deterioration—the last link snaps when he miserably fails in the attempt to display his earlier prowess on the surf-board. When youth goes, the Carnival is over.

It is in this later novel that the interlocking of money with vitality is most explicit. It is especially evident in Dick's growing subjection to Nicole: he is "inundated with a constant trickle of goods and money," and is led to reflect that despite himself he had been "swallowed up like a gigolo and somehow permitted his arsenal to be locked up in the Warren safety-deposit vaults." Money here would appear in some obscure way to be the agent of feminine sexuality; by its means Dick, robbed of his male potency—the historical will to vocation, work, culture—has fallen into subjection to the natural female will to idleness and pleasure. Fitzgerald fails to stress the fact, but it is Dick's culpable folly in agreeing to marry his own patient which is the initial fault that sets in motion the entire process of involvement and degeneration; and it is interesting to note that, although he is made to hold out for some time, he is shown in the outcome as powerless to resist, not the inducements of Nicole's bank-balance but the sheer overwhelming vital force of her sexual attraction. The passage in which the virtual seduction of Dick by Nicole is described would be conclusive even were it not underlined by the character of his subsequent liaison with the ingenuous Rosemary—transparently a recapitulation of the earlier experience—in which again the woman is sexually the aggressor, employing an appealing childishness to captivate the male to whom she stands in a relationship which is ambiguously filial and maternal. The principal defect of the novel, its one-sidedness which obstructs a truthful, total presentment of the situation, is the result of that too-close approximation of the author's viewpoint to that of his hero which leads him to expose the flaw in Nicole to the full while passing silently over the flaw in Dick which leaves him so unaccountably open to victimization at her hands. In spite of this grave defect, a sharp eye may discern clearly enough Dick's actual subterrene complicity with Nicole. It is hinted in a passage describing his emotions during one of her psychotic relapses: "Somehow Dick and Nicole had become one and equal, not opposite and complementary. He could not watch her disintegrations without participating in them." Since Nicole's condition is the consequence of physical seduction at the hands of her own father, it is impossible to evade the conclusion that Dick is unconsciously implicated in the very incestuous regression which is at the root of her psychopathic (schizophrenic) condition. It is precisely the same incestuous regression which, in fact, determines the unconscious symbolism of *The Great Gatsby*—a symbolism, however, which I lack space to elucidate in the present article.

In the dark enchantment of the incestuous regression, life flows back to its own origins, history is dissolved into nature, the masculine will to creativeness is absorbed in the feminine will to reproduction, and that in turn to the will to dissolution. As for money, that, for Fitzgerald—as is revealed in the passage concerning the *"droit de seigneur"*—was no other than a *symbol for possession*. With money, the unconscious thought seems to have run, you could *possess*—your girl, the *material*s for the earthly paradise, Mother Earth, your mother. . . . The Carnival by the Sea is an *incestuous* festival.

III

There is no help for it: what emerges most patently from Fitzgerald's biography is his character as a mother's boy. "His mother's treatment," Mr. Mizener points out, "was bad for a precocious and imaginative boy, and as Fitzgerald confessed to his daughter after she had grown up, 'I didn't know till 15 that there was anyone in the world except me. . . .'" After *The Great Gatsby* he began a novel about matricide called *The Boy Who Killed His Mother*. "At about this time he also wrote a comic ballad about a dope fiend of sixteen who murdered his mother. . . . Fitzgerald used to deliver this ballad at parties, his face powdered white, a cigarette dangling from his mouth, and his hands trembling."—Not so comic.

Already in *This Side of Paradise* the components of this complex are evident enough. "Amory Blaine," runs the opening sentence, "inherited from his mother every trait, except the stray inexpressible few, that made him worth while." At thirteen he is "more than ever son to his Celtic mother," and it is at this tender age that he begins his childish amours. The fascination of femininity supplies the book's very substance, and there is occult significance in Amory's self-identification with Monsignor Darcy and in the character of that ecclesiastical personage's relationship with Amory's mother—he had been her lover. That is, through "Monsignor" the incest-wish is indirectly expressed and religiously sanctioned. Openly faced, or half-faced, only in *Tender Is the Night*, the incest motive is in fact central to all of Fitzgerald's novels. *The Great Gatsby* is a profane myth in which the religious symbols are inverted. Gatsby seeks to go *back* to happiness and innocence through an impossible union with the maternal-image, Daisy, just as, in *The Last Tycoon*, the tired and dying Monro Stahr—another stellar hero—seeks to *repeat* his experience with his dead wife through the girl he

first descries on top of a scenic set-piece of the Goddess [*sic*] Siva, Destroyer and Reproducer, which is floating on the surface of the flooded
lot. The reason why this novel is a comparative failure and the other
a consummate success lies in the disjunction between the real and the
apparent themes in the one and their perfect mutual assimilation in the
other.

In such a situation of unconscious infatuation by the maternal image
as Fitzgerald exemplifies, the sheer assertion of masculine will becomes
a primary need of the personality. It is, I think, important to realize
that Fitzgerald felt all his life that he had failed even in the primitive
achievement of masculine independence. In *The Crack-Up* he drew
a parallel between the precipitating cause of his current dereliction and
certain experiences of his youth. Together with the crucial Zelda episode
he bracketed the loss of some coveted offices at Princeton and a humiliating failure to be appointed on active service overseas in 1918. "Some
old desire for personal dominance was gone," he wrote of the latter
discouragement, and of the former: "There were to be no badges of
pride, no medals after all. It seemed on one March afternoon that I had
lost every single thing I wanted—*and that night was the first time that
I hunted down the spectre of womanhood that, for a little while, makes
everything else seem unimportant.*" [2]

Failure of this primitive assertion of masculinity (which, among
primitive peoples, is accomplished through the initiation-ceremonies
and ordeals of adolescence through which the boy is prepared for adult
membership of the tribe) is at once a failure to achieve that indispensable
measure of individuality upon which depends the corresponding power
to individualize the "other," failure to assert the predominance of the
"reality-principle" over the "pleasure-principle" (Freud), and failure to
sever the infantile emotional bond with the mother and with the values
of childish innocence. In consequence of the *enchanted* or *charmed* subjection to the diffused attraction of a generalized, maternal femininity,
the sexual relation has a fatal tendency to regress to a childish stage
which is also incestuous, being "innocent" and "guilty" simultaneously
or by turns.

The Great Gatsby is a parable of Innocence and Experience, and Fitzgerald's history must be interpreted in the light of the alternation of
these terms and the oscillation between them: he lacked comprehension
of the third, unitive term in the series—Imagination. Innocence is here
the pristine integrality of the asexual childish selfhood represented by
the beautiful little boy in *Absolution* "with eyes like blue stones, and
lashes that sprayed open from them like flower-petals." Experience is the
abandonment of innocence through entry upon the adult, sexual,
moneyed life, the world of the Warrens and Buchanans who are, in the

[2] These italics are Mr. Savage's.

total sense of the word, *in possession*. The Gatsbys and Divers are romantics in contradiction with themselves, in that they wish to make of
experience a means to the renewal of innocence: and what was the
daemoniac gaiety of Fitzgerald's life but an attempt, not merely to ride
two horses at once, but to ride two horses going in opposite directions:
to live, in the context of adult, responsible experience with the innocent
irresponsibility of the child? In a short story entitled *Babylon Revisited,*
a repentant reveler whose escapades have brought about the death of
his wife and the alienation of her family, returns to the Paris of his
past follies in an endeavor to regain custody of the child surrendered
through his neglect into the hands of his wife's hostile sister; but his
plans are ruined by the irruption into the family circle of two drunken
companions of his former life. The biblical associations of "Babylon"
are obvious enough; but was it not Robert Graves who once pointed out
that in the old nursery-rhyme which runs:

> How many miles to Babylon?
> Three-score and ten.
> Shall I get there by candle-light?
> Yes, and back again,

"Babylon" is most probably an elided form of "Baby-land." Certainly
there is a marked infantile quality in the escapades of which the returned reveler is reminded by his former fellows. "We *did* have such
good times that crazy spring, like the night you and I stole the butcher's
tricycle, and the time we tried to call on the president and you had the
old derby rim and the wire cane. Everybody seems so old lately, but I
don't feel old a bit." Reading the note in which this occurs:

> His first feeling was one of awe that he had actually, in his mature
> years, stolen a tricycle and pedalled Lorraine all over the Étoile between
> the small hours and dawn. In retrospect it was a nightmare. Locking out
> Helen [the drunken act which had resulted in his wife's death] didn't fit
> in with any other act of his life, but the tricycle incident did—it was one
> of many. How many weeks or months of dissipation to arrive at that con-
> dition of utter irresponsibility?

It is the basic incest-pull which, accentuating the disparity between
innocence and experience and splitting the personality between irrecon-
cilable halves, results in the disorientation of the self from itself and
the eventual surrender to despair. Yet, had Fitzgerald obtained his medals
and badges of pride, worn his overseas cap overseas and, establishing
himself in Experience, staked out his masculine claim to possession, he
still would not have thereby constituted himself a self. To become a
self, to move from conscious or unconscious despair into faith, is to

relate the temporal to the external and thereby to act, not because the action will bring pleasure or avoid pain, nor yet because it is in accordance with some socially-imposed pattern of rights and duties, but because the act has intrinsic meaning through its immediate relation to the Truth of which it is an incarnation. This is imagination. What Zelda did for Fitzgerald in accepting his love was to open the possibility, through a personal relationship, of a movement towards the self in fidelity and truth; in rejecting him, by a disavowal of responsibility, she negated this possibility; and in taking him again when he had enough money to enable her to continue to live with the irrefragible egotism of a child, she implicitly rejected the potential principle of meaning and truth and enthroned the pleasure-principle at the heart of their relationship. There followed the relentless operation of a fatal dialectic of self-destruction which they both were powerless to surmount or comprehend. There is a world of pathos in the contrast between Mr. Mizener's description of the eighteen-year-old maiden—"she was beautiful and witty . . . and there was nothing she did not dare do"—with the distracted figure released for a visit from the sanatorium, who quarrels with her drunken husband, walks out and is found at the station, "exquisitely dressed, a thoroughly sophisticated woman, except that she was wearing a hat like a child's bonnet with the strings carefully knotted under her chin. She was reading the Bible."

The Maturity of Scott Fitzgerald

by Arthur Mizener

The central question about Fitzgerald's work is probably a question about its maturity of perception. Though critics seldom argue this question at any length, their conclusions about it in fact differ widely. It is made more difficult to deal with than it otherwise might be by the tendency to confuse a judgment of Fitzgerald's habitual conduct and opinions with a judgment of his work. Fitzgerald's life and opinions cannot be wholly separated from his work and ought not to be; the connections are too intimate. The problem is how to separate our judgments of the two, because if we do not separate those judgments, we are all too likely to end by having our judgment of the former determine our judgment of the latter. The result is about as unfortunate if we admire Fitzgerald personally as it is if we dislike him.

Disentangling these two judgments is not made any easier by the deep ambiguity of modern feelings—perhaps particularly modern American feelings—about youthfulness. As Glenway Wescott pointed out, Fitzgerald was "our darling, our genius, our fool" in an age which had the courage of its conviction that nearly everything was well lost for youthfulness: even in death, nothing about Fitzgerald appeared old except his hands. Since there are always people who believe—whether with delight or resentment—that as we were young and easy we were in the best state known to man, there are always critics who see Fitzgerald's work as the life story of a prince of the apple towns. Many of those who do not nonetheless find it difficult to keep their judgment of what Fitzgerald wrote unaffected by their feelings about a man who always appeared, even at his worst, in a bright glow, like an actor on a stage. Without perhaps exactly believing in his greatness, they are moved by the meaning of what they take to be his life. This is what we ordinarily call the romantic attitude. It is represented at its best in Fitzgerald criticism by Lionel Trilling's essay on Fitzgerald's "heroic awareness" and his "exemplary role." The dyspeptic version of this attitude is Westbrook Pegler's reference to the "cult of juvenile crying-drunks" who dominated

"The Maturity of Scott Fitzgerald," by Arthur Mizener. From *The Sewanee Review*, LXVII (Autumn, 1959), pp. 658-675. Copyright 1959 by The University of the South. Reprinted by permission of the University of the South.

the age when Scott Fitzgerald's "few were gnawing gin in silver slabs and sniffling about the sham and tinsel of it all."

Judgment of Fitzgerald's work is confused in another way by the critics who assume that a fiction embodies no more understanding than its author is able to formulate in expository language, as abstract theory about life or art. Fitzgerald himself knew well that the natural mode of expression for his understanding was a fiction and that he knew a great deal in his stories that he did not know any other way. Characteristically he expressed this knowledge as an observation of behavior rather than as a theory by noting his habit of "sometimes reading my own books for advice. How much I know sometimes—how little at others." At their worst, critics who demand of a novel an argument are likely to demand an argument which conforms to some dogma of their own, as does the critic who says that Fitzgerald "was fatally attracted by what he took to be the true romance of great wealth" and was not so interested as the critic requires in "what life somewhat nearer the center of the American economy was all about." At their best such critics notice that "*The Last Tycoon* is far and away the best novel we have about Hollywood." Perhaps it is, but this kind of sociological understanding is at most a minor aspect of *The Last Tycoon's* perception. A similar assumption underlies the description of Fitzgerald's literary career as a gradual shift from the technique of the novel of saturation to the technique of the novel of selection. Fitzgerald was not the kind of writer—if there are any—for whom understanding consisted in the command of a technique. These judgments of Fitzgerald's perception represent what we ordinarily call a neo-classic attitude: somewhere not very far back of them is a conviction that fiction is a theory to advantage dressed.

This confusion among the judgments of the maturity of perception in Fitzgerald's work is not helped by the comparative—in some instances almost absolute—neglect of the work he did when his sensibility had fully matured. Much of that work was done after 1936 and the neglect of it is not altogether the critics' fault: most of it is difficult to get hold of, and when a critic does find some of it his natural impulse is to see it in the context of Fitzgerald's early work, with which he is familiar, rather than in the context of Fitzgerald's late work, with which it belongs. It is particularly easy to do so because in one respect, in the perception of romantic sentiment, Fitzgerald's sensibility matured quite early. The author who could precisely measure the difference between an original passion and that same passion deliberately renewed after a six months' break, as the author of "'The Sensible Thing'" measured it, is not in that respect immature. "'The Sensible Thing'" was written in 1924, when Fitzgerald was twenty-eight years old.

But the ending of "'The Sensible Thing,'" in which Fitzgerald tries to place the story's acute insight into George O'Kelly's feelings, is comparatively ineffective, a sort of bluff such as Fitzgerald disarmingly asserted he resorted to in *The Great Gatsby* when he was unable to imagine the relations between Daisy and Gatsby from the time they were reunited at Nick's tea party to the quarrel at the Plaza; "the lack," he said, "is so astutely concealed by . . . blankets of excellent prose that no one has noticed it." In much the same way, instead of placing the acute perception of George's feelings in a similar perception of experience as a whole, Fitzgerald resorts at the end of " 'The Sensible Thing' " to a seasonal metaphor which is exploited with a good deal of rhetorical charm but embodies only the vaguest sense of experience.

If, then, the perception embodied in " 'The Sensible Thing' " is mature in one respect, and an important respect, it is nevertheless not fully mature. Its limitations are easy to see if we compare " 'The Sensible Thing' " with even an early example of Fitzgerald's late work like "Outside the Cabinet-Maker's," written in 1928. "Outside the Cabinet-Maker's" begins with a wealthy man's wife going into a cabinet-maker's to buy a very special doll's house for their daughter's Christmas, leaving the man and the daughter waiting in the car. "Listen," the man says to the little girl, "I love you." " 'I love you too,' said the little girl smiling politely." Then to keep the little girl entertained, the man begins to improvise a fairy tale around the commonplace events of the drab street—the apartment across the street, the casual pulling-down of a shade, the ordinary passers-by. The fairy story is kept commonplace, too. Behind the drawn shade the Princess is held prisoner; the King and Queen are imprisoned by an Ogre thousands of miles within the earth; the Prince is seeking the three stones which will set them all free. The little girl becomes so completely absorbed in this story that she even forgets her manners. When her father interrupts the story to say, "You're *my* good fairy," she says, "Yes. Look, Daddy! What is that man?"

When the mother returns, the little girl suddenly takes the story away from her father and gives it her own ending. As she does so, something that has been implicit all along emerges clearly. The father drops the story with the remark that he is sorry they cannot stay to see the rescue.

> "But we did," the child cried. "They had the rescue in the next street. And there's the Ogre's body in that yard there. The King and the Queen and the Prince were killed and now the Princess is Queen."
>
> He had liked his King and Queen and felt they had been too summarily disposed of.
>
> "You had to have a heroine," he said rather impatiently.
>
> "She'll marry somebody and make him Prince."

"He had liked his King and Queen," but in the interest of making the Princess the story's heroic character, the little girl has killed them off without a qualm; and because she is the Princess who, in some dim future, will *make* a man Prince, she has killed off the Prince, too.

Rhetorically, "Outside the Cabinet-Maker's" never raises its voice; its details are very ordinary and domestic; and its child is no little Pearl. Yet it conveys a feeling of the pity and terror of experience which the author nonetheless accepts so quietly that those big Aristotelian words seem almost incongruous. The story's ruthlessness is not bred of unlawful passion as little Pearl's is; it is not really even the little girl's. It is life's, and everyday life's at that. Moreover, despite the ruthlessness with which the little girl destroys the mother and father of the fairy story, she *is* her father's good fairy. At the height of his story, as the little girl stares intently at the drawn blind of the Princess's prison, "for a moment he closed his eyes and tried to see with her but he couldn't see—those ragged blinds were drawn against him forever." All he can do is to buy her the doll's house which he cannot help knowing is only an expensive piece of cabinet-making and not a fairy castle, and make up for her fairy tales "whose luster and texture he could never see or touch any more himself." He can see and touch only through her; at the same time he knows, without resentment, that this dependence gives him no right to her devotion. He is, half comically, annoyed by her summary disposal of the King and Queen, but he knows the story is really hers and that her ending is unavoidable. In the last sentence, Fitzgerald says that, as they drove away from the cabinet-maker's in silence, "the man thought how he had nearly a million dollars"—to spend, as it were, on doll's houses and fairy stories. It is not, I think, even irony, though possibly there is a certain amount of private irony about wealth and talent in this detail of a story so close in many other respects (but not in this one) to Fitzgerald's own.

"Outside the Cabinet-Maker's" is a story completely imagined and fully realized. Only a writer who understood that the valuable meaning of experience is in the familiar, even the homely, could have conceived it; only a writer who could remember what it felt like to see and was completely reconciled to blindness could have presented that little girl's murderous innocence without romantic irony; only one whose knowledge consisted of observed experience could have kept these particulars at once so easy and so precise in meaning. "Outside the Cabinet-Maker's" is not the work of a man bemused by the true romance of great wealth, though the people in it are wealthy and charming. Neither is it a fictionalized social analysis of Wilmington, where it takes place, or an exercise in allegorical fantasy. Its motive is an understanding—I think a lucid and subtle understanding—which exists as an action.

The kind of perception which is illustrated by "Outside the Cabinet-Maker's" is present in the best of Fitzgerald's work from the late 1920's. So too is the kind of technical skill its expression requires. Like this one, Fitzgerald's technical achievements are almost always direct consequences of expressive needs. He could learn from others, but only when he had an immediate need for what they could teach him. When he had such a need, he could learn from almost anyone. If he refers to Conrad's example in the letter to Kenneth Littauer about *The Last Tycoon,* he also refers, in his notes for the book, to H. G. Wells. He was even capable of learning from a movie magazine, as he did when he wrote "Author's House," in 1936, when he was well into the final period of his career.

"Author's House" begins with a wry assertion that the writer has read frequently in the movie magazines about the houses of Hollywood stars and seen photographs of them "explaining how on God's earth to make a Hollywood soufflé or open a can of soup without removing the appendix in the same motion," but that he never hears about authors' houses and that he plans to supply the deficiency. He ends with a fine extension of this ironic comparison when the visitor he is showing around the house says, "It's really just like all houses, isn't it?" "The author nodded. 'I didn't think it was when I built it, but in the end I suppose it's just like other houses after all.'" The best moment in "Author's House" deals with young manhood. The author takes his visitor up to the glassed-in cupola and throws open a couple of windows, and "even as they stand there the wind increases until it is a gale whistling around the tower and blowing the birds past them."

> "I lived up here once," the author said after a moment.
> "Here? For a long time?"
> "No. For just a little while when I was young."
> "It must have been rather cramped."
> "I didn't notice it."
> "Would you like to try it again?"
> "No. And I couldn't if I wanted to."
> He shivered slightly and closed the windows.

We know something about what it was like to live up there, because Basil Duke Lee did so. At the end of the stories about Basil, when he finally accepts the loss of his fatal Cleopatra for whom he decides he would not gladly lose the world—that Cleopatra with the marvelous name of Minnie Bibble—Basil walks out on the veranda of the New Haven Lawn Club.

> There was a flurry of premature snow in the air and the stars looked cold. Staring up at them he saw that they were his stars as always—symbols of ambition, struggle and glory. The wind blew through them, trumpeting that high white note for which he always listened, and the thin-blown clouds, stripped for battle, passed in review. The scene was of an unparalleled brightness and magnificence, and only the practiced eye of the commander saw that one star was no longer there.

Writing nearly a decade later, the author of "Author's House" has not forgotten what it was like to live up there, convinced—as Fitzgerald put it in *The Crack-Up* about his own youth—that you could dominate life if you were any good. But he knows that he not only does not but cannot live up there now. This is the full acceptance of a loss that one completely understands, a clear perception that "if all time is eternally present,/All time is unredeemable." It is the characteristic perception of Fitzgerald's late work, a perception that must have been peculiarly difficult for Fitzgerald, for whom the past was always very intensely present. But it is of course the difficulty which gives the perception its value.

In the companion story to "Author's House," called "Afternoon of an Author," Fitzgerald describes an afternoon's visit to the barber's by an author so worn out that the trip is for him a major adventure. He describes it almost gaily, certainly quite impersonally. At the end, when the author arrives back at his apartment,

> He went through the dining room and turned into his study, struck blind for a moment with the glow of his two thousand books in the late sunshine. He was quite tired—he would lie down for ten minutes and then see if he could get started on an idea in the two hours before dinner.

Effects like this one require very delicate control. This is, if you will, a technical achievement of a high order. It is nothing so gross as symbolism; it is scarcely even a detectable emphasis of diction. The passage's integrity is its precise representation of immediate experience: nothing the author sees beyond the immediate experience is allowed to stretch or distort that representation. Yet we are made to feel that it is an image of a whole way of life and, at least ultimately, of an aspect of all lives. This is only a moment, a very ordinary moment, experienced, we understand, as casually as we all experience ordinary moments, when we have the experience but miss the meaning. But the moment is, as it is realized here, quite truly "a new and shocking/Valuation of all we have been," though without in any way ceasing to be what it originally was. I have been deliberately quoting Mr. Eliot because I think Fitzgerald's late work shows us, in a homely and unostentatious way, even an amused way, what Mr. Eliot is describing in the *Quartets,* insofar as the *Quartets* are concerned with how we know the truth. It is typical of Fitzgerald's late work that Cecilia should say of her experience, on the first page of *The Last Tycoon,* "It can be understood, too, but only dimly and in flashes." "Ridiculous," she might have added, "the waste sad time/Stretching before and after."

This resemblance extends in part to the two writers' conceptions of reality. About Fitzgerald's author, who could be struck blind by the glow of even the afternoon sunshine but, because he was "quite tired," would have to rest before taking up the struggle to realize this experience in words as his job in the world requires him to—about this man there is something pitiable. But the attitude of "Afternoon of an Author" is not pity. The essay moves almost as if its author were unconscious of the pitiableness of his character; or, rather, as if he were aware of it but had long since written it off as irrelevant. If "What might have been and what has been/Point to one end, which is always present," then every end is like this one, this afternoon of an author, a new beginning.

One could trace this attitude and the skill with which it is realized in any number of Fitzgerald's late stories, in "I Didn't Get Over," "The Long Way Out," "Design in Plaster," "The Lost Decade," "News of Paris." But the most interesting manifestation of them is his last novel, *The Last Tycoon*, which shows on a large scale both the attitude and the style of his late work, even though it is unfinished, even though, as Fitzgerald's notes show, he intended to rewrite nearly all he had written.

We can say of *The Last Tycoon* that luck or accident had given Fitzgerald the nearly perfect image for his sense of experience, even if we have to say that this same luck or accident also prevented his finishing the book. The essential quality of experience for him—I think perhaps he thought it particularly a quality of American experience—was the queerness and, occasionally, the miracle of it, no less what they are for occurring always amidst commonplaceness, fakeness, sheer badness, and a good deal of evil—and, perhaps we should add, during a continuous earthquake. For this sense of experience, Hollywood provided him with an almost perfect instance, and Cecilia, with her odd upbringing to make her "[accept] Hollywood with the resignation of a ghost assigned to a haunted house," was the perfect narrator. Like every place else, Hollywood is commonplace and a little beat up with being lived in, but nonetheless haunted, and Fitzgerald's story must be told by some one able to see that.

The relevance of what Hollywood is to what experience seemed to Fitzgerald is clearly illustrated by the important scene when Stahr first meets Kathleen. The scene begins in fact with an earthquake, during which, as Fitzgerald observes, "small hotels drifted out to sea" (*small* hotels only, of course) in the most ordinary way imaginable. This is no process shot; the earthquake is quite real and would do the same thing anywhere. What it could not literally do anywhere is what it does in the studio back lot. When Stahr and his assistants get there, they see "a huge head of the Goddess Siva . . . floating down the current of an impromptu river." Incongruously, "two refugees had found sanctuary along a scroll of curls on its bald forehead." The tone here—the ironic exaggeration of "refugees" and "sanctuary," the grotesqueness of "impromptu" and "bald"—is deliberate and characteristic. We are not allowed to forget for an instant the ordinary and temporary—even fake—materials out of which this event is made; the point is driven home by Fitzgerald's adding that the idol "meandered earnestly on its way, stopping sometimes to waddle and bump in the shallows," like a frumpish old lady who means well but is badly muddled. Then Robbie, the cutter, says, "We ought to let 'em drift out to the waste pipe, but DeMille needs that head next week," and shouts at the refugees, "Put that head back! You think it's a souvenir?" And in the midst of all this, off that ludicrously waddling head of the goddess, steps the living image of Stahr's dead wife. It is, incidentally, typical of the way Fitzgerald's imagination warms to its work that he had originally thought of the floating object as "a property farmhouse"; the head of Siva, with all that it implies, was an invention of the moment of composition.

This kind of particularized and precisely controlled realization of the miracle—the often absurd miracle—at the heart of the ordinary, even fake, is the essential achievement of Fitzgerald's late fiction, and Hollywood made it possible for him to convey that perception without forcing his materials in the slightest. How strictly he held himself accountable for the actuality of his material is evident from the frequency with which people repeat Edmund Wilson's praise of *The Last Tycoon* as a picture of Hollywood. But this verisimilitude, though vital to the novel's success, is only a part, and the less significant part, of its achievement, just as the brilliant account of Long Island society in *The Great Gatsby* is a vital but relatively minor part of its achievement. The particularized world of *The Last Tycoon* is an image of experience.

The queerness of experience is everywhere in the novel, inherent in the crass and ordinary life of Hollywood. With some irony but more seriousness, Fitzgerald had made the mad priest of "Absolution" say of the amusement park that was his image of the ideal life, "but don't get up close because if you do you'll only feel the heat and the sweat and the life." But the late Fitzgerald does not share Father Schwartz's sentimental regret for the enchanted, distant prospect of the world's fair or his conviction that actual life consists wholly of unendurable heat and sweat. He has got up close and found that it is, if thoroughly sweaty, also wonderfully strange and even funny. When Martha Dodd, the faded star of silent pictures, remembers her days of fame, she says with a wistfulness all the more moving for its incongruous expression: "I had a beautiful place in 1928—thirty acres, with a miniature golf course and a pool and a gorgeous view. All spring I was up to my ass in daisies." When Cecilia, hearing some one moaning in the closet of her father's office, rushes over and opens the door, her father's secretary, with the wonderful name of Birdy Peters, "tumble[s] out stark naked—just like a corpse in the movies"—except that she is faint and covered with sweat from the heat of the closet.

This sense of the queerness of commonplace existence spreads through the book's vision of life beyond Hollywood. When the pilot in Nashville tells "the awful-looking yet discernibly attractive" drunk that they will not take him on the next flight, he says earnestly, "Only going up in ee *air*." "Not this time, old man," the pilot says. And Cecilia observes,

"In his disappointment the drunk fell off the bench—and above the phonograph, the loudspeaker summoned us respectable people outside." When Kathleen, who has constantly disconcerted Stahr by her European, her almost peasant inclination to calculate what there is for her in their relation, finally tells Stahr her story, it turns out, in the most plausible way in the world, that she has spent a large part of her adult life as the mistress of a king.

But perhaps the most beautiful image of the book's sustained sense of the everyday queerness of experience is the scene of the consummation of Stahr and Kathleen's love. The scene makes clear another element of Fitzgerald's perception, the element that dictated the earthquake at the beginning of their love, that earthquake which set everything visibly afloat and moving. Indeed, everything in the novel is afloat and moving, in an earnest and fumbling way which is at the same time a rapid drift toward the waste pipe. Nothing stands still and no one can afford to wait for things to be just right. Even while Stahr decides to wait a day before proposing to Kathleen, for instance, Kathleen's fiancé is unexpectedly on his way to marry her, and the next thing Stahr knows he is looking at a telegram that says: *I was married at noon today. Goodbye; and"*— Fitzgerald's sense of the everyday absurdity of things notes—"on a sticker attached, *Send your answer by Western Union Telegram."*

Stahr and Kathleen had consummated their love on a visit to a house Stahr was building at Malibu. Characteristically, it was only half finished, surrounded by concrete mixers, yellow wood, and builders' rubble. But Stahr had given "a premature luncheon" the week before and had "had some props brought out—some grass and things." Kathleen laughed and said, "Isn't that real grass?" "Oh, yes," Stahr said, "—it's grass." Just before they leave this half-finished house with its quite real but of course temporary lawn and furnishings, Kathleen reminds Stahr that perhaps he only thinks he loves her because she looks like his dead wife; he says simply, "You look more like she actually *looked* than how she was on the screen," and Kathleen gets up, goes over to a closet, and comes back wearing an apron.

> She stared around critically.
> "Of course we've just moved in," she said, "—and there's a sort of echo."

Within this queer, half-finished, floating world with its ghostly echoes, which constitutes the unavoidable condition for everyone, Stahr works to build something. As a young man, Fitzgerald had thought that if you are any good you dominate life; Stahr, who began life leading a street gang in the Bronx, does dominate it for a while, by the exercise of imagination and will. Fitzgerald calls him "the last of the princes" and Stahr calls himself "chief clerk." Both are right. Stahr is a genuine aristocrat, in contrast to phonies like Brady who keeps a painting of Will Rogers in his office to suggest his "essential kinship with Hollywood's St. Francis," and the Café-Society aristocracy of Hollywood—"from Wall Street, Grand Street, Loudoun County, Virginia, and Odessa, Russia." "[Stahr] had a long time ago run ahead through trackless wastes of perception into fields where very few men were able to follow him." He knows as few men do what has to be done, and knows too the unavoidable conditions in which it has to be done. When Boxley, the British novelist Stahr has hired as a script-writer, says complainingly, "It's this mass production," Stahr says, "That's the condition. There's always some lousey condition." To using the complex technique of the movies and the muddle of Hollywood to make something under his condition, Stahr devotes all his energy, as the fine scenes of one of his working days show.

But this is not the only condition, for Stahr has also to dominate an economic organization. On one side, he is under attack from people like Brady who do not want to create something but only to make something for themselves. "I want," Fitzgerald said in one of his notes for the book, "to contrast [Stahr's attitude] sharply with the feeling of those who have merely gypped another person's empire away from them like the four great railroad kings of the coast." On the other side, Stahr is under attack from organized labor and the Communists. In part these two attacking groups work together: Brady's plot to murder Stahr involves Wylie White of the Writers' Guild and Robinson, the cutter. But Brimmer, the Communist organizer, can understand Stahr and even feel sympathy with him. "I never thought that I had more brains than a writer has," Stahr tells him. "But I always thought that his brains *belonged* to me—because I knew how to use them. . . . Do you see? I don't say it's right. But it's the way I've always felt—since I was a boy." And Brimmer says, "You understand yourself very well, Mr. Stahr." When Stahr says to him, "You don't really think you're going to overthrow the government," Brimmer says, "No, Mr. Stahr. But we think perhaps you are." And Stahr, remembering all the Bradys of his world, the American business world, cannot be sure Brimmer is wrong.

Stahr *is* a tycoon, a great Prince, because he is not just a tycoon in *Time* magazine's sense but the image of genuine authority in a democratic society. The particular form authority has taken in him is necessarily the form required for authority by the comparatively old-fashioned capitalism in which he grew up. That was the condition, and he may well be the last tycoon of that kind there will be. But the essential qualities of the great Prince which he possesses will be needed by any society if it is to be any good. Brimmer knows that; it is the source of his sympathy with Stahr. On the other hand, the contrast between Stahr and Brady represents a contrast which Fitzgerald plainly felt runs, not only through modern American business society, but through the whole of American history. His imagination was haunted by the difficulty of recreating, over and over again, the tradition of responsibility that

Stahr instinctively represents. The tradition is there, but the people who are capable of realizing it cannot see it: the fluidity of American society keeps them unaware of it, so that they are forced, against the odds, to recreate it from scratch each generation. There is, then, great irony in calling Stahr a tycoon. He is, in all essentials, truly a great Prince, but these are the last terms in which he could conceive of himself because he is a great Prince, not as the real tycoons were, with the support of a whole society and its dominant tradition, but in spite of them.

This aspect of Fitzgerald's understanding is stressed at regular intervals. The book opens with an example of what this ignorance can mean. A producer named Manny Schwartz, who has been defeated in Hollywood, arrives by pure accident on the steps of The Hermitage at the moment he has decided in despair to commit suicide. He too was once a prince, if a minor one. "I have decided," he says to Wylie White when he stays on at The Hermitage. "Once I used to be a regular man of decision—you'd be surprised." And then Fitzgerald says:

> He had come a long way from some Ghetto to present himself at that raw shrine. Manny Schwartz and Andrew Jackson—it was hard to say them in the same sentence. It was doubtful if he knew who Andrew Jackson was as he wandered around, but perhaps he figured that if people had preserved his house Andrew Jackson must have been someone who was large and merciful, able to understand.

The tradition is there in American society, but for the people who need it most it is very difficult to know.

About a quarter of the way through the book, a Danish prince who is visiting the studio sees an extra dressed as Lincoln in the studio commissary. "This, then, he thought, was what they all meant to be." Then, with Fitzgerald's acute sense of the queer way the miracle lives in the commonplace in American society, he adds: "Lincoln suddenly raised a triangle of pie and jammed it in his mouth, and, a little frightened, Prince Agge hurried to join Stahr." "Stahr," as Boxley thinks later, "was an artist only, as Mr. Lincoln was a general, perforce and as a layman." Such has always been the character of American life.

About halfway through the book, Stahr was to have visited Washington, but he has an attack of grippe there and moves around the city in a high fever, so that he never gets acquainted with it and its meaning as he wanted to, just as Schwartz never found out who Andrew Jackson was. This parallel between the moral and economic conflict in Hollywood and the conflicting moral and economic traditions of American society, and this reiteration of a fluid society's a-historical blindness make Fitzgerald's novel an image of American experience, not only in our time, but through the country's history.

We cannot tell, of course, what the exact emphasis of the novel's conclusion would have been, but Stahr is a dying man all through it and is

killed in the crash of a transcontinental plane at the end, after having
been defeated—though he does not stop fighting—in his battle for control of the studio. In any event, Stahr is the last *tycoon*. Fitzgerald shows
us all his limitations, the bad side of his paternalism, the laissez-faire
attitude which forces him to connive at building a company union. The
novel pretty clearly implies that the forms within which Stahr, as a man
of his time, has learned to work are doomed. In this sense Stahr is the
last *tycoon,* the last of the typical rulers of a doomed and on the whole
unregretted social order. But from Brimmer the Communist and Wylie
White the intelligent rascal to Jim, the young boy of the epilogue, those
who can understand know how vital to any kind of society Stahr's real
gifts are. In this sense, though Stahr is the last prince of this particular
dynasty, he is only the latest ruler of a great tradition that runs back
through Lincoln and Andrew Jackson and will produce in the future
people who, in another style, become Princes, as Lincoln became a
general, perforce and as laymen. For this, as Prince Agge saw, was what
the best of them all meant to be. Perhaps, then, we may guess at the
effect Fitzgerald would have aimed at in his treatment of Stahr's end
from the effect he produced at the end of "Afternoon of an Author."

Fitzgerald too had been through some trackless wastes of perception.
It seems to me difficult to deny that *The Last Tycoon* is an extended
exercise of a perception of great distinction in marvelously close contact
with actual life. The notes Fitzgerald wrote to himself about the novel
formulate this perception only in the crudest general way, as does the
note about the railroad kings "who gypped another person's empire
away from them." This is expository shorthand, similar in character to
Dr. Johnson's queer habit of writing a poem in his head and then jotting
down only the first part of each line; the important part was the poetry
in his mind—"some unfinished/Chaos in your head," as Fitzgerald called
it. It was when Fitzgerald created an action, a fiction, that his full perception was realized. If we look at the perception realized in *The Last
Tycoon* without allowing ourselves to be influenced by our judgment of
Fitzgerald's personal life or of his opinions, what we see is a remarkable
awareness of the actual, in all its ordinariness and all its strangeness,
together with an acceptance of what we are so complete and unqualified
by romantic irony that it can take even heroism like Stahr's, with mild
amusement, as a kind of vice. There is certainly nothing juvenile about
such a perception, and even less that suggests Fitzgerald's novels are
illustrated ideas. This is, in fact, the kind of perception that the mature
imagination achieves.

Chronology of Important Dates

September 24, 1896	Born in St. Paul, Minnesota
1911-1913	Attended Newman Academy, Hackensack, New Jersey
1913-1917	Attended Princeton; left before graduation
1920	*This Side of Paradise;* married Zelda Sayre
1921	*Flappers and Philosophers*
1922	*The Beautiful and Damned; Tales of the Jazz Age;* Frances Fitzgerald born in St. Paul; moved to Great Neck, L. I.
1923	*The Vegetable*
1924	Moved to the Riviera
1925	*The Great Gatsby*
1926	*All the Sad Young Men*
1927	Script-writing in Holloywood; moved to "Ellerslie," near Wilmington, Delaware
1930	Zelda Fitzgerald broke down mentally in Paris
1931	Script-writing in Hollywood
1932	*Save Me the Waltz* by Zelda Fitzgerald; moved to "La Paix," Rodgers Forge, Maryland
1934	*Tender Is the Night*
1935	*Taps at Reveille*
1937	Moved to Hollywood as script-writer; fell in love with Sheilah Graham
December 21, 1941	Died in Hollywood; buried in the Rockville Union Cemetery, Rockville, Maryland

Notes on the Editor and Authors

LIONEL TRILLING is a professor at Columbia University and the author of *Matthew Arnold, The Liberal Imagination, The Opposing Self* and other influential critical work. His essay on Fitzgerald is from *The Liberal Imagination*.

WILLIAM TROY, the critic, taught at Bennington from 1935-1944. His essay on Fitzgerald appeared in *Accent*.

WRIGHT MORRIS, the American novelist, is the author of *The Deep Sleep, The Huge Season,* and a number of other well-known novels. His essay on Fitzgerald comes from his book on the American novel, *The Territory Ahead*.

JOHN ALDRIDGE, the novelist and critic, is the author of *The Party at Cranston* and *After the Lost Generation,* of which his essay on Fitzgerald constitutes a chapter.

EDWIN FUSSELL is a professor at the Claremont Graduate School and is at work on a book on the frontier in American literature. His essay on Fitzgerald appeared in *ELH, A Journal of English Literary History*.

ANDREWS WANNING is a professor at Bard College and a specialist in contemporary literature. His essay on Fitzgerald appeared in *The Partisan Review*.

MALCOLM COWLEY, the poet and critic, is the author of *Blue Juniata, Exile's Return, The Literary Situation,* and other well-known books. He edited the standard collection of Fitzgerald's short stories. He has written widely about Fitzgerald; the essay in this book appeared in *The New Yorker*.

LESLIE FIEDLER is a professor at Montana State University and the author of *Love and Death in the American Novel*. The essay on Fitzgerald in this book comes from his collection called *An End to Innocence*.

CHARLES E. SHAIN is President of Connecticut College. Previously he taught at Princeton University and Carleton College, where he wrote *F. Scott Fitzgerald,* from which the selection in this book comes.

EDMUND WILSON, the American critic, is the author of *Patriotic Gore* and many other influential books. The essay on Fitzgerald in this book was originally written for *The Bookman* and published in *The Literary Spotlight*. Mr. Wilson reprinted it in *The Shores of Light*.

JAMES E. MILLER, JR. is a professor at the University of Nebraska and the author of *The Fictional Technique of Scott Fitzgerald,* from which the essay in this book is taken.

DONALD OGDEN STEWART, the playwright and parodist, wrote the parody of Fitzgerald printed in this book as a chapter of his *Parody Outline of History* in 1921.

JOHN HENRY RALEIGH is a professor at the University of California and the author of *Matthew Arnold and American Culture*. His essay in this book is the second of two he wrote on *The Great Gatsby* for *The University of Kansas City Review*.

TOM BURNAM is a professor at Colorado State College. His essay on Fitzgerald was written for *College English*.

A. E. DYSON is professor at the University College of North Wales at Bangor. His essay on Fitzgerald appeared in *Modern Fiction Studies'* Fitzgerald number in the Spring of 1961.

MARIUS BEWLEY teaches at Fordham and is the author of *The Complex Fate* and *The Eccentric Design,* in which a revised version of the essay in this book is a chapter. The essay as it is printed here appeared in *The Sewanee Review.*

D. W. HARDING is a professor of psychology at Bedford College of The University of London. His essay in this book originally appeared in *Scrutiny* as a review of *Tender Is the Night.*

D. S. SAVAGE, the English poet and critic, is the author of *The Withered Branch* and *The Personal Principle.* His essay on Fitzgerald was published in *The Arizona Quarterly.*

ARTHUR MIZENER is a professor at Cornell. He is the author of a biography of Fitzgerald. His essay in this book appeared in *The Sewanee Review.*

Selected Bibliography

A full and reliable bibliography of Fitzgerald criticism by Maurice Beebe and Jackson R. Bryer appeared in *Modern Fiction Studies,* VII (Spring, 1961), 82-94.

Books

Kazin, Alfred (ed.). *F. Scott Fitzgerald: The Man and His Work.* The World Publishing Company, 1951.

Miller, James E., Jr. *The Fictional Technique of Scott Fitzgerald.* Martinus Nijhoff (The Hague), 1957.

Mizener, Arthur. *The Far Side of Paradise.* Houghton Mifflin, 1951; Vintage Books, 1959.

Piper, Henry Dan. *Scott Fitzgerald: A Candid Portrait.* Holt, Rinehart, and Winston, 1963.

Turnbull, Andrew. *Scott Fitzgerald.* Charles Scribner's Sons, 1962.

Essays and Selections

Berryman, John. "F. Scott Fitzgerald," *The Kenyon Review,* VIII (Winter, 1946), 103-112.

Chase, Richard. "Three Novels of Manners—*The Great Gatsby,*" in his *The American Novel and Its Tradition.* Anchor Books, 1957, 162-167.

Cowley, Malcolm. "Introduction," *The Short Stories of F. Scott Fitzgerald.* Charles Scribner's Sons, 1951, vii-xxv. "F. Scott Fitzgerald: The Romance of Money," *The Western Review,* XVII (Summer, 1953), 245-255.

Graham, Sheilah, and Frank, Gerold. *Beloved Infidel.* Henry Holt, 1958, 173-338.

Geismar, Maxwell. "Orestes at the Ritz," in his *The Last of the Provincials.* Houghton Mifflin, 1943, 287-352.

Harding, D. W. "Scott Fitzgerald," *Scrutiny,* XVIII (Winter, 1951), 166-174.

Harkness, Bruce. "Bibliography and the Novelistic Fallacy," *Studies in Bibliography,* XII (1959), 59-73.

Hoffman, Frederick J. *The Twenties.* The Viking Press, 1955, 100-119.

Mizener, Arthur. "Introduction," *Afternoon of an Author.* Charles Scribner's Sons, 1958, 3-12.

Piper, Henry Dan. "F. Scott Fitzgerald: A Checklist," *The Princeton University Library Chronicle,* XII (1951), 196-208.

Thurber, James. "Scott in Thorns," *The Reporter*, IV (April 17, 1951), 35-38.

Weir, Charles. "An Invite with Gilded Edges," *The Virginia Quarterly Review*, XX (Winter, 1944), 100-113.

Wescott, Glenway. "The Moral of Scott Fitzgerald," *The New Republic*, CIV (February 17, 1941), 213-217.

TWENTIETH CENTURY VIEWS

Forthcoming Titles